# PORTRAIT OF THE MORAY FIRTH

*Also by Cuthbert Graham*

PORTRAIT OF ABERDEEN AND DEESIDE

# Portrait of

# THE MORAY FIRTH

by

CUTHBERT GRAHAM

ROBERT HALE · LONDON

© *Cuthbert Graham 1977*
*First published in Great Britain 1977*
ISBN 0 7091 6018 6

Robert Hale Limited
Clerkenwell House
Clerkenwell Green
London EC1

PHOTOSET BY WEATHERBY WOOLNOUGH
AND PRINTED IN GREAT BRITAIN BY
LOWE & BRYDONE LTD., THETFORD, NORFOLK

# CONTENTS

# ACKNOWLEDGEMENTS

Visits to every one of the localities described in this book, over a period of fifteen years, and discussions with permanent residents in each, in the course of my journalistic work, suggested to me the idea of attempting to depict what I believe to be one of the most fascinating regions in Britain at a period when it is changing rapidly under the impact of government growth policies.

No book of this kind could be written without indebtedness to the copious local literature, particularly on the past of the area. I feel particularly indebted to the writing of Mr Ronald G. Cant on the history and architecture of Moray, to the late Dr Evan M. Barron's books on Inverness and to the Banff Preservation Society's guide to the architecture of Banff. When any authority is quoted in the text, full details of the literary source are given in the bibliography.

On archaeological topics I am specially indebted to the late Dr W. Douglas Simpson and to Mr Stewart Cruden; on dialect matters to Mr David D. Murison, editor of the *Scottish National Dictionary*, and for brief verse quotations to Mrs Flora Garry and the late John C. Milne.

I would like to thank Mr K. J. Peters, Managing Director of Aberdeen Journals Ltd, and Mr Peter Watson, Editor of *The Press and Journal* for kind encouragement and Mr Peter Grant, City District Librarian of Aberdeen, and Miss Moira Wilkie, Reference Librarian, for unstinting aid. All my photographer colleagues and particularly Mr Ian Hardie and Mr David Sutherland have assisted my coverage of the region, while my wife Enid has helped to revise the typescript.

# ILLUSTRATIONS

*Between pages 114 and 115*

*pages 230-231*

MAP (based with permission on the Ordnance Survey)

# CHAPTER I

# BIRTH OF A GROWTH AREA

LIKE Caesar's Gaul, the northern half of Scotland is divided into three parts. There are the north-eastern Lowlands, so Spartan yet so dear to so many, beginning with the luxuriance of the Howe of Strathmore, crossing the Great Highland Fault and the tail end of the Grampians (more correctly called the Mounth) and running out into the weather-beaten, wind-swept plain of Buchan; recovering mellower fertility in the Laich of Moray and the green peninsulas of Easter Ross. There are the Highlands, hugging to their stony bosoms dark lochans and sequestered glens and pinewoods and shaggy moors, stretching north and away from the Great Glen to the Strath of Kildonan. And finally, there is a third world, distinct from the other two, which begins on the far side of that great bun of a hill, the Ord of Caithness and opens out into that sea-girt land so long grabbed by the Norsemen: more flat and windswept than the Buchan plain. It is the glory of the Moray Firth that it partakes of each of these realms by driving a deep, watery wedge into the heart of these northlands.

'Moray Firth' is a term with as many meanings as an onion has skins. Taken at its widest, it is the largest opening on the east coast of Britain—a great triangle of water, 96 miles deep from north to south, 95 miles wide from west to east on its landward coastline, and 78 miles across on its third or open sea side between Duncansby Head in Caithness and Cairnbulg Point in Aberdeenshire. Its inland apex is at the mouth of the Beauly River.

Although the largest of Scotland's firths, its shores are less heavily populated than those of the Clyde, the Forth or the Tay, though exceeding the much narrower Firth of Lorne. It is a strange paradox that in the past its most exposed and

weather-beaten coasts, those of its outer extremities, have seen
the greater human development in the fishery districts of
Fraserburgh, Macduff, Buckie, Lossiemouth and Wick, while
its inner reaches, around the apex of the triangle where the
wide waters proliferate into the smaller inlets of the Inverness,
Beauly, Cromarty and Dornoch Firths, have lain like a
sleeping beauty awaiting the kiss of life.

Of course, wherever the rock weathered down into a rich
tilth upon a sheltered shelf of land between the mountains and
the sea, agriculture has been intensively practised here for
centuries. The Laich of Moray, with the cathedral city of
Elgin, has sometimes been called the Garden of Scotland, and
across the water in the strangely misnamed Black Isle and the
more northerly peninsula of Easter Ross the quality of the
farming is world famous. But man cannot live by bread alone,
especially when the tractor and the combine harvester make
farming very far from labour intensive, as it was once upon a
time.

To people this delectable land to more than a minimal
extent, other kinds of industry were necessary. Sporadic attempts were made to provide it. Before the union with
England destroyed its first era of prosperity the little town of
Cromarty was a notable trading port. At the end of the
eighteenth century it enjoyed a remarkable industrial revival
which collapsed when the power loom, the steamship and the
Railway Age passed it by. In World War I the Cromarty
Firth became a major base of the British High Seas Fleet, but
the Cromarty Firth's naval importance passed when it became
too vulnerable to air attack.

The Navy had built up its main supply centre at Invergordon, scene of the Mutiny in 1931, but in the years after
World War II the flotsam and jetsam of abandoned naval
occupation gave the deserted base, with its batteries of oil
tanks and its silent streets, an air of dereliction.
Unemployment in the area was heavy. It was one of the
running sores which led to the establishment by Act of
Parliament in 1965 of the Highlands and Islands Development
Board, pledged to staunch the fatal drain of population from
the Highlands and to bring about the economic and social
regeneration of the region.

In its first report, published in 1967, the Board declared:

We will do our utmost to generate major growth points, involving substantial increases of population, wherever the natural advantages of the area seem to warrant it; the Moray Firth is unquestionably the most important of these areas.

Before the Board was established, the inner Moray Firth area had been identified by various bodies, including the Scottish Economic Planning Council as an area with substantial development potential and the White Paper on the Scottish Economy endorsed that view. Our aims in promoting Moray Firth development are:

> to establish a major centre of job opportunity for those from within and without the Highlands, offering conditions in all respects comparable with the best likely to become available in the United Kingdom.
> to establish a major centre which can offer within the region a full range of modern, commercial, social, cultural and other activities, as well as job opportunity . . .

At one sweep this elevated the Moray Firth to a unique status within the Highlands. It was to be the hinge of Highland regeneration by its role as the sub-region selected, in the Board's own words, "to help balance the economic structure of an area in which the distinctive feature is the very small representation of manufacturing industry".

The "major centre" which the Board had in mind to provide "modern commercial, social, cultural and other activities, as well as job opportunities" was Inverness, which had always claimed to be "the Capital of the Highlands". It lay on the southern base of the Firth, near its apex. But the development itself was to be widely spread.

What made the Highlands and Islands Development Board and the other government agencies so confident that the Moray Firth could do the job? They were already negotiating with the Occidental Petroleum Corporation of Los Angeles about the possibility of a petro-chemical complex at Invergordon as a major step towards the development of the Moray Firth area. As conceived at that stage the complex would have produced fertilizers, plastics and various other organic and inorganic chemicals, in addition to a substantial output of refined oil. As it happened, this was a project which never materialized. But why Invergordon? Why the Cromarty Firth?

As the Board put it, this area has great potential because it possesses resources that are highly attractive to modern industry, the three most important being: 1. a sheltered deepwater harbour capable of taking the very large tankers of up to 200,000 tons and all the biggest bulk carriers likely to be built; 2. ample supplies of fresh water; and 3. the very unusual situation where suitable areas of flat land lie adjacent to the deep water.

The petro-chemical complex—ironically enough when one considers the subsequent energy crisis and the discovery of oil in the North Sea—proved to be a chimera. But the Board had in mind other possibilities for the area, including mineral processing industries, as well as those based on the natural produce of the surrounding country districts.

One of these, mineral processing, proved to be the trump card and in due course the British Aluminium Company built its smelter in Invergordon. Before that happened however there had been much research, not only into the industrial potentialities of the inner Moray Firth, but also into the extended infrastructure it would require to support a greatly increased population.

Following an industrial credibility study, a consortium of consultants, the Jack Holmes Planning Group, was commissioned to assess the capacity of the Moray Firth area for development and "to prepare a plan for urban land use and an infrastructure arising from industrial expansion at Invergordon".

In March 1968 they submitted their report "The Moray Firth: a Plan for Growth in a sub-region of the Scottish Highlands". The Holmes Report was sensational in its implications. It covered the area from Tain to Nairn and demonstrated that this area, with a present population of around 75,000, could house a population of 250,000 to 300,000 in comfort and in pleasant surroundings.

The daring of this as a forecast of the future is apparent when one realizes that the entire Highland Region from John o' Groats to the Mull of Kintyre had at that time a total population of 269,000. Yet here were the planners saying that a relatively tiny corner of it, along the 'Highland Edge', could in the foreseeable future support a population of up to 300,000, and could give that population an environment and a way of life that might be the envy of the rest of Britain.

In their sixth report in 1971 the HIDB recorded: "The results of the 1971 Census show an appreciable population increase since 1966—an increase of over 5,000, compared with barely 5,000 in the previous 45 years from 1921. About a third of the gain has been due to natural increase and two-thirds to immigration, i.e. since 1966 some 3,700 more people have moved into the area than have left it."

But—there was still anxiety. "There is still substantial unemployment in the sub-region, particularly in Easter Ross, where over 1,000 people, or 13%, were unemployed at the end of the year (1970). This unemployment," said the Board

> is due partly to the ending of the peak construction phase at Invergordon [where the new smelter was now completed]—and partly no doubt to the fact that local men and women have their eyes fastened on greater opportunities in this area than they see in the South. These opportunities will arise, both out of the Board's drive to attract additional conventional manufacturing firms to the area, and from on-shore developments in support of oil exploration and exploitation in the North Sea.

At that time the Board calculated that one fabrication yard for the construction of fixed platforms for North Sea oil wells "could employ up to 900 people and there are likely to be several in this category". This now appears quite an understatement. By the summer of 1974 in the race to meet the deadline for the launching of their first platform at the Bay of Nigg, Highlands Fabricators, the consortium formed by the American firm of Brown and Root and the British firm of Wimpey, were employing a maximum of 3,200 men, while at the other side of the Moray Firth 2,000 men were fabricating another platform at Whiteness Head, near Ardersier. Invergordon itself had entered the oil race with the firm of M. K. Shand coating the pipes for undersea pipelines.

In this situation the chairman of the Board, Sir Andrew Gilchrist, estimated in the foreword to the HIDB's eighth report that "whereas we are authorised to inject capital into the Highland economy at the rate of about £11 million per annum ... the oil-related industry is probably injecting capital into the same area at a rate conservatively estimated to be about £30 million per annum, and this proportion is rising fast". Early in 1973 it was agreed that 4,000 new houses would be required for incomers to the inner Moray Firth area in the next three years.

The Holmes Report made detailed recommendations for the siting of industry and new residential communities in the inner Moray Firth based on an assessment of the special advantages of the sub-region: its climate, its land-forms, its scenic beauty and its communications and transport potential. It waxed lyrical on what it called "incomparable assets" in climate and scenery. "Splendid hills," it stated, "lie on one side, the coast with all its interest and variety on the other, and all the many distant views are enhanced by the unusual qualities of the atmosphere. It is probably true that nowhere else in the United Kingdom enjoys scenery of this character *as well as a dry and sunny climate* . . . "

This is true. As one approaches Inverness along the Firth on the A96 road from Nairn the line of the Highland Edge comes nearer and nearer. At first the ridge of Ben Wyvis generally snow-streaked, soaring above the lower land of the Black Isle that lies between, dominates the whole picture. Then as the road curves to the south-west the low hills around Inverness, a succession of rounded pyramids, occupy the foreground. But behind them when one reaches the narrows at Kessock and enters the area of the Beauly Firth rise range upon range of other mountains around Strath Farrar and Strath Conon in weird and tumbled magnificence.

That one should be able to enjoy this without the usual penalties of hill fog and heavy rainfall in the 'dry' area of the Firth is benediction enough—but it is accompanied also, on the south side of the Firth in particular, by incomparable sunsets, and on both sides of the water by a translucent quality of light.

How 'dry' in fact is the inner Moray Firth? Compared with Stornoway in the Outer Hebrides with nearly 50 inches of rain a year, Nairn has on average only 26 inches. Fortrose in the Black Isle is even milder and though only about ten miles farther west across the Firth it has only 33 days of air frost in a year compared with Nairn's 60. The average duration of sunshine in the whole area is that of Coventry. The coast near

Culbin is reckoned to be one of the driest parts of Scotland and this has accounted for the movement of sand-dunes in the past. In addition to this the lowland occasionally experiences *Föhn* conditions in winter and spring, with temperatures 10 to 20 degrees higher than at Aberdeen. The mild conditions and relatively low rainfall are attributable to the mountain massif to the west and south, which moderates the influence of the prevailing westerly and south-westerly winds.

How about the land-forms? The Moray Firth as a whole can be regarded as a drowned river system. All along the bottom of the Firth near the centre is a deep trough or channel known among fishermen as the Trink—meaning 'the trench'. Where the bottom is not rocky this hollow is about half a mile wide and sinks to a depth of 15 fathoms below the ordinary sea-bed. It is thought to mark the course of a large river which in the Pleistocene era, when Britain was united to the Continent, must have had its origin in the Beauly River.

After receiving all the present rivers of the firth—the Wick and Berriedale from Caithness, the Helmsdale and Brora from Sutherland, the Oykell and Alness and Allt Grand and Conon from Ross, the Ness from Inverness, the Nairn, the Findhorn, the Spey and the Deveron from the southern shores of the Firth—as tributaries, this enormous stream flowed north-westwards to join the Atlantic beyond the Shetland Islands.

When the sea advanced to form the present outer Moray Firth the softer rocks of the Old Red Sandstone at its hinge weathered down to form the swampy lowlands at the foot of the Highland Edge, and large portions of the tributary valleys themselves became tributary firths: the Beauly, Cromarty and Dornoch Firths, each with their distinctive beauties, but Cromarty, stemming from the mighty River Conon, deeper than the others, and so the natural magnet for industries dependent on deep-water carriers and tankers.

At some periods the 'drowning' of the Moray Firth water-ways was much more extensive than it is today, hence the manifold traces of raised beaches which delight the geologists. Another feature, calculated to rouse images of a terrestrial cataclysm can be seen by taking a ruler to the map and running it along the coast of the Black Isle peninsula from North Kessock opposite Inverness to its northern tip at the South Sutor of Cromarty, and, then, leaping over the narrow strait to the North Sutor, along the coast of the Easter Ross peninsula to Tarbatness. This whole line of coast, for the most part fringed by cliffs or by narrow beaches in front of terraced hills, can be seen to be in exact alignment with the Great Highland Fault farther south which slices through the Highlands from Inverness to the Firth of Lorne and contains the Caledonian Canal. One theory is that it was caused by a mighty dextral wrench.

Basing their plan for new settlements on the lie of the land, the authors of the Holmes Report were guided by two principles which they called the Window Concept and Travel-to-work. There was really nothing new about this. Hard economic necessities had imposed both these principles on Moray Firth communities in the past. Only now they were to be applied, of free choice, to industrial communities of quite a different kind, and as a means towards a gracious and pleasing way of life.

# CHAPTER II

# THE INHERITANCE

BEFORE man had reached the shores of the Moray Firth nature had provided a dramatic stage for his operations. The name 'Moray' itself, which appears first in the Pictish Chronicle, seems to mean simply 'beside the sea'. To the Vikings it·was Breidafiord—the Broad Firth. What it was called by those first men who came and sheltered in caves, as at Inchnadamph, before the Great Ice had departed, no man can tell, but they, as much as the German observer Kurt Wittig in our own day, must have been impressed by the landscape of the far north of Scotland, "where the strange mountains rise so abruptly out of the waiting moors, lying there like animals watching you".

These weird heights of Caithness and Sutherland are carved out of the Moine schist of the very ancient bedrock that dominates the whole country north of the Great Glen, but nearer the coast to which they form the spectacular backdrop the northern and western two-thirds of the Firth are fringed by a shelf of the Old Red Sandstone. This gives way along the eastern flank to Dalradian rocks in long sections of cliffed plateau. Originally they were clays, sands and limestones but as a result of metamorphism they have been converted into slates, phyllites, schists, gneisses and quartzites.

Broadly speaking, the two outer wings of the Firth are guarded by long sequences of hard and spectacular cliffs ranging from 100 to 300 feet in height. In striking contrast is the 'soft centre'. This, all the way from Golspie to Portgordon, consists of sand and shingle spits and barriers, extensive sandy forelands and sandy marshes with often whole series of raised beaches and, some way inland, the line of former cliffs cut in the shingle of a former beach.

Once cleared, drained and cultivated, the low-lying Old Red Sandstone lands of the Firth, in Caithness, Easter Ross and the Laich of Moray, became a miracle of fertility—save immediately along the coast itself where glacial detritus had accumulated and overlaid the fertile soil and in the form of blown sand and unstable dune formations could lead to 'little deserts' like that of Culbin.

Between the Old and the New Stone Ages the Mesolithic hunters and squatters, who were the first men to populate Scotland, certainly penetrated the Moray Firth countryside, probably about 4000 BC. A Mesolithic settlement was identified at Keiss in Caithness by Laing and Huxley last century. But these food-gatherers could never have been present in large numbers. It is with the arrival of the Neolithic people, the first farmers, that the whole area became dotted with their mysterious monuments—the chambered tombs.

The Moray Firth seems to have drawn the chambered tomb builders like a magnet. Three great groups of these mysterious structures are distinguished—the Orkney-Cromarty group, by far the largest, the Clava group and the Long Cairn group found mainly in the east—in Aberdeenshire and Banffshire. Modern research seems to suggest that the Neolithic settlers who brought the religion of the chambered tomb with them entered Scotland from the west, for the earliest and most primitive varieties of these structures—which however were widespread throughout Western Europe—are found around the shores of the Irish Sea. At a comparatively early period they had reached the northern shores of the Moray Firth.

Caithness has 67 chambered tomb sites; in Sutherland 58 have been identified; while Ross-shire has 42. Inverness-shire has over 50, and 6 have been identified in Nairnshire. No tally seems to be available for Moray. Four phases, beginning with the fourth millennium BC, have been distinguished in the long story of the chambered tomb in Scotland. New forms of elaboration were devised as time passed and the characteristic form in Caithness takes its name from Camster in which a roughly oval chamber is divided into three sections divided by two pairs of orthostats (large upright stones).

Chambered tombs are essentially rooms formed by dry masonry in which successive burials took place. They were sealed off but could be reopened for additional interments and it has been shown that long and elaborate ceremonies took place on these occasions. An important innovation attributed to the second phase of the chambered tomb era, around 3000 BC, was the building of passage graves in which the approach to the tomb took the form of a long stone-built passage. Where the burial chamber is encircled by a ring of stones or stone circle it is known as a ring cairn.

Around 2860 BC, it is believed, long cairns, very large and massive mounds of loose stones, began to be imposed on chambered tombs, perhaps by an entirely new race of incomers to the country, but while some long cairns were built up around tombs others do not appear to have burial chambers within them at all. Long cairns of this type are found on the eastern flank of the Moray Firth—at Longmanhill and at Hill of Foulzie near Macduff, at Tarrieclerack near Buckie and at Cairncatto in Buchan.

But by far the most spectacular and interesting evidence of the religion of the dead which gave rise to the chambered tombs around the Moray Firth is provided by the Clava group, largely concentrated in the inner hinge of the Firth and its tributary river valleys, the Beauly, the Ness and the Nairn. The group takes its name from the Clava Cemetery a little over a mile to the south of the battlefield of Culloden, deep in the valley of the Nairn River.

In this valley no fewer than twenty-five stone circles have been found and eight of them are within a distance of a mile on the plain of Clava. Now that the very late date of the group seems to be established, it is thought that it represents a coming together, a coalescence of three originally quite separate cultures.

Another age dawned over the Firth about 600 BC. The climate turned cooler and wetter. Celtic Iron Age immigrants arrived. Petty wars became endemic and brought with them those unique fortified tenements, the brochs.

The northern half of the Moray Firth coastline and its immediate hinterland, from Duncansby Head to Golspie, is thickly sprinkled with the shattered remnants of these amazing towers, originally 40 feet high, cylindrical in form, with walls 15 feet thick at the base, enclosing a central open courtyard 30 feet in diameter. In Caithness alone there are around 150 of them and they continue more sporadically southward in Sutherland. The outside walls are smooth and tapered near the base becoming vertical near the top, while inside there are galleries and corbelled mural chambers where no doubt the inhabitants stored their treasures or slept. In the courtyards were fresh-water wells, fireplaces and drainage systems, confirming the notion that brochs were the multi-storey flats of the Iron Age. The Pictish Dark Age that followed is an age illuminated only by the wonderful efflorescence of Pictish art in sculptured stones. These fall into three classes: first, incised symbols on roughly dressed boulders, then symbols carved in relief on more carefully dressed stones and accompanied by the Christian cross, and finally in Stage Three, the Celtic cross alone. All three forms are found along the Moray Firth but before Stage Three was reached the brief early Christian era had been sorely threatened and in some areas overwhelmed by Viking raids.

Nevertheless the cross slabs in some areas of the Firth are among the finest anywhere in the country. There were three magnificent specimens in the Easter Ross peninsula—at Nigg (almost within a stone's throw of the North Sea oil platform site), at Hilton of Cadboll and at Shandwick, while on the other side of the Firth, within half a mile of Forres stands the Sueno Stone—23 feet in height, bearing its cavalcades of horsemen and ranks of infantry and a finely enriched cross.

It is the fashion to date the conversion of the Picts to Christianity from the visit of St Columba to King Brude MacMaelchon in 564 at Inverness. But it has been pointed out that this famous visit, despite the colourful legends that cluster around it, may well have been more diplomatic and political than missionary. St Moluag from Lismore, St Maelrubbha from Applecross and that remarkable constellation of saints, Drostan and his disciples Colm, Medan and Fergus, have left their names plentifully sprinkled on early church sites on both sides of the Moray Firth, which they crossed from Caithness to Buchan to found the Celtic Abbey of Deer.

If the fortunes of war on the southern shores of the Firth swayed to and fro in the years of Viking pressure, on the northern shores the matter was settled once and for all by outright conquest. In AD 875 the Norse Earl of Orkney Sigurd I, and Thorstein the Red occupied the whole of Caithness and Sutherland down to the Oykell River and they remained a Norse province for 350 years. This situation in which the fertile lands of Moray became a buffer state between the Norse power in the north and the growing unity of the Scottish kingdom south of the Great Glen and the mountain barrier of the Mounth and the Cairngorms, had dramatic consequences.

The necessity of strengthening local defences against the Norse incursions resulted in the emergence of a semi-independent kingdom, the Province of Moray extending from the Dornoch Firth to the Spey and upper Banffshire. Time and again the Men of Moray as they were called produced rival claimants to the Scottish throne and their pretensions had to be put down by force. Dynastic complexities added to the confusion for the Mormaers of Moray were as often as not the representatives of alternative lines of succession. This was certainly the case in the well-known instance of Macbeth. By his wife Gruoch he inherited a claim to the Scottish throne and an undying grudge against King Duncan, who had slain Gruoch's brother to establish his own position.

Having made himself indispensable to King Duncan as the successful captain of his hosts against the Danes (who were now competing with the Norse for what they could grab of eastern Scotland), Macbeth used his power to bring about his sovereign's death at Bothgowan, near Elgin, on 14 August 1040. But the price of Macbeth's triumph was a working alliance with the most potent of the Norse earls of Orkney and Caithness, Thorfinn the Mighty.

Macbeth was very far from being the melancholy and sinister figure depicted in Shakespeare's play. He was a great king "renowned alike for his piety, ability to govern and his skill and valour in the field". But in 1057 destiny caught up with him in the shape of Malcolm Canmore who overtook and slew him at Lumphanan and established the dynasty which achieved the final unification of Scotland with the aid of Norman feudalism. It was of course a gradual process.

Probably to help in consolidating his position Malcolm married Thorfinn's widow, Ingebjorg, herself of high Norse blood, but this lady died in a few years and left him free to woo and marry Margaret of England, sister of Prince Eadgar, who after challenging William the Conqueror in an abortive rising had been shipwrecked with his kin and followers at St

Margaret's Hope, near Dunfermline—then virtually the Scottish capital.

The effect of St Margaret's influence—for she became the patron saint of the united Scotland—was, in the long run, to carry the country into the European Catholic tradition and to confirm Norman feudalism as its system of government. Against this irresistible trend the Men of Moray fought in vain for nearly two centuries more, and in the end were swept from the stage of history at the same moment as the Norse influence on their northern flank finally came to its end.

Malcolm Canmore, after slaying Macbeth's heir Lulach the Fatuous at Essie in Strathbogie in March 1058, did not return to the north of his kingdom until twenty years later when a rebellion in Moray compelled him to assert his authority there. His successor Alexander I (1107-24) established the Bishopric of Moray with the consent of the Mormaers who still ruled over the province as a semi-independent territory. It stretched in those days almost from sea to sea, including a vast area of the Highlands which afterwards became detached from it as the earldom of Ross. The earliest see of the diocese was at Birnie, where a fine Norman parish church, the only one in the whole region, still survives.

In 1130 when Alexander's son David I was absent in England, Angus Mormaer of Moray and grandson of Lulach, with his brother Malcolm, Earl of Ross, rose in arms against him and marched as far south as Stracathro in Angus where his army of 5000 was soundly defeated by Edward, Constable of Scotland.

Gradually, as the Canmore kings in successive reigns carried out the policy of drastic resettlement of the country, known as the Plantation of Moray, the seat of disaffection moved more and more to the west and north. In 1181 in the reign of William the Lion a new revolt was launched by Donald Bane MacWilliam, a descendant of Ingebjorg, with headquarters at Inverness. He was slain in battle but in 1211 his son Guttred occupied Ross and there were two more MacWilliam revolts in 1215 and 1228, in the latter of which Inverness was burned.

Details are tedious, but it is interesting to note how the Plantation of Moray appeared to one of the chroniclers.

"At this time", he says,

the rebel nation of the Moravienses . . . would for neither prayers
nor bribes, neither treaties nor raids leave off their disloyal ways
or their ravages among their fellow-countrymen. So having
gathered together a huge army the King removed them all from
the land of their birth—as of old Nebuchadnezzar had dealt with
the Jews—and scattered them throughout the other districts of
Scotland . . . so that not even one native of that land abode there,
and he installed there his own peaceful people.

While no trace—with the possible exception of the sculptured stones—remains of the old Celtic Moray which the
Plantation extirpated, the great landmarks of the resettlement
are with us today. It involved the establishment of royal
castles at Banff, Elgin, Nairn, Blervie (near Forres), Redcastle
(in the Black Isle) and Dunskaith (in Easter Ross). Duffus
Castle, at first a royal stronghold and then the capital mes-
suage of the great family of Freskin de Moravia, gives today
a better idea of what these early motte and bailey structures
were like. It had originally been a timber tower on the top of
a low hill surrounded by a moat enclosing an artificial island
nearly ten acres in extent and with a bailey or subsidiary
courtyard, an acre in extent, defended by a wall 15 feet high.
At some later time, probably in the fourteenth century, the
timber tower was replaced by one of stone, three storeys high.
But the weight of this immense mass proved too great for the
foundation and the whole of the north-west corner slid away
in the most dramatic manner. These ruins, dominating a great
extent of the Laich north of Elgin, are today cared for by the
Department of the Environment.

Bolstering the civil power which carried out the Plantation
were the religious foundations. In 1125 the small priory of
Urquhart was settled by Benedictine monks from Canterbury.
In 1150 Kinloss Abbey was established by King David I for
Cistercians from Melrose. But the most spectacular developments had to wait till the first half of the next century, when
under Alexander II the whole of the north of Scotland was
pacified and reorganized.

This final pacification involved not merely the scotching of
the MacWilliam rebellions but the expulsion of the Norse
earls of Orkney from the mainland. Once the Norse power
had extended as far south as Dingwall but in the twelfth

century their influence upon events in Caithness became increasingly sporadic and tenuous. In 1201 when Earl Harald Maddadson landed at Scrabster to impose his will on the people of Thurso, who had given their allegiance to the Scottish King William, John, second Bishop of Caithness, went to intercede between them. Lomberd, one of Harald's followers, promptly cut out the Bishop's tongue while the Norse Earl overran the county.

King William came to Caithness with an army and confronted Harald's forces at Ousdale. Realizing that discretion was the better part of valour Harald now sued for peace and got off with a fine. But the next outrage was not passed over so lightly.

In 1222 Bishop John's successor, Bishop Adam, was barbarously put to death in his palace at Halkirk. He had exacted an unpopular tax on butter and when some malcontents complained of this to the Norse Earl, now Harald Maddadson's son John, he remarked: "The devil take the bishop and his butter. You may roast him if you please!"

The aggrieved tithe-payers took this as a licence to demonstrate their defiance and 300 tenants, led by two sons of Simon Harbister from Harpsdale, set fire to the episcopal residence and burned it to the ground—with the Bishop inside. The Pope was appalled to hear of this barbarity and the Scots king, Alexander II, took prompt and ruthless action. According to the Orkneyinga Saga he "caused the hands and feet to be hewn from eighty men who had been present at the burning so that many of them died".

Earl John, whose casual remark had led to the burning of the Bishop, was himself murdered in a Thurso cellar by a band of outlaws from Orkney in the year 1231 and with his death all Norse pretence to succession to the Orkney earldom was effectively at an end. This event preceded the shattering Norse defeat at Largs by thirty-two years, so that while the Norse overlordship continued in the Western Isles till then, and in Orkney itself until 1455, where Scots held the earldom as vassals of the Norwegian kings, their hold in the mainland had been eliminated for ever.

Bishop Adam was succeeded by Gilbert de Moravia, whom Alexander II created his treasurer in the north, and whose power was virtually absolute throughout the entire Moray

Firth area. As Bishop of Caithness he removed the see from Halkirk to Dornoch. At the same time his relative Andrew de Moravia, appointed Bishop of Moray, was entrusted with the building of Elgin Cathedral, and Gilbert himself performed the act of consecration on 19 July 1224.

The next two decades saw a further proliferation of religious foundations. The Valliscaulian Priory of Pluscarden was founded six miles to the south-west of Elgin. Its foundation charter was granted by Alexander II in 1236 and the oldest work in the transepts and lady chapel, which strongly recall the contemporary portions of Elgin Cathedral, must date from this period. Another Valliscaulian Priory was established by Sir John Bisset of Lovat in 1232 at Beauly. Dominican convents were set up at Elgin and Inverness in 1233. Between the diocese of Moray and the diocese of Caithness lay the newly created diocese of Ross where in 1235, in a lovely corner of the Black Isle, the cathedral of Fortrose superseded the ancient chapel of St Moluag at Rosemarkie.

The significance of this train of events has been finely summed up by R. G. Cant. In Moray, he says,

> the key struggle for the allegiance of Scotland—between Celtic conservatism and medieval progress was fought out .... At the time the process must have caused intense misery to many people; worse, it must have seemed to involve a disastrous betrayal of native traditions and native interests. But in the long run it meant that Moray received the benefits of medieval civilisation—law and order, religion and culture, trade and agriculture—almost as fully as anywhere in Western Europe. And in due course the new order of society took roots, acquired an indigenous character, so much so that within a century and a half, Moray under its new leaders, was to form the main centre of Scottish national resistance to absorption in the English kingdom from which so many of these new leaders' own ancestors had originally come.

Mention has already been made of the great family of Freskin de Moravia. His descendants Gilbert and Andrew de Moravia were the bishops who presided over the foundation of Elgin Cathedral. At the end of that century another Andrew de Moravia, better known as Andrew Murray, became a partner with William Wallace in the first Scottish victories in the War of Independence.

Although it emerged well from the Wars of Independence, Moray suffered during the reigns of the early Stuart kings from the peculiar plague represented by the "overmighty subject". In 1390, Alexander Stewart, son of Robert II, irked by the Bishop of Moray's anathema against him for deserting his legitimate wife, Euphame, Countess of Ross, and cohabiting with his mistress Mariota de Athyn (by whom he had five sons), descended from his mountain fastness, the Castle of Lochindorb, in Brae Moray, and burned and sacked the towns of Forres and Elgin, giving Elgin Cathedral to the flames.

The lurid story is told in Sir Thomas Dick Lauder's novel *The Wolf of Badenoch*—Stewart being Earl of Buchan and Lord of Badenoch. By an irony of history a second Alexander Stewart, the illegitimate son of the Wolf of Badenoch, appeared in the role of defender of the low country from the ravages of Donald, Lord of the Isles, whom he halted at the Battle of Harlaw in 1411.

More trouble came in the mid-fifteenth century from the mighty family of Douglas who had inherited the Earldom of Moray and were in life-or-death conflict with the monarchy. By a superhuman effort King James II overcame and obliterated the House of Douglas and annexed the earldom of Moray to the Crown.

Compared to other parts of Scotland the Reformation and the Wars of the Covenant in the seventeenth century passed over the Moray Firth with relatively little skaith. True, armies moved across the area; battles were fought, as at Auldearn (1644) and Carbisdale (1650), but on the whole there was little participation by the men of Moray and little disturbance of its daily life. At this period the people of the Laich were moving in advance of the general trend of developments in Scotland, preoccupying themselves not with politics and religion but with economics and social betterment.

The merchants and burghers of Elgin were embellishing the town with its superb arcaded street architecture. Cromarty was enjoying its golden age and trading ports were being developed at Findhorn, Burghead and Lossiemouth, where in 1698 the magistrates of Elgin set up their harbour at the mouth of the Lossie. The same tale of non-involvement could be told of the Jacobite conflicts in the first half of the eighteenth century although both the Young Pretender and 'Butcher' Cumberland hurried across the region to the final confrontation at Culloden, the last great battle on British soil.

The pace of economic advance accelerated spectacularly in the decade of the 1760s though it had been under way long before that. In 1728, for example, the York Buildings Company purchased standing timber on Speyside, most of which was sold in London. Later in the century the Duke of Gordon sold trees in the Rothiemurchus forest to two wood merchants, Osbourne of Hull and Dodsworth of York, for £10,000. The timber was assembled in Loch Morlich and floated down the Rivers Luineag and Druie to the Spey and thence to the coast, where the logs were sawn up at a new settlement called Kingston (from Kingston-on-Hull) and a shipbuilding industry was created. This was also a great age of tree-planting. All along the Firth from Banffshire (where in mid-century the Earl of Findlater planted his estates round Cullen) through Moray (where the Earl of Moray created the forest of Darnaway) to Ross-shire (where the forestry pioneers were Sir William Gordon and his son), the hitherto naked moors and hill slopes were converted into flourishing plantations.

Meanwhile throughout the lowlands around the Firth, and particularly in the Laich of Moray itself, farming was becoming diversified. The main cereal crop had always been oats but now barley was being grown in quantity and wheat was soon extensively sown. By this time Moray was famous as the granary of Scotland. Crops were heavy and every year surplus oats were exported to the Highlands, to the central belt of Scotland and even to London.

Moray was always conscious that its good fortune was conditional, that it lay like a jewel inspiring the envy of the wild men from the hills in the west and the hungry pastoralists in its own upland hinterland. When Isaac Forsyth came to publish a *Survey of the Province of Moray* in 1798 he gave a lurid account of the Seven Ill Years in the 1690s which left a mark on men's memories that was passed on from generation to generation.

"Agriculture", he wrote,
fell so low by the end of the last century as to be wholly unable

to withstand the seven unfavourable seasons when these took place. In the higher parts of the country the practice of agriculture was in that short period wholly abandoned. Thousands of people, leaving their homes, perished in the highways and streets through insupportable hunger. The magistrates of Elgin established a police for burying in every dismal morning the bodies of those miserable wretches that had fallen a prey to the famine under the piazzas in the course of each melancholy night.

After Culloden the clan system which had prevailed in the Highlands for four centuries was destroyed. It was in its beginnings an adaptation of Norman feudalism to the peculiar economic situation in the remote mountainous country where pastoralism and the pursuit of game was along with fishing the only source of human sustenance. Clans were not 'tribes'. They were associations of fighting men under a chief whose territories fluctuated depending on the chief's ability to hold land, either legally as a feudal vassal of the king, or illegally by the strength of his own armed prowess in face of other legal claims. Once a chief had become established in a certain area elaborate genealogies were usually devised for him tending to demonstrate ancient lineage and long traditional rights of possession, but his power depended on the number and fighting qualities of his followers or clansmen.

This can be demonstrated over and over again in the story of the clans who flourished and declined on the Highland frontiers of the Moray Firth. They included the Campbells of Cawdor, the MacKenzies of Seaforth, the Grants of Strathspey, the Frasers of Lovat, the Macphersons of Cluny, the Munros of Foulis, the Rosses and the Mackintoshes and the MacKays. Virtually all of these clan chiefs, as their fortunes rose, came to have substantial landholdings on the fertile lowlands fringing the Firth.

About 1724 it was estimated that the various clans on the borders of the Moray Firth could command fighting men in the following proportions: MacKenzies 2,500; Grants 800; Mackintoshes 800; Frasers 900; MacKays 800; Munros 350; and Rosses 500.

The danger of the existence of these small standing armies became glaringly apparent in the two Jacobite Rebellions.

After Culloden the government took measures to disarm the clans and destroy the military power of their chiefs. Those who had refrained from attacking the Hanoverian regime were left in possession of their lands, but shorn of their 'heritable jurisdictions' they became landowners pure and simple. The clansmen or followers of the chiefs became merely tenants or squatters. Whereas it had been policy on the part of the chiefs to attract large numbers of fighting men to their territories and offer them small parcels of land or other means of subsistence, so long as their presence had a power-and-status value, only sentiment remained after the Disarming Act. And sentiment did not prove strong enough to perpetuate a hopelessly out-dated and inefficient economy.

Once content to remain in their Highland territories lording it over their clansmen the chiefs sought the distractions of court life in London or high society in Edinburgh. They sent their sons to be educated in English public schools and to make the Grand Tour of Europe. They began to look to their rent-rolls to support this altered way of life and they discovered that bigger rents could be obtained from their straths and glens by converting them from over-crowded peasant holdings, rearing diminutive black cattle into great empty sheep-walks pasturing vast flocks of Cheviot sheep imported from the Borders.

This was the origin of the movement known as the Highland Clearances which had such a tragic impact not only upon remote glens but also upon the Moray Firth as a whole. From it arose the lamentations of a whole people. Looking back upon the days when their services were valued, the descendants of the clansmen could see the past, not as it actually happened but as they fondly imagined it. They had been taught to consider themselves as the 'kindred' and the 'children' of their chiefs. They had been taught to see themselves as the descendants of 'conquerors' who had won an inalienable right to the land in which they were settled. To them the rebuke of the Canadian Boat Song was well merited:

We ne'er shall tread the fancy-haunted valley,
  Where 'tween the dark hills creeps the small clear stream,
In arms around the patriarch banner rally,
  Nor see the moon on royal tombstones gleam.

When the bold kindred, in the time long vanish'd,
  Conquered the soil and fortified the keep,—
No seer foretold the children would be banish'd
  That a degenerate lord might boast his sheep.


By no means all the chiefs were 'degenerate lords' in this
sense. Many of them ruined themselves in the effort to
maintain the old economy and to provide for the poverty-
stricken peasants in the overcrowded glens. Strenuous efforts
were made to introduce 'second strings' of auxiliary industry
to supplement the living of settlers whose pitiful holdings were
incapable of sustaining the growing population no longer
thinned out by war and rapine.

The Forfeited Estates Commissioners had a vision of fostering a great home-based linen industry. Spinning schools
were to be set up in numerous centres. Alexander Shaw, a
merchant in Inverness, in one year (1766) bought 17,854
pounds of flax and sold 4,582 spindles of yarn, distributed 173
spinning wheels and claimed to have taught 174 girls. Two
years later he reported that spinning was "spreading over the
Highlands very fast", while Lord Kames declared that there
were "more than enough spinners for all flax that probably
will be raised in Scotland for many years to come". Duncan
Grant of Forres, another merchant manufacturer, employed
spinners in Strathspey, Badenoch and Strathdown.

This was only one of the great white hopes entertained for
keeping the families of the now unemployed warriors of the
Highland fringe on their native heath, but by the time Boswell and Johnson toured the region in 1773 the great tide of
voluntary emigration had set in and soon the Highland
Clearances were to empty the glens not by voluntary
emigration but by rude force.

Parallel with, and in some sense consequent upon, the
Highland Clearances, there arose two great and characteristic
industries of the Moray Firth, herring fishing and malt distilling, which were to greatly change the physical appearance
both of coast and of hinterland. Another more delayed consequence of the Clearances was the transfer of large numbers
of the peasant population from one flank of the Firth to the
other—from the north-west to the south-east. And along with
this went a revolution in the means of communication: the

making of the 'new ways through the glens', the great inland
waterway of the Caledonian Canal, the new post roads and
turnpike roads, and ultimately the railways.

When this revolution was completed in the second half of
the nineteenth century the sheep-based economy of the
Highlands had already given way to the even more
depopulating economy of deer forests and game preserves. A
pattern had been set which was to persist well into the present
century, when it was patently in decline, and new industry
and a new system of communications had to be invoked to
revitalize a countryside that was feeling the chill of death.

From a very early period small white-fishing communities
had dotted the coastline of the Firth, a few men and boats
operating in a small way from virtually every creek and inlet.
They dwelt in cottages and small crofts made available to
them by the landowners, who also provided small capital
grants for boats and gear and exacted in return a share of the
catch, sometimes disproportionate to the hard toil and servi-
tude endured by the fishermen.

But the herring industry when at last it was organized
effectively in the early years of the nineteenth century im-
pinged upon the ancient semi-feudal system, which held the
white-fisher in its grip, with the force of an earthquake.
Equipped with larger boats to pursue the herring shoals, joined
by other seamen from distant ports, offered tempting contracts
by curers in advance of the catch, the more adventurous local
fishermen experienced a great widening of horizons and the
opportunity of amassing capital of their own for the first time.

This chance of new-found wealth came all the more
dramatically to the fishing havens that had been created on
the coasts of Caithness and Sutherland to rehouse the dispos-
sessed peasants from the glens in the interior, evicted through
the Clearances.

This is the theme of Neil Gunn's novel *The Silver Darlings,*
a brief quotation from which may indicate the atmosphere
that prevailed around 1813:

In a moment the latest news of the rise of the fisheries was
flowing like a torrent. "The Moray Firth is burning, from
Fraserburgh, along the whole south coast, Macduff, Banff,
Buckie, Lossiemouth, Brochhead and a score of villages besides.

We've got to go ahead. No half measures now. The money will
be flowing like the river. As one man said in Wick: the creels of
silver herring will turn into creels of silver crowns."

It was in fact the ancient royal burgh of Wick that had
been the prime pioneer of the herring boom. Scotland's po-
tentiality as a base for herring fishing was apparent in the late
eighteenth century when between 1787 and 1797 there were
2,049 vessels fitted out for the herring fisheries in Scotland,
with 33,606 men—as compared with 55 vessels and a mere 701
men in England.

By the 1790s Wick was exporting well over 12,000 barrels
of herring a year, despite the fact that there was only a natural
harbour suitable for very small boats and the bulk of the
herring catchers were amateurs. How amateur is explained by
the Old Statistical Account of 1793:

> There are hardly any real fishermen. Such however is the desire
> of gain that pervades all sorts of tradesmen here that they betake
> themselves to the herring fishing when they think it likely to
> turn to better account than their own peculiar business. Weavers,
> tailors, shoemakers, house and boat carpenters, blacksmiths,
> masons, etc., in this and neighbouring parishes, repair to the
> fishing boats, go to sea in the night, the only time for catching
> herrings, and spend all the day in sleep . . .

The British Fisheries Society, a semi-government agency,
now stepped in, built a proper harbour and a 'new town'
called Poultneytown after one of the Society's directors, and
the herring catch rose from 12,000 to nearly 200,000 barrels
per annum. The indigenous population of 2,000 was swollen
by 7,000 at the height of the season, including crews from
Norway, Holland, France, Cornwall and Ireland.

The progress of the herring boom throughout the Moray
Firth as a whole can be traced by the fact that gutting and
curing yards were opened at Fraserburgh in 1810, Helmsdale
in 1813, Macduff, Banff, Portsoy, and Cullen in 1815,
Burghead in 1817, Lossiemouth in 1819, Peterhead in 1820
and Lybster in 1830.

The malt whisky distilling industry so largely concentrated
in the counties of Banff and Moray on the southern shores of
the Firth had an origin even more romantic in its way than
the birth of the nineteenth-century herring boom. From the

The big float-out on 16 August 1974 as Highland One, the first of three oil production platforms designed for B.P.'s Forties Field, is launched from the yard at Nigg Bay. In the foreground is the town of Cromarty with hundreds of cars lining the grassy foreshore.

Tin-hatted workers from the Nigg yard stream ashore at the jetty at Cromarty after completing a shift at the fabrication yard.

Tourists explore the passage graves in the Clava chambered tombs.

Inverness: *above* at dusk, like a Paris of the north. Looking down the river towards the Inner Moray Firth from the Castle Hill; *below* the castle and, left, the Bridge Street shopping complex and Bridge House, the H.Q. of the Highlands and Islands Development Board.

Elgin: the great western towers of the cathedral.

Wick: the fishing harbour.

The foreshore at Cairnbulg on the extreme south-eastern tip of the
Moray Firth.

Kinnaird Head, Fraserburgh. The lighthouse was built as a castle in 1569. The top storey was removed in 1787 and replaced by the lantern chamber. In front of the lighthouse can be seen the Wine Tower dating from the first quarter of the sixteenth century.

In the Great Hall of Cairnbulg Castle. Above the fireplace is a portrait of Mary Queen of Scots.

Rosehearty: detail from the Pitsligo Aisle with its Jacobean Scottish carved woodwork.

The village of Pennan under its soaring green cliffs. It is a designated conservation area.

Banff: Mr and Mrs Raymond Harrow in the courtyard of their home at No. 1 High Shore, a little castle in the heart of the town.

Middle Ages whisky had been the 'water of life' in the Highlands but a succession of mistaken and wrong-headed Acts of Parliament ensured that Highland malts would achieve a pre-eminence which put them in the forefront.

By the second decade of the nineteenth century this legislation, which encouraged legal distilleries to sacrifice quality to quantity, had resulted in the connoisseurs of the drink giving preference every time to the products of the illicit "small stills" in the Highlands, particularly those which flourished in Glenlivet in upper Banffshire, where around 200 small farmers or crofters had been making illicit Scotch for decades.

So constructed that they could be easily hidden from the gaugers or customs officers, these "sma' stills" as they were called produced a spirit so obviously superior to the 500 gallon stills of the large Lowland distilleries that even the king himself, in this case George IV, had to be supplied, via the cellars of Sir Peter Grant of Rothiemurchus, with the "true Glenlivet". To circumvent this Gilbertian situation the Government was at last persuaded to produce in 1825 an Act to Eliminate Illicit Distilling.

It was based on a realistic assessment of the situation by the Duke of Gordon, who in 1822 had told the House of Lords that whisky was the national and traditional drink of the Highlands, that the Highlander could not be prevented from distilling it and that it was natural for him to wish to do so. He went on to give a pledge that if realistic legislation was passed, providing an opportunity for the legal distilling of whisky of as good quality as that produced by the illicit stills, he and the other landed proprietors in the Highlands would do their utmost to suppress illegal distilling and to encourage their tenants to license their stills.

The new Act accordingly fixed a flat licence rate of £10 for stills of 40 gallons capacity upwards, thus setting a minimum of 40 gallons in place of the totally unrealistic 500 gallons of the previous Act of 1814, which had merely intensified the long-persisting smuggling traffic in remote glens. Before the Act was on the statute book, one of the duke's tenants, George Smith of Drumin in Glenlivet, had begun building a new distillery on the site where an illicit still had formerly operated and became the first man to take out a licence.

Smith's priority in the legal distilling of whisky in Glenlivet was vindicated by the High Court in Edinburgh in 1880 when the product of the distillery he founded became the only whisky entitled to call itself 'The Glenlivet'. But other whiskies may use the name provided it is prefixed by another name, as in Glen Grant-Glenlivet, Glenfarclas Glenlivet, Longmorn-Glenlivet and so on. Twenty-three other distilleries availed themselves of the honour, some of them twenty miles distant. The area south of the Moray Firth coast between the Findhorn and Deveron rivers contains the great bulk of the malt distilleries in Scotland, though they continue to be sprinkled along the coast of the Firth as far north as Wick. There are over 100 and their numbers are still increasing.

Although whisky is the fifth largest employer of labour in manufacturing in Scotland, distilling is not a labour-intensive industry. It remains a rural industry, the distinctive pagoda-like towers which indicate its presence being set down in moorlands, glens and small towns, yet its economic importance as a dollar-earner is immense. It is exported to 180 countries and the stocks of maturing whisky now stand at over 1,000 million proof gallons—enough to assuage the thirst of the Scots for over 300 years if they had to drink it all themselves.

Before we pass from the inheritance of the Moray Firth to its present-day actuality, a final word requires to be said about the bias given to its development by the exigencies of railway finance and engineering in the second half of last century. Along the southern shores of the Firth the railway system, unimpeded by great natural obstacles, followed a normal course, although today, after the ravages of the Beeching 'axe', only two main lines remain, the old Highland Railway from Inverness to Perth via the Slochd pass to Aviemore on the Spey and thence by the Drumochter pass into Perthshire, and the Aberdeen to Inverness line slanting across country via Keith and Elgin.

Although these lines had to traverse upland and mountain country, they pursued a relatively direct course taking the shortest route between two points. But it was a different story when the Highland Railway came to be constructed from Inverness northwards to Wick. As the crow flies the distance from Inverness to Wick is about 80 miles, yet because of the deep indentation of the coastline, and because the only places of any size lie on that coast, the railway had to take a route 161 miles long.

Early ideas about opening up the country were based on the notion of having a steamer service across the Moray Firth from Nairn to Nigg at the entrance to the north shore of the Cromarty Firth, from which one railway would run to Invergordon and another to Tain, each tapping the rich farming lands of the Easter Ross peninsula. If that had materialized the route to the far north would have been greatly shortened, and the major industrial developments of the present day, like the Nigg platform site and the Invergordon smelter, would have been much more accessible from Aberdeen and the east coast, but in the event, it was left to the wealthy Highland landowners, Sir Alexander Matheson of Ardross and the Duke of Sutherland, to finance the line.

The bridging of the firths and the rivers involved costly engineering works, including great viaducts and bridges: the Ness Viaduct and swing bridge over the Caledonian Canal at Clachnaharry, the massive masonry viaduct over the River Conon at Conon Bridge, the viaduct over the Kyle of Sutherland, with its five masonry arches and a girder span of 230 feet, not to mention expensive rock cuttings. Two great detours into the Highland hinterland were necessary, the first along the southern shore of the Dornoch Firth from Tain to Lairg, the second from Helmsdale up the Strath of Kildonan and across the desolate, depopulated moorland of Caithness to avoid the impossible gradients and deep chasm-defiles of the coastline beyond the Ord of Caithness.

When all this had been accomplished, Dornoch, the county town of Sutherland with its popular golf courses, was left without a rail connection, while no railway penetrated the fertile acres of the Black Isle. Branches were built from the Mound to Dornoch and from Conon Bridge to Fortrose to meet the deficiency but, like the great multiplicity of branch lines on the south side of the Firth, did not survive the Beeching era.

Today, indeed, the southern coastlands of the Moray Firth are rail-less east of Elgin, where once Lossiemouth had been served by the earliest railway in the north, and a great coastal

loop crossed the mouth of the Spey between Kingston and
Garmouth to serve Portgordon, Buckie, Findochty, Portknockie, Cullen and Portsoy to rejoin the main line to
Aberdeen at Cairnie, north of Huntly. Banff and Macduff had
been served by a branch passing through Turriff and linked
with the Aberdeen-Inverness line at Inveramsay, while
Fraserburgh was one of the two termini of the Buchan and
Fortmartine Railway which also served Peterhead and linked
up with the main line at Dyce, just north of Aberdeen. The
lower Findhorn and the Spey north of Aviemore were also
served by a vanished rail network, while Dufftown, the upper
Banffshire whisky capital, stood midway on a line linking
Keith with Craigellachie.

All these lines had of course their heyday before the motor
car became ubiquitous, but they also reflected the needs of a
countryside much more populated than it is today, a countryside where farming was a labour-intensive industry, where
grain for the distilleries and fish for the southern markets
inevitably travelled by rail. The reawakening in the Highlands
and the industrial boom in the inner Moray Firth has come
just in time to reprieve the railway system north of Inverness
and to reopen closed stations like Alness and Muir of Ord.

At the same time it has overloaded the existing roads and
necessitated a reorientation of the line of communications to
the north. The old A9 from Inverness to Invergordon, which
followed the same route as the Highland Railway, skirting the
inner tips of the Beauly and Cromarty Firths, will be bypassed
by a new major trunk road which will leap across the Inner
Moray Firth to North Kessock opposite Inverness, slice across
the heart of the Black Isle and cross the Cromarty Firth by a
causeway to Evanton, several miles north of Dingwall. Farther
north still, there is the prospect that the trunk road to the far
north will be spectacularly shortened by a new bridge at the
entrance to the Dornoch Firth, linking Tain and Dornoch
directly in place of the present long detour via Ardgay and
Bonar Bridge. Destiny has reshaken the multi-coloured pieces
in the kaleidoscope and a new pattern with sharper, cleaner
lines is emerging.

# CHAPTER III

# THE THREE CAPITALS

FROM WHICH base should one begin to sample the attractions of the Moray Firth? A very good case could be made out for starting outside the region altogether with the city of Aberdeen, the only really large town in Scotland north of the mountain barrier which insulates the Firth from the main body of Lowland Scotland. In that way one would have the advantage of a gradual approach to its peculiar atmosphere and charm, an approach sharpened by contrast with long miles of rugged rolling uplands, undramatic and often treeless, and redeemed only from stony wilderness by centuries of strenuous peasant toil.

Nothing in fact can be so exhilarating as to climb up over the spartan uplands of Aberdeenshire or Banffshire till one reaches the windswept plateau overlooking the cliffed coast somewhere between Fraserburgh and Cullen, and then to descend to sandy coves between the rocks, at Aberdour perhaps, or Sandend, or Tarlair where a breeze from the north-west is ruffling the manes of the waves' white horses while, on a really good day, the thin blue line of the Sutherland hills is faintly visible on the water's far horizon.

This is what the Moray Firth means to the Buchan farmers to whom its mellower influence is like a touch of holiday heaven. In one of the classics of Aberdeenshire's local literature, William Alexander's *Johnny Gibb of Gushetneuk*, there is a description of a family picnic early in the nineteenth century when in the midst of a midsummer lull in endlessly toilsome farming operations, the farmer loaded up a cart and crossed the hump of land that normally shut him off from the Firth. His feelings on sighting the Promised Land, transposed from

Alexander's salty prose into equally salty dialect verse by Flora Garry, are expressed in this pregnant stanza:

Oh, blue's the lift abeen the Firth this bonny Simmer day
An blue's the water reeshlin ower the san's on Deveron Bay.
The win' blaas saft doon Langmanhill an rare's the caller guff
O' tar an'raips an' dilse alang the sea-wynds o' Macduff.

—which can be roughly translated: "Oh blue the sky above the Firth, this lovely summer day, and blue the water rustling o'er the sands of Deveron Bay. The wind blows soft down Longmanhill and rare is the fresh smell of tar and ropes and seaweed in the steep lanes of Macduff." There is the real Moray Firth magic. Another equally exhilarating line of approach is to fly from the Aberdeen Airport at Dyce to Wick, the capital of the Firth's Viking province, Caithness in the far north. Here one has the chance of seeing, as the plane crosses the Aberdeenshire coast west of Fraserburgh, a sandy shelf extending far out to sea under the water which seems so clear that it interposes but a cloudy veil above the spotless sea-bed. Then the tumbled hills on the north shore of the Firth show their ragged edges, but only briefly, till the plane taxis in over the flat green plain to the airfield with lighthouse and ruined castle on one flank and the sprawling town and its latest industrial estate on the other.

But of all the centres from which the Firth can be approached, the most magical is the Highland Capital—

## INVERNESS

It has been called the Paris of the north, which for a town of such modest proportions may seem needlessly pretentious. What makes the analogy with Paris inevitable is the way Inverness focuses upon its majestic river, the Ness. Edinburgh, with the great leonine ridge of Arthur's Seat at one end and the Castle Rock at the other, has some claim to be the most theatrical city in Britain, if not in Europe. But it has no noble river flowing through its heart. Perth on the other hand has such a river in the Tay, but neither Perth nor Edinburgh have the mountain backdrop which adds the final touch to Inverness's magnificence of setting.

Climb up to the castle forecourt in Inverness and you have the majestic river at your feet, spanned by many bridges, fringed by delectable green hills like Tomnahurich, backed by higher hills like Craig Phadraig. Turn to the north and your horizon is bounded across the gleaming Firth by the tremendous, usually snow-tipped, knife-edge of Ben Wyvis (3429 feet). Turn west and you are facing up the Great Glen in the same attitude as the great black bronze statue of Flora Macdonald placed there in 1899. I have often wondered why the glamorous saviour of Bonnie Prince Charlie is scanning the Highland horizon with so keen a glance. But it appears that, although in this commanding situation, she is actually looking along the line of the cleft which divides Scotland from sea to sea, the sculptor, Andrew Davidson, intended to depict her 'on the watch' outside her home, Kingsburgh House in Skye, while the prince was in hiding there, and she is scanning the country for his pursuers.

Not only does Inverness have a spectacularly scenic situation which will always give it interest, it is today an organism in an exciting stage of growth. In the Middle Ages it had a population of around 2,000. By 1961 it had reached a figure of 29,508. By 1971 the dramatic upsurge consequent upon the industrialization of the Moray Firth had brought the total up to 34,670 and the Jack Holmes Group's blueprint for the future envisages it growing by another 35,000.

The results of the rapid growth in the 1961/71 decade were not to everyone's taste. An old Invernessian's survey of the changes lamented the loss of much that was old and familiar and its replacement by a series of the 'concrete boxes' that pass for modern all-purpose buildings. He regretted the disappearance of the picturesque suspension bridge in the centre of the town "which at once identified Inverness in any photograph" and its replacement by a streamlined new one "so smooth and featureless as to be not so much a bridge as a road across a river". He deplored the fact that the castle "stands reduced in scale and importance by the monstrous shop and office complex nearby".

It would be useless to deny that there is much truth in this criticism. Yet in the same decade some really admirable

restoration work took place and this can be taken as an earnest
of even better things to come.

But first let us get the existing situation in proportion.
There can be no better starting point than the castle. It is not
really a castle surviving from antiquity but a castellated
structure of the nineteenth century. Yet its site on the Castle
Hill is probably the most historic spot in the whole of the
northern Highlands. The river divides the town into two
parts. The houses stand partly in the valley and partly on a
wooded terrace 100 feet high that winds along the glen that
links Loch Ness and the inner Moray Firth at the seven-
mile-long river's mouth. The Castle Hill is a spur of this
terrace just at the point where it gives way to the flat plain of
the river's estuary. On the Castle Hill a royal castle stood from
the twelfth century, undergoing many transformations and
rebuildings until it was blown up by Prince Charles Edward
in 1746.

The ruins of the old castle gradually disappeared and were
succeeded in 1834 by the south-west part of the present
structure, built as a court house for the sheriff and assize
courts. In 1846 the north-eastern part was added to form a
prison. It was later taken over by Inverness County Council
for offices and their council chamber.

There have been various conjectures as to the probable site
of even earlier castles in Inverness. There is an Iron Age
vitrified fort on the summit of Craig Phadraig (556 feet), the
picturesque hill to the north-west of the burgh, and this was
at one time believed to be the fortress of King Brude of the
Picts, who was visited by St Columba in the second half of the
sixth century. Brude was surrounded by priests and Druids
deeply hostile to the new faith, but as Adamnan tells it, the
strong personality of Columba, more than equal to all his
opponents, triumphed, and he appears in the end to have been
accepted as the guide and counsellor of the king. It is most
unlikely, however, that the negotiations took place on the
summit of the windswept hill. Brude's residence must have
been elsewhere.

Another site on the river terrace, variously called the Auld
Castle Hill or the Crown, has been suggested as the site of
Macbeth's castle in Inverness, the place apostrophized by
Duncan in Shakespeare's play in the words:

This Castle hath a pleasant seat; the air
Nimbly and sweetly recommends itself
Unto our gentle senses.

We know now, of course, that King Duncan was not murdered here, but slain at Bothgowan near Elgin, but Invernessians have been quick to point out that the "nimble and sweet air" of their town is confirmed by its favourable climatic records.

Mention was made in the previous chapter of Donald Bane MacWilliam's revolt against William the Lion in 1181. It was as a result of this that the king established a castle on the Castle Hill of Inverness and during his reign he gave four charters to the burgh. The first, a tiny parchment, beautifully written and well preserved, was lost for several years but recovered through a private collector who bought it with other documents at a sale.

In 1312 King Robert the Bruce held a parliament at Inverness which was attended by envoys from Norway and at which various matters in dispute between the two kingdoms were settled. Between 1380 and 1500 Inverness was burned and sacked no fewer than five times. In 1411, the year of the Red Harlaw, one solitary burgess of Inverness, James Cumming, donned his armour and stationed himself at the far end of the narrow bridge which then spanned the river in front of the castle, to dispute the entry of Donald, Lord of the Isles, on his conquering way in defiance of the royal power. Needless to say the gesture was in vain, but it demonstrated once again that throughout its history Inverness was loyal to the king who was the source of its being. In 1427 James I held a parliament at the castle at which he dealt out summary justice to a number of Highland chiefs, but in 1491 the burgh again fell victim—for the last time—to the ever-troublesome Lords of the Isles.

Between 1530 and 1540 the Earl of Huntly rebuilt the castle. In 1562 it refused to admit Mary Queen of Scots, as the governor had received no instructions to that effect from the Earl of Huntly, and until this little matter was cleared up the Queen lodged in an old house at the foot of Bridge Street opposite the castle, ever afterwards known as Queen Mary's House—until it was engulfed in the massive new block which now houses various shops and the headquarters of the Highlands and Islands Development Board. The castle itself survived into the eighteenth century, being extended by General Wade and renamed Fort George. A print of 1690 shows it as a strong, square building, while another print of 1744 shows it as a complex and greatly extended structure, with a tenement-like eighteenth-century wing, no doubt used as a barracks.

The presence of the castle dictated the medieval layout of the burgh. It was girdled by a palisade on the south, east and north sides, but no palisade was necessary on the west where the Castle Hill descended abruptly to the river. The medieval streets corresponded very closely to the Castle Street, Church Street, Bridge Street and Eastgate of today.

Let us descend from the castle and crossing the top of Bridge Street to the Town Steeple let us enter Church Street. While the riverside is undoubtedly destined to be the future show-place and climax of amenity in Inverness, this does not mean that the old historic streets to the east of it will be forgotten. In the past decade it is Church Street that has been recovering its pride in the past.

First the Steeple itself. This characterful landmark was built in 1791, is 150 feet high and has a four-stage steeple on top of a three-storey tower. It adjoins what is now the Prudential Building, built in a Renaissance style in 1794 as the burgh courthouse. Both buildings were recently singled out for a much-needed facelift and cleaned at a cost of £30,000 as part of an extensive programme of "environmental improvement" aided by an 85 per cent grant offered by the Government.

Next along Church Street the massive Caledonian Hotel is unabashedly modern but beyond it is sixteenth-century Abertarff House, the only remaining castellated mansion in the burgh. Built in 1593, it is now revealed in gleaming white harl as a T-plan structure with picturesque crow-stepped gables and a sturdy round stair tower corbelled out to square in a bulky cape-house projecting from the centre of the front. It has made a splendid permanent headquarters for An Commun Gaidhealach (The Gaelic Society) since 1966. A constant stream of tourist visitors passes through the showroom and literature centre on the ground floor, admiring the wide old fireplace which came to light in the course of restoration, bearing on its decorative lintel a set of initials and the date 1681.

In the cape-house room at the top of the turnpike stair the director of An Commun presides over his organization's campaign to further the continued use and the increasing general interest of Gaelic language and culture. There has been a long tradition of Gaelic study in Inverness. Shortly after the inception of the Inverness Royal Academy in 1757 (the royal charter came a little later in 1793) "a class was opened for the teaching of the Gaelic language at the desire of the Highland Society of London who provided a salary of £15 for the teacher". Today, the director, Mr Norman Burns, informed me, it is realized that the speaking of Gaelic just cannot begin too early, and with this in mind Inverness has opened a Gaelic play-group for pre-school toddlers which is held in the hall attached to St Andrew's Episcopal Cathedral.

The next most venerable building in Church Street is the Dunbar Centre with its seven-window frontage, arched centre door, crow-stepped gables and handsome row of decorative dormers, bequeathed to the community in 1668 by Provost Alexander Dunbar.

It became in turn an almshouse for old men, the old grammar school of Inverness, a hospital for the wounded of the royal army after the Battle of Culloden, a library and a women's school. It is now once more dedicated to the service of old folk as a residential club for senior citizens.

Immediately to the south of the Dunbar Centre on the east side of Church Street is Bow Court, dating from 1729, recently admirably restored and reconstructed by the Ruthven Development Company so that its fine ground-floor arcade, centred by a pend arch, now hung with a wrought-iron gate, is occupied by an art salon and craft shop, while the upper storeys contain six exclusive three-roomed flats. Bow Court was at one time occupied by the Inverness Incorporated Trades guilds, and later by the Academy rector, with accommodation for boys boarded for tuition. Later it passed to the Old High Church trustees, who sold it to the development company.

Still farther south in Church Street is Cumming's Hotel, another well-restored historic building. The cumulative atmosphere generated by these well-cared-for old houses is a credit to the town, while the Old High Church itself, entered by a gateway and flight of steps on the west side of the street, dates in its present form from 1770, although its tower and steeple are much older than that. It stands on the site of the medieval parish church, still surrounded by its crowded graveyard. Separated from the ancient parish kirk by Friar's Lane were the lands and monastery of the Black Friars, covering in medieval times six acres and extending east from the river to Chapel Yard, yet another old burial ground. Between the Old High Church graveyard and the Chapel Yard is a third tiny cemetery, known (erroneously) as Greyfriars Churchyard. Within it, now standing up against a wall, is a much-weathered tomb-slab, believed to be that of Alexander Stewart, Earl of Mar, mentioned in the previous chapter as the illegitimate son of the Wolf of Badenoch. After acquiring the earldom of Mar by forcibly seizing the widowed countess and marrying her at Kildrummy Castle, he went on to achieve 'respectability' and renown by defeating Donald, Lord of the Isles, at the Battle of Harlaw and was thereafter created Justiciar of the North with headquarters in Inverness, where he died in 1435.

Also standing in the little Greyfriars burial ground is a striking single Gothic pillar of red sandstone. It is perhaps all that remains to us today of the monastery of the Black Friars. In the Chapel Yard itself are headstones dedicated to the officers of the royal army stationed in Inverness after Culloden. Here too is an imposing sepulchre of the Macleods of Macleod, mutilated in 1746 by partisans of Bonnie Prince Charlie angered by Macleod's refusal to join the Jacobite forces.

In this historic quarter of the town one is always stumbling against reminders of the fact that Inverness saw the last days of the 1745 rebellion—first under Jacobite occupation and then under the heel of the victorious 'Butcher' Cumberland. Between Dunbar's Centre and Bow Court is a narrow street called School Lane and in the walling here is a heraldic panel bearing the arms of Katherine Duff, Lady Drummuir, wife of Provost Alexander Duff who seized the town in the Jacobite interest in 1715. Lady Drummuir's house, now demolished, was occupied in 1746 by the Dowager Lady Mackintosh. It was at that time the only house in Inverness which had a room without a bed in it. So there before Culloden, Bonnie Prince Charlie took up his abode. This would have been wholly agreeable to Lady Mackintosh, whose sympathies were undoubtedly with the rebels. But after the battle of Culloden her house was immediately requisitioned by the Duke of Cumberland and Lady Mackintosh used to say: "I have had two King's bairns living with me in my time, and to tell the truth I wish I may never have another."

Originally Church Street stood alone with, (apart from the parish kirk and the Black Friars' monastery) long gardens or cultivated strips running down on the west to the riverside. This area is now built over with a succession of short streets, Bank Lane, Fraser Street, Church Lane and Friars' Lane linking Church Street with the Bank Street – Douglas Row esplanade. The reach of the river opposite the monastery took the name Friars' Shott, the place where the monks held the fishing rights. Here under the Inverness development plan a new road bridge will span the river carrying a new road to the west. Halfway between Friars' Shott and the main Ness Bridge the river is spanned by the Greig Street suspension bridge, a pleasant footbridge.

This no doubt suggested to the planners another civic improvement. A new road system will be laid out in the extensive area bounded by Young Street (the continuation of Bridge Street on the west side of the Ness Bridge) on the south and Friars' Shott on the north, with Huntly Street (which forms the river esplanade on its west side) and Kenneth Street (which runs parallel to it a couple of streets farther west) as the east-west boundaries. All this will form a pedestrian precinct with Greig Street and the Greig Street suspension bridge bisecting the area.

Huntly Street is a delightful promenade along the west bank of the river, marred only by the seedy deterioration in one part of it, where Balnain House, a large Georgian mansion, stands derelict. But there are plans to restore this very handsome building and standing as it does between two churches, with plenty of space between, the area will be landscaped to form an open courtyard with Balnain House in the middle as a visitor centre. The Ness in this quarter of the town is lined with churches on both sides, their spires and steeples reflected in the water. Its character is somewhat stark and formal, but the whole aspect changes on the other (or south) side of the Ness Bridge.

Here trees and gardens come into their own. With the castle on its hill on the east side and St Andrew's Episcopal Cathedral on the west, Inverness here achieves its climax of amenity, and only a short distance up the river, with parks and public open spaces on both sides, one reaches the Ness islands, a never-failing source of pleasure. From both banks footbridges connect with a cluster of wooded islets in the centre, linked up by rustic bridges to form a sylvan retreat overarched by fine old trees, criss-crossed by winding paths and plenteously provided with seats giving vistas up and down stream, ceaselessly serenaded by the music of the rushing waters.

Stand on Ness Walk on a sunny evening in June and look up or down the swift-flowing river; watch the strolling crowds hasten their steps to welcome the pipers marching to the Northern Meeting Park, and you are glad to be alive.

The cathedral is a Gothic revival, Late Decorated structure in rich red stone. There are nave arcades with polished granite circular columns supporting arches with clerestories above. The nave roof has scissors trusses with wooden ceilings. At the springing of the nave arcades are sculptured heads. The altar and reredos are of Caen stone, embellished by coloured marbles.

Built between 1866 and 1869, the cathedral has an unusual font, designed as a kneeling angel, modelled after Thorwaldsen's in the museum at Copenhagen. One transept contains the organ and the other a lady chapel. The magnificent canopied choir stalls and screen, with a hanging rood, were designed by Sir Robert Lorimer. The architect of the cathedral was Alexander Ross, an Inverness man. One of the many gifts with which the interior is embellished is a set of five gold engraved icons presented by the Czar of Russia.

Eden Court, in nearby Bishop's Road, the former bishop's palace, was converted into a fine civic theatre complex which opened in April 1976. The green room is the former chapel, and the auditorium has 814 seats for plays, opera, ballet and concerts and rather fewer for films. It is an exciting multi-purpose building and the immense height is most notable on the stage, which can be varied in size for different productions.

Scottish Opera, the Scottish National Orchestra, the Scottish Ballet and the Oxford Playhouse Company participated in the opening season.

In Ardross Street, flanking the cathedral, is the Northern Meeting Park, venue of the annual Northern Meeting (Highland games), famous for the most important piping contests in the country and for military tattoos and other regimental ceremonial.

To complete the tally of public parks, we have facing each other across the river Bellfield Park, on the east side, mainly well stocked public gardens with tennis courts and putting greens, and on the west the much larger converted estate, the Bught, with sports ground and stadium, ice rink, riding stables and a municipal caravan park. To the north of the Bught is the massive Royal Northern Infirmary, founded in 1804. The Inverness war memorial, facing the east bank of the river, is centred by a Celtic cross.

At Ness Bridge, despite its smooth modern simplicity, it takes no great effort of imagination to appreciate that all down the centuries the river crossing here was the strategic crux of the northern Highlands. The timber bridge which stood here in the Middle Ages collapsed, with a crowd of a hundred people on it, in 1664. It was succeeded in 1685 by an extremely picturesque seven-arched bridge of stone which appears in many old prints. This was carried away by a flood in 1849 and a suspension bridge with tall piers succeeded it and survived until the sixties of this century. The redevelopment scheme at the end of that decade produced the massive Bridge Street complex of shops and offices on two levels, which also includes the public library and art gallery and museum, each excellent of their kind.

The Inverness Museum is worthy of attention for it contains many illustrations of the Highland way of life: costume and tartans, weapons and targes, items the visitor should know about but is unlikely to see elsewhere in a casual tour of the country. There are also six fragments of different symbol stones to illuminate the strange, mysterious themes of Pictish art. Water-colours of old Inverness buildings and streets are displayed on the staircase.

Despite its sprinkling of historic buildings of earlier periods, central Inverness is mainly a Victorian town, so it is no surprise to find that the Town House, which occupies the site between Castle Street and Castle Wynd fronting the small square called the Exchange at the junction of Bridge Street, High Street and Church Street, is an over-elaborate Tudor Gothic-style creation dating from the late 1870s. Its interior has many interesting portraits including one of Thomas Telford, the engineer of the Caledonian Canal, a full-length study of President Forbes of Culloden in his robes as a senator of the College of Justice—a fitting memento of the statesman who did much to tide the community over the crisis of the '45 Rebellion—and a likeness of his ancestor, Duncan Forbes, founder of the Culloden family, who was Provost of Inverness in 1626.

There are also portraits of Bonnie Prince Charlie (by C. J. Mackintosh) and of Flora Macdonald, as well as six windows showing the armorial bearings of numerous clans. It was in the council chamber here in September 1921 that an emergency meeting of the British Cabinet under Lloyd George was held which produced the 'Inverness Formula' for the settlement of the Irish question. Among those signing the roll, retained in a frame, were Winston Churchill and Stanley Baldwin.

In front of the Town House is the old town cross. Enclosed in one of the steps which form its pedestal is the famous Clachnacudain, a slab of sandstone also called the Stone of the Tubs. It originally stood on the pavement and was the rendezvous of women and girls passing to and from the river with their water-buckets. Here they paused for a gossip or a teasing encounter with the lads of the town. At this spot in May 1650 the Marquess of Montrose on his way to trial and execution in Edinburgh, and seated on a pony led by his captors, took a drink of wine, diluted with water, offered to him by the magistrates. Provost Duncan Forbes, aforementioned, said to him: "My Lord, I am sorry for your circumstances," to which he replied, "I am sorry for being the object of your pity."

From the east end of High Street two short streets, Inglis Street and Hamilton Street, lead to Academy Street, on the east side of which is the Station Square with its handsome Cameron Highlander memorial. Directly opposite, Union Street, a broad shopping thoroughfare, leads west to George Street, while to the north of this is the Market Arcade, a covered shopping precinct with great over-arching roof in the Victorian manner, which demonstrates how well the principles of pedestrianization were understood—even in the days when traffic pressures did not make it inevitable.

The central bus station in Inverness is in Farraline Park, a square approached by a short side street on the east side of Academy Street a little farther north than the railway station. The backdrop to this square is the handsome classical frontage of the former Dr Andrew Bell's School (1840), now used to house the Little Theatre and the Burgh Police Courtroom. At its northern end Academy Street joins George Street at the Chapel Yard and from this point Chapel Street and Waterloo Street lead to the Waterloo Bridge over the Ness, beyond which lies Inverness Harbour and the Longman industrial area.

As a port Inverness has a very long history. A large vessel was launched here in 1249 for a French magnate who went in it with St Louis to the Crusades. Timber from the Highland forests, along with skins and hides, was an early export. Today the Thornbush Slipway on the west bank of the river and the commercial harbour on the east bank are important. Perhaps the best-known industry is the production of automatic electric-welding machines for use in the motor car, ship-building and steel industries, but there are also woollen manufacture and whisky distilling.

The industrial estate on the former Longman airfield is a thing of more utility than beauty. Here marooned amidst a regiment of oil tanks is all that remains of a great fort constructed by Cromwell's soldiery in 1652, only to be demolished in 1661, with the exception of Cromwell's Tower—a clock tower in two stages with a shapely ogee roof. Not far from here is the Inverness Technical College, recently extended at a cost of over £1,000,000, to meet the demands of the Moray Firth industrial boom. It provides courses for over 3,000 students, drawn from the whole Highland area, from Campbeltown in the south to Orkney in the north, and from Nairn in the east to Stornoway in the west.

The Longman lies on the broad peninsula extending into the inner Moray Firth east of the estuary of the Ness, and along the north-eastern flank of the industrial estate runs the line of the new A9 highway bypassing Inverness and crossing the Firth to North Kessock. This is only part of the new road system designed to be in full operation by 1990. The A9 trunk road and the A96(T) from Aberdeen meet at a great round-about on the eastern outskirts of the town. From this a town centre road will follow the line of the existing A9 as far as Eastgate, the eastern extension of the High Street, where roads leading west, south-west and south will meet at a new exchange point, the main western road proceeding to another exchange point east of the projected Friars' Shott Bridge. All this should greatly relieve the present intense pressure on the narrow streets in the centre of the burgh.

One contemplates these changes with mixed feelings. At present visitors to Inverness greatly enjoy the crossing of the Firth from South to North Kessock by ferryboats which run with admirable regularity and afford in doing so magnificent views up the hill-fringed Beauly Firth on the west and down the equally spectacular Moray Firth on the east. To take an evening jaunt across the water in time to see the splendour of a sunset over the calm seaways, to stand on the quiet North Kessock shore and see the throbbing heart of the Highland capital put on its dusk-time dress of a myriad twinkling lights, this is something not easily forgotten. When one is whisked across the strait on a super-highway, foregoing the intimacy of the friendly little ferryboats, will it be quite the same?

So far we have considered the beauties with which Inverness is endowed by its broad, majestic river and the Beauly and Moray Firths. But there is a third element, the man-made Caledonian Canal, which has been with us now for so long that it is almost a force of nature. The Great Glen fault, slicing across Scotland from the Firth of Lorne on the west to the Moray Firth on the north-east, for a distance of over 60 miles, had long suggested to speculative observers that its constituent chain of lochs, Loch Dochfour, Loch Ness, Loch Oich and Loch Lochy, might be linked by canal to provide continuous navigation from sea to sea. Edward Burt, the army officer stationed at Inverness in the period between the two Jacobite rebellions, toyed with the idea of a canal but dismissed it because he thought the winds channelled between the mountains along the Great Glen would render navigation too hazardous. More serious and professional plans for a canal long preceded the actual proposals of Thomas Telford in 1801.

Work on the canal began in 1804 and continued until 1822, costing in all £1,311,000.

North-west of Huntly Street on the west bank of the Ness, Telford Road leads to the Muirtown Bridge over the entrance to the canal and to Clachnaharry Basin where vessels wait to enter the first reach of the canal by Muirtown Locks. Mechanization of the four locks here was completed in 1963 and by 1969 the entire canal had been modernized in this way, shortening the passage to Corpach, near Fort William, 60 miles away, by two hours. Traffic on the canal today includes pleasure cruisers, fishing boats (which thus eliminate the stormy passage of the Pentland Firth on their way to the west coast) and cargo shipping of all kinds. The canal is administered by the British Waterways Board. Beyond the basin itself lies picturesque old-world Clachnaharry village, with Clachnaharry House as the canal offices.

On its way to Loch Dochfour and Loch Ness the canal passes those two delightful little hills Tomnahurich and Torvean, both obviously mounds of glacial detritus. In 1793 the ministers compiling the Old Statistical Account of Inverness wrote: "The most remarkable hill in this parish is Tomnahurich near the town on the west side of the river. It is a beautifully insulated mount, nearly resembling a ship with her keel uppermost. This hill in the year 1753 was enclosed and planted, chiefly with Scots firs. The elevation from the channel of the river is 250 feet." In 1878 a company was formed to convert the hill into a cemetery. They did so with such good effect that it is now claimed to be the most beautiful burial ground in the world. The summit offers a magnificent view.

Torvean, a ridge with a round peak, is slightly higher, rising to 275 feet. There are traces of ramparts around it some 40 feet from the top. At Torvean's base the workmen making the canal uncovered a massive silver chain, 18 inches long, consisting of thirty-three circular double links and weighing 104 ounces. The hill is said to take its name from St Bean or Baithene (536-600), the second abbot of Iona. Farther to the west terraced slopes lead up to the ridge of Leachkin and Craig Phadraig where the summit fort, said to date from 300 BC, was recently excavated. The hill is 556 feet high and is now being partly reafforested by the Forestry Commission.

Behind Inverness Castle the 100 foot terrace slopes gently upward to what is called the Hill district of the town, largely residential. Approached by Eastgate and Stephen's Street is Inverness Royal Academy. It became 'Royal' by Royal Warrant and Charter of Incorporation in 1793 after a century in Academy Street, to which it gave the name before moving to the original part of the present building in 1895. There have been three major extensions since then. Of its roll of nearly 1,000, many pupils come from such great distances that they must be boarded away from home and there are two large hostels, Drummond Park for boys and Hedgefield for girls.

The south-eastern outskirts are spreading rapidly towards Strathnairn and there has been massive residential development in the Hilton district but little has happened since to modify the predictions made in the Holmes Report of 1968.

Born 800 years ago as a bulwark of royal authority against self-assertive and often rebellious powers in the Highland hinterland, at first a 'frontier town' on the edge of anarchy, Inverness has become more and more in a true sense the capital of the Highlands. Today it functions as an administrative capital and regional service and entertainments centre. It is now the headquarters of the huge Highland Region with an area of around 10,000 square miles and a population of 179,000. It houses the head office of the Highlands and Islands Development Board and offices of the Forestry Commission, Highland Regional Hospital Board, North of Scotland Milk Marketing Board, Department of Agriculture and Fisheries and regional offices of many major nationally known commercial concerns. As a shopping centre it compares with Perth, Stirling, Falkirk and Dumfries.

Expansion to a population of 65,000 is envisaged by peripheral extension on the slopes which enclose the town up to an altitude of 300 feet. The views from these sites give a total panorama sweeping from Strathconon and Ben Wyvis across the Black Isle to the outer Moray Firth in the east.

From the many and sad vicissitudes of its past, from burnings and ravagings, from economic declines and ruinous desolation, Inverness has come at last into the full sunlight of prosperity and popular esteem. No other resort in the northern half of Scotland offers so much beauty in its immediate environs and so much choice as a springboard for exploratory tourism in every direction by road, by rail, by water and by air. Its outer peripheral attractions are described in Chapter VII.

## ELGIN

If Inverness is the capital of the Highlands, Elgin is the queen of the Laich, or low country of the province of Moray, a very different sort of countryside. It reigns over what William Lithgow, writing in 1628, described as "the delectable planure of Murray ... enriched with corns, plantings, pasturage ... a second Lombardy or pleasant meadow of the north". That is why I am treating it here as the 'second capital' of the Moray Firth although a casual tourist might be content to define it as "just a pleasant country town". It has not grown in recent years so spectacularly as Inverness. But then it had come to its full glory in centuries when Inverness was suffering humiliation after humiliation and much more than Inverness it has retained a rich heritage of historic buildings, of long-settled amenities and of civic self-confidence. It is the city of Elgin and until May 1975, when the reorganization of local government swept away such proud distinctions, its chief magistrate was entitled to the style of Lord Provost.

How Elgin was regarded by Scots from less favoured areas in the seventeenth century may be gathered from the Latin eulogy written by Arthur Johnston and thus picturesquely translated:

> To Elgin's Praise the ancient Bajae yields
> Hesperian Gardens and brave Tempe's Fields;
> Both Sea and Land doth still Thy needs supplie,
> That Fishes, This Cornes doth afford to Thee.
> Corcyra, Apples unto Thee hath sent,
> Damascus, Prunes, Cerasus Cherries lent.
> The Bees seem to have left their Attick hyve,
> And come to Thee their Honey-trade to dryve.
> The silver streams of Lossie here doth glyde,
> By crooked paths into the sea they slide.
> With Stately Castles Thou'rt environed,
> Within with pleasant Buildings garnished.

All there is lovely and delights the Eye,
But the torne Walls and Rubbish when you see
Of that Great Temple, which e're yet appears,
Bid Scotland now bedew Her Cheeks with tears.

The "Great Temple" of the second-last line is Elgin Cathedral, the most delicate and beautiful of all Scotland's great medieval churches, whose "torne Walls and Rubbish" in the seventeenth century were a reproach not to Elgin alone but to Scotland's follies at the time of the Reformation. The mighty cathedral, majestic in ruin, still shows on the skyline of Elgin when seen from afar, with its western towers. At a closer approach it seems to be swallowed up in the lesser buildings in the foreground. There are of course various routes of approach. From the A96 highway on the west one comes to Elgin through the Oakwood, a thickly forested belt, and the cathedral is then hidden by the bluff of the Lady Hill where the ancient royal castle once stood. It was along the line of the High Street from the foot of this hill, eastwards to the Little Cross that marked the bounds of the cathedral precincts, that the ancient burgh was laid out.

The defensive strength of the little town may not be so apparent today but as the early kings of Scotland saw it the site was protected to the west, north and east by the winding course of the River Lossie and to the south by a peat-moss, while in the centre was a ridge of level land and above it a small but steep hill forming a natural fortress. In this after his fatal wounding at Bothgowan by Macbeth in 1040, King Duncan may have died, and in 1135 after his triumph over the rebellious Men of Moray, David I, Duncan's grandson, built the castle and laid out the burgh on the level ground below. Castle and town lay in the very heart of the fertile Laich.

It was still being mentioned as one of the major strongholds of Scotland in the fourteenth and fifteenth centuries and among its buildings a chapel of St Mary survived until the sixteenth century, hence the name Lady Hill. The ancient burgh was rectangular in form with the High Street running down the middle and two parallel streets, the North Back Gait (now Blackfriars Road and North Lane) and South Back Gait (now South Street) bounding it to north and south.

Just as it does today, the High Street widened towards its eastern end to provide a site for the market place and church, and also for the tolbooth or burgh jail (not of course represented in the present layout). The burghers (privileged settlers in the king's new town) were each allotted 'tofts' or 'tenements'—holdings of land,—ten paces in width and extending north or south to the burgh limits. It is estimated that in the twelfth and thirteenth centuries there were 100 such tofts and a population of some 500 or 600. Croft lands beside the Lossie on the area called Borough Briggs and mills on the river itself were an essential part of the early burgh's economy. Hence today we have the Kingsmills, Bishopmill and Sheriffmill areas and while the mills themselves have been repeatedly altered, the sites with their 'cruives' or caulds may still be seen.

Despite the fact that the greater part of modern central Elgin was built in the nineteenth century, so many historic buildings do survive that it is possible to interlace the story of the burgh's history with these and so enjoy the advantage of a traditional approach to sightseeing.

The most venerable antiquity in the town is the famous Elgin Pillar, a Pictish cross slab, originally unearthed near the parish Kirk of St Giles on its island site in the centre of the High Street but now appropriately preserved at the north side of the west end of the cathedral choir. It dates from about AD 900. On the front is a cross standing on a rectangular base and ornamented with an interlaced pattern. In the four angles of the cross are figures thought to represent the four evangelists, while in the space below is an interlaced design with four animal heads meeting in the centre. On the back of the slab is a hunting scene above which are a series of decorated symbols.

The next most ancient survival is of course the cathedral itself, founded in 1224. Today it is approached at the eastern end of the Cooper Park, the magnificent 40-acre stretch of civic parkland lying north of the High Street which had been acquired from the Earl of Seafield by Sir George A. Cooper and after suitable landscaping was presented to the community of Elgin in 1903. From the Little Cross towards the eastern end of the High Street, North College Street skirts the south-east corner of the park and leads directly to the western portal of the cathedral, the great towers of which dominate the eastern half of the park.

This is where one enters the cathedral and this is its most impressive façade. The design of this superb twin-towered frontispiece recalls the great cathedrals of northern France, although the main portal, the tower windows and the delicately profiled buttresses that rise almost to the full height of 92 feet belong to the Scottish variant of Early English Gothic known as 'First Pointed' and date from the thirteenth century. Of later date were the twin doorways within the · portal and the large traceried window above them. They belong to the period of reconstruction following the conflagration of June 1390 when the Wolf of Badenoch wreaked his spite upon Bishop Alexander Burr by burning the cathedral and the whole town of Elgin.

A cry of sheer agony was joined to the eloquence with which that aged prelate petitioned King Robert III for reparation of the wrong committed by the king's unruly brother and his "wyld Wykked Heland-men". His cathedral was, he said, "the special ornament of the realm, the glory of the kingdom, the delight of foreigners and stranger guests; an object of praise and glorification in foreign realms by reason of the multitude of those serving and the beauty of its ornament, in which we believe God was rightly worshipped, not to speak of its high belfries, its sumptuous furniture and its innumerable jewels".

Lost in that merciless blaze were also "18 noble and beautiful manses of canons and chaplains" and besides the cathedral itself, "all the books, charters and other valuable things of the country therein kept".

The cathedral is 263 feet long and the western towers contained four storeys and were originally capped by lead-covered wooden spires. One can still reach the first floor by a stair at the south-east angle of the southern tower. The interior walls of this tower still show the effect of the heat caused by the burning timbers of the floors and the spires. The first bay of the nave was framed between the walls of the west towers, but beyond this a vast luminous space opened out 82 feet wide defined by the range of pillars supporting the six arches of the main arcades, each with three clerestory lancet windows above, and beyond them on each side a further range of pillars and arches separating the inner from the outer aisles, both vaulted. The bays of the outer aisles contained chapels (ten in all) lit by traceried windows set within a gabled roof at right angles to the main roof, as in the great French cathedrals.

At the far end of the nave was a rood screen and an altar of the Holy Cross, the timber screen being "painted in excellent colours illuminated with stars of bright gold". The crossing was also screened off at the east end with a choir screen of stone, and between the two screens the "croce kirk" formed by the crossing and transepts was 102 feet long. Above it rose the central tower, the largest of the three, which collapsed on Easter Sunday 1711.

The oldest work in the cathedral is in the south transept. It belongs to the transition between Romanesque and Gothic and was probably part of the ancient church of the Holy Trinity which stood on the site before the cathedral was transferred there in 1224. The choir, 108 feet long, is the best preserved part of the cathedral. The vaulted south aisle, containing tombs of bishops and nobles of the neighbourhood, was named after the altar of St Mary at its east end and its beautiful carved detail is still pristine, firm and delicate. Just west of the north aisle a short passage leads into the chapter house, also vaulted and largely entire, where the canons met to discuss their corporate business, the dean presiding from the centre of the five stone canopied stalls on the north wall. At the far east end of the choir stood the high altar.

From the outside this eastern end of the cathedral still presents a noble sight, richly decorated and built in the late thirteenth century. The eastern gable consists of two tiers, each of five pointed windows, surmounted by a large rose window. Dr Douglas Simpson has pointed out that in the two tiers of lancets each of them is framed in a tall rectangular panel formed by slender projecting fillets, horizontal and vertical. Since the fillets are carried through the bases and caps of the lancets, Dr Simpson concludes that the design had been copied by the masons from an architect's drawing—the architect being in all probability Wilars de Honcort, who made a habit of drawing all his designs within a geometrical framework —and so faithful were the workmen to their model that they reproduced in stone the artist's 'construction lines'!

Where it towers over the green banks of the River Lossie encircling it on the east, the cathedral of Moray, "the lanthorn of the north", in ruin as it is, and minus its great central tower 198 feet high, still succeeds in convincing us that it is the supreme example of Scottish church architecture in the great building period of the thirteenth century.

In its heyday the cathedral was surrounded by a residential precinct called the College of the Chanonry, containing the residences or 'manses' of the canons, twenty-five in number. This college was surrounded by a precinct wall on three sides, half a mile in length, the fourth side, protected by the open bank of the River Lossie, being left open. There were four 'ports' or gateways of which the only survivor today is the handsome masonry arch of the Panns Port, on the south-east, by the Lossie, which takes its name from the Canons' Meadows. It was also called the Water Yett and was defended by a portcullis and massive wooden doors. A short fragment of the precinct wall, originally 12 feet high, adjoins the Panns Port, and there are two other fragments to the south-west.

Of the canons' manses the most substantial relic is the so-called 'bishop's palace' to the north-west of the cathedral. Like a ruined castle in miniature, this house now consists of two wings, linked by a square staircase tower. They originally formed the east and south sides of a courtyard entered from the north. It has handsome crow-steps and one of the skew-puts is dated 1557. It was never in fact the bishop's palace (for the bishop continued to live in the old bishop's palace at Spynie) and has been identified as the precentor's manse.

Beyond the 'bishop's palace' to the north-west is a white-walled old house called The College. Although much altered, this L-plan house with a vaulted ground floor, moulded windows and corbelled chimney stacks has been identified as the original deanery. Another house called South College contains part of the vaulted under-storey of the archdeacon's manse—once the home of John Bellenden, "father of Scottish prose literature".

The ruination of Elgin Cathedral after the Scottish Reformation of 1560, when all corporate services within the building ceased, is one of the great tragedies of Moray's history. In 1568 the Regent Moray gave orders that the lead roof should be removed to provide materials of war. Unlike

St Machar's Cathedral in Aberdeen, no use was found for the building as a Reformed place of worship and its neglect was total.

For some time, indeed, a use could be made of the chapter house for it proved convenient for Regality Courts and for meetings of the Six Incorporated Trades of Elgin in the early eighteenth century, but after the great central tower had fallen the rest of the building was used as a quarry and stones were taken from it to build the first Elgin Academy. By 1807 when the ruins had become a dump for rubbish public conscience was aroused. An enclosing wall was built and a keeper appointed. One famous keeper called John Shanks carried out initial work of repair and after 1833 the Crown took the building into its care.

Elgin's interest in its own history has long roots. It received great impetus from the publication of a seminal book, *The History of the Province of Moray* by Lachlan Shaw, senior minister of Elgin in 1775, and the tradition thus formed was furthered by Isaac Forsyth, a bookseller, who started the first circulating library in the area in 1789, published a *Survey of the Province of Moray* in 1798 and helped to found the Morayshire Farmers' Club in the following year. Elgin's first newspaper, *The Courier,* appeared in 1827, and in 1836 came the Elgin and Morayshire Scientific Association, one of the parent bodies of the Elgin Society, for whom a fine museum, in a pleasant Italianate style of architecture, was designed by Thomas Mackenzie in 1843. The Elgin Museum, opposite the Little Cross, at the entrance to Cooper Park, is still administered by the Elgin Society today and while still enshrining the results of 140 years of local research, has been splendidly modernized and is used as a cultural and educational centre.

The Little Cross itself deserves a second look. It was originally built in 1402 as part of a penance by Alexander, Lord of the Isles, for damage which he had inflicted in a raid on the cathedral precinct. Probably it was used as a market cross for the community which grew up to serve the needs of the cathedral clergy. It was rebuilt in 1773 in the form of a tall column set on a flight of steps and capped by a sundial, which owing to severe weathering had to be replaced by a facsimile in 1941.

Immediately opposite the Museum and the Little Cross on

the other side of High Street is Greyfriars Lane leading
southwards to Greyfriars Street, off which stands Greyfriars
Church and Monastery now used by a community of the
Sisters of Mercy. The church, a long aisleless building with
some fascinating detail, was restored in 1896 by John Kinross
for the third Marquess of Bute and handed over to the
Roman Catholic Church. The conventual buildings were at
the same time rebuilt on the old foundations and incorporated
some fragments of the original. The church is of great beauty
and has been described by Mr Ronald G. Cant, one of
Scotland's foremost medievalists, as being "more like a true
medieval interior than any other in Scotland". It has simply
plastered walls and a richly decorated screen.

To find the next oldest structure in the town it is simplest
to walk along Greyfriars Street to the west and crossing
Commerce Street continue along South Street, passing all the
openings on the north till one reaches the narrow lane called
Thunderton Place. Here some three-quarters of the way back
to High Street, on the right or east side, is the King's House,
better known as Thunderton House, a hotel which represents
part of what was once the most splendid mansion in Elgin.
The King's House was the Great Lodging in which the
Scottish kings or their representatives in Moray held court.
From the early fourteenth to the mid fifteenth century it
belonged to the earls of Moray, then to the Dunbars of
Westfield, and from 1650 to the Sutherlands of Duffus. In the
eighteenth century it became the town house of the Dunbars
of Thunderton and took the name by which it has been
familiarly known ever since. It had originally a forecourt
facing towards High Street and a garden extending to South
Street. It was occupied by Prince Charles Edward on his way
to Culloden. Though much altered, the shell of the surviving
building belongs to the sixteenth and seventeenth centuries.
There is a notable line of decorative dormers to the south and
other carved details are built into the walls, some in the
courtyard and some in the garden behind No. 1 North Street.
Carved 'savages' which formerly flanked the entrance are now
in the Elgin Museum.

High Street has over a dozen historic houses of great charm,
of which the most striking are those graced by open arcades
or piazzas on the ground floor, once the predominant style

and all dating from the seventeenth century. Typical of these is No. 7 on the north side close to the Little Cross. This is Braco's Banking House, a three-storey house with crow-stepped gables, stone slab roof and pedimented dormers and an arcade of three arches adapted as a shop. The dormer pediments carry the initials ID and MI, for John Duncan and Margaret Innes, his wife, and the date 1694, with the initials and date repeated on the skewputts. The house takes its name from the fact that from 1703 to 1722 it was the banking house of the magnate William Duff of Dipple and Braco, ancestor of the earls of Fife. There is a court behind, entered from No. 5 High Street, containing a charming row of two-storeyed whitewashed houses, also with stone slab roofs and crow-stepped gables.

Plainer and more austere, but still a remarkable period building, is Nos. 15-19 High Street, the former home of the Kilmolymock Lodge of Freemasons, dated 1728. It was restored in 1971 by the Elgin Fund, a conservationist body founded in 1963 by E. S. Harrison, a former lord provost of Elgin, and his fellow directors of the Johnston Mills. This large three-storeyed block has crow-stepped gables and moulded chimney heads, with a carved face on one of the skewputts. It, too, has a courtyard behind formed by two crow-stepped wings and entered from a pend or arched passage on the High Street.

In 1975 for European Architectural Heritage Year, adjoining four-storeyed houses with a long crow-stepped wing to the back at Nos 21-25 High Street were also restored, as were Nos 30-32 High Street, while on the opposite side of the street, between Commerce Street and the County Buildings, a long range of buildings, including two with piazzas, forms part of an ambitious development by the Elgin Fund. This is the Red Lion Close scheme, taking its name from the Red Lion Inn where Johnson and Boswell dined in 1773.

With his usual keen eye Johnson remarked on the piazzas in the High Street: "In the chief street of Elgin, the houses jut over the lowest story, like the old buildings of timber in London, but with greater prominence; so that there is sometimes a walk for a considerable length under a cloister or portico, which is now indeed frequently broken, because the new houses have another form, but seem to have been uniformly continued in the old city."

When the Red Lion Close scheme is completed four of the arches in the arcade at Nos 42-46 High Street, which had been built up, will be restored to their original glory. This is a large three-storeyed house with crow-stepped gables, moulded chimneys and stone-slab roof. The wallhead is finished with a moulded cornice and the skewputts are inscribed 1688 IW. The close behind, entered through a vaulted pend, contains several old houses. Farther along, Nos 50-52 High Street is similar with a four-arched arcade and its skewputts bear the date 1694 and the initials AO JH (for Andrew Ogilvie, merchant and Dean of Guild of Elgin, and his wife Janet Hay). The group as a whole is of first-class architectural importance and its restoration will greatly enhance central Elgin. At No. 103 the largely rebuilt Tower Hotel has a round tower projecting to the street. The tower is topped by a square cape-house with crow-stepped gables and carries a heraldic panel with the initials AL IB and the date 1634. AL was Andrew Leslie of the Glen of Rothes and IB Jean Bonyman his wife.

As you pass along the High Street do not fail to explore its many pends or closes, narrow openings either arched or open to the sky. So many of them contain little hidden gems of antiquity that it is worth while. To take just one example, at the end of the close behind No. 78 High Street, there is a small L-plan house with crow-stepped gables, moulded doors and windows. A fireplace within is inscribed THOMAS RUSSELL 1694.

The heart of Elgin burgh is of course that widening out of the High Street already mentioned as the original market place where stood the church and tolbooth from the earliest times. Here stood, also, just to the east of the church, the Mercat Cross, called the Muckle Cross, a raised balcony twelve feet high, from the centre of which rose a tall shaft topped by the Scottish lion. The lion has survived but the cross of today, on the same old site, is a restoration built in 1888. In 1786, intended as base for the market place, was laid down the raised paving called the Plainstones still there today. The original parish church, the Muckle Kirk of Elgin, was rebuilt in the thirteenth century and again in 1390 when like so much else in the town it was severely damaged by the Wolf of Badenoch in his vengeful incendiary raid. In 1826 it was demolished and in the following two years replaced by St

Giles' Church of today.

This is a case where, however much one may regret the loss of a historic building of great age and character, one can but applaud the style and grandeur of the neo-classic structure which superseded it. The architect was Archibald Simpson of Aberdeen and he created a church in the manner of a Greek Doric temple with a portico of six fluted columns on the west and a graceful tower to the east, the upper stages of which were adapted from the Choragîc Monument of Lysicrates at Athens. When it was built the old tolbooth still stood on the Plainstones to the west of it, obscuring the full effect of the portico, but this too was demolished in 1845 and replaced by a fountain designed by Thomas Mackenzie of Elgin, which stands there today adding to the classic dignity of the town's civic centre.

The neo-classic theme which gives such character to modern Elgin was reinforced by two public buildings at either end of the High Street. The first of these, at the west end, is Dr Gray's Hospital, which in point of time actually preceded the replacement of the Muckle Kirk. Alexander Gray, a native of the town who had made a fortune in India, left £20,000 when he died in 1816, to provide a hospital "for the sick of the Town and County of Elgin".

In the following three years Gray's Hospital arose on a commanding site facing along the whole length of the High Street. The architect was James Gillespie Graham who designed a great three-storey front topped by a balustraded parapet and centred by a Tuscan portico and handsome dome. Gray's Hospital remains today one of the great centres of healing in the north. Five years later, in 1824, Elgin received an even more spectacular legacy when General Anderson —who like Dr Gray made a large fortune in India— bequeathed the princely sum of £70,000 (his entire estate) to found an institution "for the support of old age and the education of youth". From part of this sum the governors erected a magnificent building designed by Archibald Simpson and built in 1831-32. It stands well back from the street at the east end of High Street on the south side, and consists of a two-storeyed H-plan structure with large pedimented wings and a recessed Ionic portico with a domed belfry as its central feature.

The original exit from Elgin to the north was by Lossie Wynd towards the eastern end of the High Street, but in 1820 a new street called North Street was formed leading north and then east from the west end of the Plainstones. Forming a fine terminal feature for the view along North Street from the burgh centre is Holy Trinity Episcopal Church (1825-26) designed by William Robertson of Elgin. Moss Street, originally the Moss Wynd, leads to the south and to the railway station. Near the station end on the east side is St Columba's Church, a handsome modern structure in the Norman style designed by MacGregor Chalmers and opened as an adjunct to St Giles in 1906. Among its treasures it contains the old pulpit of the Muckle Kirk, exquisitely carved and canopied and bearing the date 1684.

Nearer the centre of the town are the two churches which were the fruit of the Disruption of 1843, the High Church (at the corner of South Street and North Guildry Street) and the South Church (facing North Guildry Street) with Gothic pinnacles and a steeple 130 feet high, which dates from 1853. The Lady Hill, site of the medieval castle, with its park-like grassy sides and summit, was crowned in 1839 by a tall column commemorating the last Duke of Gordon and offers today a pleasant viewpoint from which to survey the town.

No one can live in Elgin without coming to have a special regard for the Cooper Park. Its history—and its future —demand some further comment.

For centuries it was a wide expanse of private parkland containing five noble residences. Within it, close to the Elgin Museum, stood the town house of the Marquess of Huntly. A little to the north of this was the town house of the Mackenzies of Pluscarden. On its eastern tip was the already mentioned precentor's manse or bishop's palace. Finally near the centre, on the position it still occupies, was Grant Lodge, the town house of the Grants. It was built around 1750 and later enlarged by Francis William, sixth Earl of Seafield. When the whole area was acquired from the Seafield Estates by Sir George Cooper and presented to the people of Elgin, Grant Lodge became available as a public building and today it is the central library for Moray.

Bitter controversy broke out in Elgin when a by-pass road to carry the A96 was routed through the south-eastern seg-

Cullen: the old church dating from 1236 with additions in 1536 and 1545.

Portknockie: the houses on the clifftop overlook a harbour that once held 100 steam drifters.

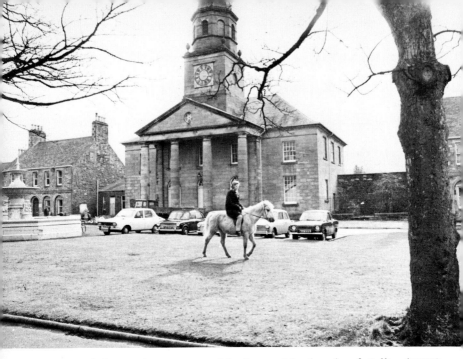

Fochabers: The Square, with the parish church of Bellie (1798) designed by John Baxter.

A corner of the Old Harbour, Portsoy, with, on the right, the Old Corff House (salmon curing factory), now converted into a pottery and a workshop for Portsoy marble (serpentine) souvenirs.

Lossiemouth: the modern harbour with its fleet of dual-purpose
seine netters.

Boys of Buckie high school at rowing practice in their school launch with the town and harbour behind.

A Gordonstoun girl signalling on the sands in a surf safety exercise on the shore of the Moray Firth.

Gordonstoun school pupils in a cliff rescue exercise at Cove Bay near Hopeman on the Moray Firth.

Bellringers summon the Benedictine monks to a service at Pluscarden Abbey.

The Laich of Moray from the York Tower on the Knock of Alves with the hills of Ross-shire in the background.

Forres: part of the town as seen from the top of the Nelson Tower.

An aerial view of Nairn with the Moray Firth and the Black Isle in the background.

Kilravock Castle and the River Nairn. On the right is the keep (1460) and on the left the south wing (1553).

ment of the Cooper Park with the object of relieving the heavy traffic congestion in High Street. Some fine old trees were doomed and the Elgin Society and other objectors pointed out that the donor of the park had expressly stipulated that it was "never to be alienated from the purpose for which it was given". But trunk road policy triumphed over local considerations and after a public inquiry lasting twenty-one days the relief road scheme was given the green light. The wide open spaces of the park north of the bypass remain unharmed and motorists passing through will enjoy a better glimpse of the cathedral and a refreshing view of Elgin's green lung.

The Gaskin Report on the economy of the Grampian Region, marked out Elgin for substantial industrial growth and population expansion and the arrival of the North Sea oil boom has accentuated this trend. Elgin is by far the most important service centre between Aberdeen and Inverness. Its present modest population of 16,400 will certainly see an upward swing in the coming decade. But mere size cannot be the criterion of importance here. As a market town, as a woollen manufacturing centre, as a headquarters of the distilling industry, as a saw-milling and forestry centre it has its own busy economic life, but above all it is the gateway to some of the most lovely countryside in the British Isles—a countryside in which the lush and fertile Laich of Moray is sheltered by the rugged uplands, the pinewoods and the moorlands rising to mountain massifs in the south that guard the superb upper glens of the Spey, the Lossie and the Findhorn.

## WICK

Like Elgin and Inverness, Wick is also a capital. It stands in this relation to the third of the distinctive regions that border the Moray Firth. It has three avenues of approach, each of which illuminates its peculiar strategic importance. By air, which means dropping down out of the clouds to the flat green peninsula to the north of the town, it is the last airport on the mainland of the United Kingdom, the springboard to the islands beyond. There is a quiet, intimate air about the

modest runways and the pleasant, friendly passenger con-
course. But to reach it one will have had a glimpse on the hop
across the Firth of the long, jagged, cliffed coast of Caithness,
or, coming from Orkney on the north, of the ceaseless angry
surges that beat upon Stroma in the middle of the Pentland
Firth.

By the A9 trunk road one will have already become
acclimatized to the windswept shelf of farming land above
jagged cliffs which will have shown their true stature at the
point of entry into this land apart, the 750 foot Ord of
Caithness. But perhaps the most revealing entry of all is by rail
across the all-pervading dead level of the plain of Caithness,
featureless, flat, green, cultivated land where the rugged
uplands of the Highland Fringe seem but a distant memory
and the remote peaks of Morven and Scaraben stand up like
a mirage across thirty miles of moorland or farmland, and the
only touch of the exotic is provided by the dykes and fences
of dark red wafer-thin Caithness slabs.

You may think there is really nothing here to excite the
eye. But a thousand years ago the Vikings regarded it
differently. To them it was a magnet, a granary, capable of
feeding with rich crops their hungry, more mountainous
homeland in Norway. Caithness is part of the Viking saga-
land; its place names are warp and weft of the Orkneyinga
Saga. And something of this ancient glamour still remains in
the modern Caithness capital for all its dedication to fishing
and commerce. A wedge of the Caithness plain penetrates deep
along the widening banks of the Wick Water to Telford's
Bridge at the heart of the town.

The Bridge is really the hinge of Wick. North of it lies the
ancient royal burgh and south of it Poultneytown founded in
1808, but now the larger portion. East of it lies Wick Bay
with its three harbours and west of it an attractive riverside
quarter opening straight out into the Caithness plain.

The ancient High Street of Wick running roughly west to
east is linked to the Bridge by Bridge Street which dates from
the early nineteenth century and contains the Sheriff
Courthouse, the Town and County Hall and the Police
Station. The Town Hall with its dome and chiming clock has
been remodelled internally and has an interesting collection of
paintings including a reputed Raeburn, a landscape by Ben-

jamin West, a fine view of the old harbour and a portrait of James Bremner (1784-1856) the civil engineer, often regarded as Wick's greatest son. In his building yard at Poultneytown he built over fifty vessels and as an engineer planned, built or improved nineteen harbours, including the new harbour of Poultneytown. He had a special fame as a salvager of wrecked or sunken ships of which his tally was 236, including the *Great Britain,* then the largest ship in the world (3,500 tons), which he refloated from the strand at Dundrum Bay in Ireland in August 1847.

The narrow and winding High Street is full of interest and off it run the little lanes or wynds, which, as we saw in the case of Elgin, were typical of medieval Scots burghs. Wick, which had been a Norse settlement in the Dark Ages, received its charter as a burgh from James VI in 1589. Some controversy surrounds the name Wick, which is generally taken to be derived from the Norse *vik,* a bay, although a rival school derives it from the Gaelic. By the natives the name is pronounced Weik and was indeed so spelt until after 1790. James V held a 'parliament' at Wick during his voyage round Scotland in 1540 and Parliament Square to the right of Market Place, which fronts the east end of the High Street, is said to have been the site of this gathering.

The location of the old market cross is marked by granite blocks placed in the roadway where Tolbooth Lane joins the High Street. Royal proclamations are still made here and it was here in 1715 that Dunbar of Northfield proclaimed the Old Pretender, James VIII, and drank his health in the first Jacobite rebellion.

At the west end of High Street is the Old Parish Kirk and the Old Kirkyard. The churchyard dates from about 1576 while the church, the third on the same site, and dedicated like its predecessors to St Fergus, the patron saint of the burgh, dates from 1830. It is peculiar in its great width, the wide-spanning roof being unsupported by pillars and reputed to be the widest in Scotland. Part of the second church on the site survives in the form of the Sinclair Aisle containing the sepulchres of the old earls of Caithness. One interesting old carved tombstone is to be found in the aisle, but the oldest relic of the kind in the town, the recumbent effigy of a cleric in the Benedictine garb dating from the fifteenth century, has been removed from a niche in this old church and placed in the Wick Museum.

St Fergus was a far-travelled saint. After his ministry in Wick he crossed the Moray Firth to Aberdour and with St Drostan took part in the founding of the Celtic abbey of Deer in Aberdeenshire. Perhaps some reference to this is implicit in the old burgh seal of Wick, where he is depicted standing in a boat rowed by two men in top hats.

At its eastern end High Street leads to the sea at the Shore and the area known as the Camps facing the River Harbour and the Old Town Wharf, where there is a pleasant viewpoint. On the other side of the water, guarded by the North Quay, are the inner and outer harbours of Poultneytown.

Although it was the enterprise of the tradesmen of the old royal burgh which resulted in the creation of the 'new town' of Wick—Poultneytown—by the British Fisheries Society in 1808, the two communities lived under separate administrations for nearly a century and it was only in 1902 that a civic union took place, the new town council being formed of nine representatives of Poultneytown and six from the old royal burgh.

This peculiar situation resulted from the capital which the British Fisheries Society, the body charged with the fostering of the herring industry throughout the Highlands, expended in creating the 'new town'. The Society was particularly proud of Wick because in a long tale of failures and anti-climaxes it was their one really great and triumphant success. Their other 'babies' like Ullapool and Tobermory languished and declined, but Poultneytown astonished the world and became "the mistress of all the herring fisheries".

Thomas Telford designed first the Bridge of Wick, then Poultneytown itself on a rectilinear plan with the dwelling houses on the higher ground of a plateau south of the port, and the storehouses and curing yards on the narrow strip of low ground fronting the harbour, which was completed at a total cost of £14,000. By 1813 the population of the new town was 300, by 1819 almost 1,200, and by 1830 over 2,000.

By 1862 no fewer than 1,122 boats were operating from Wick during the summer herring season. In this year the foundation stone of a new harbour was laid, with the firm of D. and T. Stevenson as engineers, but the work had to be abandoned after a succession of disastrous storms and Robert Louis Stevenson, whose father was one of the partners in this abortive enterprise, wrote bitterly of the experience.

"As for Wick itself," he declared, "it is one of the meanest of man's towns, and situate certainly on the baldest of God's bays," and yet, he added, "it is a strange sight, and beautiful, to see the fleet put silently out against a rising moon, the sea-line rough as a wood with sails . . . " Stevenson had second thoughts about the meanness of Wick. In a later essay he wrote: "Out of the strong came forth sweetness. There in the bleak and gusty North I received perhaps my strongest impression of peace. I saw the sea to be great and calm, and the earth in that little corner was alive and friendly to me."

In *The Silver Darlings* Neil M. Gunn gave a more human picture of Wick in the heyday of the herring boom. It is one of "great stone walls, endless yards and cooperages, immense stacks of barrels, the smell of brine, long wooden jetties, the clanking of hammers, the loud rattling of wheels, warning yells and the cracking of whips, herring guts, crowds of screaming gulls, women in stiff rustling skirts, and everywhere men and boats . . . "

These great days are over. The centre of the herring industry has moved from the Moray Firth to the Minch and the top herring port of Europe is not now Wick but Mallaig. After the opening of the present century the industry in Wick declined rapidly and was replaced by the smaller white fishing industry which received a boost with the introduction of the seine net in the 1920s. In 1972 Wick had 496 fishermen and 162 fishing vessels, 24 of them over 40 feet of keel and the remainder smaller. The white fish catch totalled 130,074 cwt., valued at £783,875; shellfish accounted for 6,135 cwt. fetching £124,974, and herring only 1,314 cwt. worth £3,023.

But Poultneytown remains, although before the Wick and Poultneytown burgh council handed over its responsibilities to the Highland Region and the Caithness District Council in May 1975 it had very largely cleared and rebuilt the residential upper town which the British Fisheries Society had created, and was in process of replanning the harbour area with its deserted herring warehouses. So that the massive style of the old Poultneytown would not altogether disappear, some old properties were restored and internally modernized, among them a large three-storey block of tenements in Hȯddart Street, which can be seen today in rather stark contrast with the twentieth-century housing alongside it.

Another survival is the Poultneytown Academy now converted into a lively modern community centre as part of Wick's war memorial scheme. One of the first buildings in Telford's 'new town', it occupies a commanding position on the Braes where the plateau of Upper Poultneytown overlooks the harbour, and is called the Assembly Rooms. Nearer the Bridge is the Carnegie Library and Wick Museum. The library has a notable collection of local books, a series of early works by the outstanding modern Caithness artist D. M. Sutherland, and in the reading room a portrait gallery of characters in Caithness history. The museum has a complete collection of Caithness birds.

Farther south in Poultneytown is the Caithness glass factory which opened in 1959 and now attracts over 50,000 visitors a year to see the colourful glass-blowing processes by which decanters, flagons and chalices are shaped and the brilliantly designed engraving which has given this new industry an international cachet. The factory gives work to some 80 people in Wick and a total of 120 over the country.

Educationally Wick is an important centre. Its high school, with a roll of around 1,200, receives all the senior secondary pupils from the eastern half of Caithness, from Berriedale in the south to John o' Groats in the north. A new science block and games hall have just been added to the buildings.

Wick's total population is around 8,000. The commercial trade of the harbour is comparatively modest but the cargoes include coal in bulk from the English port of Goole, cement and slag from the continent and timber from the Baltic. An excellent modern fish market was opened in 1968. As the exploitation of North Sea oil continues to escalate, Wick's situation on a direct western line from important blocks of oil-field concessions may lead to greater harbour activity in support of the offshore oil industry.

Splendid rock scenery and invigorating clifftop walks are the main attractions in the environs of the town. The roads leading to South Head and to North Head on either side of the entrance to Wick Bay have each their attractions. From Braehead, overlooking the harbour, the South Head road passes the coastguard station and the Grey Bools, huge detached rocks lying on the top of the cliffs, and sweeps round to Old Wick or Auldwick. There is a tantalizing rhyme:

> Auldwick was Auldwick ere new Wick was begun,
> Auldwick will be Auldwick when new Wick is done.

It seems to have no historical justification other than a reference to the castle of Auldwick, a grim, roofless, three-storey tower, with rough masonry perforated by narrow arrow-slits, which appears to date from the twelfth century. A deep moat defended it on the landward side while its only door looked towards the sea in the direction of the north-east. The most colourful incident its history can boast refers to George Oliphant, who was occupying the castle in the reign of James IV of Scotland when he became involved in a violent feud with the Earl of Caithness. The earl and his men-at-arms attacked him when he was out hunting alone near the Loch of Yarrows. He galloped home towards Auldwick with the earl and his minions close on his heels. No drawbridge was down to receive him and his pursuers were pressing him close, so he gave his horse its head and the charger cleared the 25 foot chasm of the moat. 'Lord Oliphant's Leap' thereafter became a by-word in Caithness.

It might be best to leave the many fascinations of the coastline immediately north of Wick to the chapter on the Caithness countryside.

# CHAPTER IV

# BANFF-BUCHAN

THE THREE 'CAPITALS' of the Moray Firth lands described in the previous chapter would have little significance apart from the glorious countrysides to which they offer the key. To explore these countrysides, we now embark on a survey which is made easier by a road system based on two trunk highways, A9 Perth-Inverness-Wick (which gives access to the entire northern flank of the Firth) and A96, Inverness to Elgin and Aberdeen, which at Fochabers, a little east of Elgin, sends off an offshoot A98, also a trunk road, which serves the southern shore of the Firth from the River Spey to Fraserburgh.

Here, away at the eastern flank of the Firth, lies the hummocky green plateau of Buchan, now united for local government purposes to the administrative district rather clumsily labelled Banff-Buchan, because it incorporates the province of Buchan in Aberdeenshire with the eastern half of the county of Banff. The western half of that county is now united with Morayshire to form the Moray District, and both Moray and Banff-Buchan now belong to the Grampian Region, which also includes the remainder of the former county and city of Aberdeen and the former county of Kincardine.

The Grampian Region thus includes most of the southern flank of the Moray Firth, from Fraserburgh to Nairn. Nairn itself, with Inverness, Ross and Cromarty, Sutherland and Caithness, has been allocated to the huge Highland Region, so that the western and northern sectors of the Firth are officially in the Highlands. The visitor may well ask, do these distinctions really matter? Are they not, perhaps, merely matters of administrative convenience?

He will soon discover however that the distinction is very

real. Despite the mountainous connotations of the name 'Grampian', the culture of the region is predominantly lowland. The speech of its people is technically northern Scots, a very distinctive dialect deriving from Anglo-Saxon via Northumbria, enriched by copious infusions of words from Gaelic, French, and Scandinavian. He may perhaps be temporarily bewildered by a strong, clear, deliberate, somewhat high-pitched utterance that may at first seem to have only a distant affinity to English, though of course there will be many recognizably English words in it. "He will hear plenty of *ah's*, *eh's*, *ee's* and *f's* in odd places which will eventually make a pattern for him, for like all dialects it conforms to a system of sounds, and one too, with a long history and pedigree."

This sentence I have taken from an essay by the editor of the *Scottish National Dictionary*, Dr David D. Murison, himself a native of the region. He points out that by the fourteenth century, English, which had been established as Anglo-Saxon in the Lothians since about AD 600, had triumphed throughout the Lowlands of Scotland and the undulating plains of the north-east (which we are now calling Grampian). The language it supplanted was Gaelic which continued to be spoken in the Highlands until the old clan system was broken up finally and forcibly after the '45 Rebellion, though even in Highland parts of 'Grampian'—such as Braemar—it was spoken by old people until the period of the Second World War.

This is why, west of Nairn, the visitor will have no difficulty in understanding local speech, for here, despite the Highland heritage, the universally spoken tongue is a very charming, softly spoken school English, "the best English in Scotland"—since it was imbibed at school by the children of Gaelic-speakers who were only too anxious that their offspring should learn from the beginning only the language of commerce and success.

In the northern Scots of Grampian then, many exotic words will be heard; words from the Gaelic like *bannock* (pancake), *partan* (crab), *dulse* (edible seaweed), *girn* (to complain); words from Anglo-Saxon that has been modified by Scandinavian, such as *kirk* (church), *kist* (chest), *brig* (bridge), *rig* (ridge), *brae* (brow of a hill), *ain* (own), *hing* (hang), *strae* (straw), *gar* (to cause or compel), *big* (to build) *tyne* (to lose); words from Dutch like *cweet* (ankle), *crannie* (little finger), *dubs* (puddles) and *loon* (not a lunatic but a boy).

But, as Dr Murison points out, the real difficulties in understanding lie chiefly in the differences in the development of Anglo-Saxon vowels between the north and the south. What was once a long *ah* has become in standard English a long *oh* sound, but in Scots a long *eh,* and so we get the correspondences, go, *gae*; so, *sae*; more, *mair*; both, *baith*; home, *hame*; stone, *stane*; and so on. Anglo-Saxon said *ooh,* the Englishman says *ow* but the Scot keeps the *ooh* sound as it was, so that we get *doon* for down, *coo* for cow and *prood* for proud.

There is a small difficulty in deciding precisely where the ever-widening Moray Firth ends and merges with the broad expanse of the North Sea because of the gradual curve of the coastline of the north-east knuckle of Scotland as it veers round from a west-to-east north-facing line to the south-south-east-running east coast of the country. A classic topographical work of the late nineteenth century, Groome's *Ordnance Gazetteer,* placed it at Cairnbulg Point, four miles east of Kinnaird Head, the low rocky headland which dominates Fraserburgh harbour. Between Cairnbulg and Kinnaird lies the wide sandy sweep of Fraserburgh Bay and the fishing basins of the harbour.

Fraserburgh has a population of 10,750 and this is not expected to rise much above 11,000 in the next decade—unlike Peterhead, its old rival eighteen miles to the south-east which is in the throes of rapid industrial expansion as a North Sea oil servicing port and is expected to top 19,000 in the near future. Fraserburgh stands on a promontory facing two ways: east across the North Sea to Norway and due north to the North Atlantic and the Arctic and the Shetland Isles. At the angle between these two seafronts Kinnaird Head forms a jagged shelf of rock supporting a lighthouse of ancient origins, for it is a converted sixteenth-century castle.

It dates from 1569 and was the creation of Alexander, eighth laird of Philorth, a barony which had been the possession of the Fraser family since 1375. These Frasers were proud men and quick to wrath, as was Alexander Fraser the Seventh, the castle-builder's grandfather, who in 1530 was tried at a court in Aberdeen for slaying one David Scott in the course of a family feud. In penance for this crime he made a pilgrimage to the shrine of St John of Amiens and travelled on the continent until 1534, when he returned to the north-east of Scotland and devoted the rest of his life to the wresting of prosperity from his sea-girt lands. In 1542 King James V granted him the charter of extensive fishings and four years later the village Faithlie, the "hill of watch" at Kinnaird, became at his suit a free burgh of barony. "Whereas," says the charter granted by Mary Queen of Scots,

> Alexander Fraser of Philorth, for the convenience of his neighbours, has built a harbour upon the seashore, in which ships and vessels overtaken by storms may be able to find refuge, we erect the town of Faithlie into a free burgh of barony, granting to the inhabitants the power of buying and selling, and that there may be burgesses and baillies annually elected and that they may have a market cross and weekly markets.

When he succeeded his grandfather in 1569 Alexander the eighth built the Castle of Kinnaird and in the following year founded a new church on the site of the present old parish church of Fraserburgh and by 1576 had completed a greatly improved harbour. Three more charters—from James VI—followed in 1588, 1592 and 1601. The second charter created the town a burgh of regality with a free port, declaring that "the same shall in all time coming be called the Port de Fraser". The third speaks of "the town now called Fraserburgh" and empowers "the said Alexander to erect and endow a university".

Only the central tower—on a rectangular plan but much altered—of the castle which Sir Alexander built remains. Four floors survive, but the fifth was removed in 1787 to make way for the lantern chamber of the lighthouse.

But if the castle itself has been transformed it has a unique appendage—an isolated, square, keep-like structure called the Wine Tower which stands on the rock at the foot of the castle 'wynd' and has good claim to be considered the oldest unaltered building in the town.

What was the Wine Tower? Certainly more than a glorified wine cellar. The elaborate and stately interior construction of the tower belies this idea. It is of three storeys, all vaulted, and from the vaulted roof of the upper chamber hang three finely carved pendants while there are other pendants of smaller size in the soffits of the windows. One of the pendants bears the royal arms of James V with supporters and the crest and motto 'In Defens' in a scroll round the top, which would seem to date the tower to the first quarter of the sixteenth century. A second pendant contains the arms of the Frasers with their motto 'In God is All', while the third pendant takes the form of an angel supporting a shield and pointing with one finger at the emblems of the Crucifixion which it contains. On the window pendants are the arms of the Frasers, Erskines, Douglases and other Scottish noble families. This apartment, it is almost certain, had been used as a chapel.

The University of Fraserburgh which Sir Alexander Fraser obtained King James's permission to establish had a short and chequered career. A grant to set it up was obtained from the Scottish Parliament and the Rev. Charles Ferme was appointed Principal. Unfortunately in 1605 Ferme took part in the General Assembly at Aberdeen convened in defiance of the king's pleasure. In consequence of this he was, with seventeen other clerics, denounced by the Privy Council, carried off by the Earl of Huntly, and placed under arrest. In his absence the infant university collapsed and never recovered. A street called College Bounds, a continuation of High Street, is a memento of the incident.

The present civic centre of the town is in Saltoun Square where stands the Old Kirk built in 1803 to replace the church built in 1570-71. Alongside it stands the ancient burial aisle of the Frasers. Sir Alexander Fraser had left instructions for this structure to be built "at the south side of the kirk". So there it stands today, surmounted by its cross—a direct link with the founding of the burgh.

Here too are the market cross and the Town House and immediately to the east lie the basins of the modern harbour. As already mentioned, it was in 1546 that Fraser of Philorth built the first harbour. This was manned by a colony of fishermen who dwelt in what was called the Seatown, now Broadsea, immediately to the west of Kinnaird Head, and as late as 1789 there were only forty-two fishermen and seven boats. But by 1810 a major expansion due to the commencement of herring fishing was under way and by 1815 there were already fourteen firms curing here. What is called the Old Harbour, or Faithlie Harbour, at the north end of Fraserburgh Bay, was built between 1814 and 1830. This was followed by the North and Balaclava Harbours, and two long breakwaters were completed in 1910.

Nearly 200 fishing vessels at present operate from Fraserburgh and a harbour improvement scheme costing over £1 million is under way. There are three big fish-processing plants, the largest of which, Associated Fisheries, has the biggest freezing plant in the country.

Alongside the fishing interest a great asset to the town is the engineering complex of the Consolidated Pneumatic Tool-works. When CPT first came to Fraserburgh in 1905 it brought work to 400. Now there are 1,100 on the payroll and the employees are mainly male, a factor of importance in a fishing burgh where shore jobs are otherwise superabundant for women.

Two prominent street names in the town tell their own story. The main highway to the south—to Aberdeen and Peterhead—is called Maconochie Road after W. A. Maconochie, who at the end of last century founded the canning and food processing firm which achieved international renown in the South African War as the suppliers of a large part of the British Army's canned rations and continued the same role in the First and Second World Wars.

The other street name of international significance is Marconi Road in Broadsea at the north-western end of the town. This commemorates the fact that in the early years of the century the Marchese Marconi, inventor of wireless telegraphy, set up a research station on Broadsea Farm to test out the power then required to send wireless signals from Fraserburgh to points in the south of England. The inventor was something of a local hero and was fêted by Fraserburgh town council.

Broadsea itself deserves special mention. This remarkable old-world fishing village, now surrounded on three sides by the westward spread of the modern town, has retained all its ancient character and has been designated a conservation area. Its red-tiled cottages cluster on the clifftop and old residents can recall when the herring boats were drawn up on the beach by traction engines.

South-east of the town lies the great curve of Fraserburgh
Bay stretching for four miles to Cairnbulg Point. Unlike
Wick, Fraserburgh has no river, but its sands are superb, a fact
recalled by John C. Milne's verse eulogy in the Buchan dialect:

> O Tam, gie me auld Faithlie toon
> Whaur trees are scrunts for miles aroon
> And nae a burn wad slake or droon
> A drunken miller;
> But sands and bents that wear a croon
> O' gowd and siller.

Fraserburgh beach is the town's main holiday attraction.
Safe swimming and bathing areas are marked off by floats; a
beach rescue is on duty throughout the summer, and there is
a paddling pool and a miniature railway. A modern 25 metres
swimming pool attached to Fraserburgh Academy in Alex-
andra Terrace is open to the public in the evenings and
throughout the day at weekends and during school holidays.

Although it soon lost its university, Fraserburgh is a centre
of higher technical education for the entire Banff–Buchan
district through the recently opened Buchan Technical College
in Lochpots Road to the west of the town. Probably the most
spectacular feature of the college is the navigation room or
'bridge' at first-floor level above laboratories. The navigators'
tools here include a gyro-compass, a deviascope, a Decca
simulator, and direction finding and radar along with chart
tracing equipment—all very fitting for a school of navigation
which serves what is the most important fishing district for
inshore fishermen in Britain.

Buchan for fishermen—but also Buchan for farming. The
most popular alternative for the somewhat ponderous name
Fraserburgh is not Faithlie, the old historic name of the place,
but simply 'the Broch', meaning the burgh or town, because,
to many thousands of country-dwellers in the broad Buchan
farmlands it may be the only town they know—their town.

A little stream, the Water of Philorth, enters Fraserburgh
Bay at its eastern end. About a mile upstream is Cairnbulg
Castle, the ancestral home of the Frasers. The oldest part of
the building, the lower part of the square tower, is now
thought to date back to the early sixties of the thirteenth

century. It was probably built to resist King Haakon of Norway in the invasion attempt that was frustrated by the Battle of Largs.

This tower would have been intended merely as a strong-point of Scots resistance and was rebuilt by Sir Alexander Fraser for use as a domestic dwelling after he had acquired the barony of Philorth on his marriage to Joanna, daughter of the Earl of Ross, in 1375. For the next 240 years it was the home of the Fraser family until in 1615 it was sold by the eighth laird, to help pay debts which he had incurred by building Fraserburgh. The plan of the castle as finally completed in the sixteenth century was that of a Z-plan tower house, a pattern achieved in 1545 when the seventh Fraser laird added on to the keep a rectangular building with a circular angle tower. It remained habitable until 1785 when it began to fall into disrepair and was abandoned a decade later. Almost a century later it was restored by Sir John Duthie, a ship-building magnate, whose son sold it to Alexander Arthur Fraser, nineteenth Lord Saltoun, the direct descendant of its original owners. So once more the Frasers reign in Philorth, in the person of Lord Saltoun's daughter Flora, who married Captain Alexander Ramsay of Mar. Thomas the Rhymer's prophecy is vindicated:

> While a cock crows in the north
> There'll be a Fraser at Philorth.

The sweep of Fraserburgh Bay comes to an end at Cairn-bulg Point and upon the shingly beach beyond, in one of the most ruthlessly exposed places of human settlement in Britain, lie the twin villages of Cairnbulg and Inverallochy. The two of them have a joint population of around 1,331 and to the uninitiated eye appear a single, undifferentiated built-up area. There is only one road in across the green Buchan plain, but under this road there runs a hidden stream, now imprisoned in an underground pipe, so what looks like a single conur-bation is immutably divided.

The division is now effectively signposted by large nameplates at first on either side of the approach road and finally at the central crossroads—a precaution that is necessary since each village has its own Mid Street, Main Street and

Shore Street—long eighteenth-century cottage rows of identical pattern, now all listed buildings in a designated conservation area. It might be called curious rather than picturesque,
but given the flash of sun the austerity vanishes. There is little
colour in the stone gables, yet a dazzling contrast and beauty
in the blue of the sea, the gleam of the pebbles, and the
blinding white of the breakers as they surge to the shore. Let
there be a fanfare of washing on the lines, the gaily painted
hulls of beached boats, and the red network of lobster creels,
and the picture is complete.

The twin communities share with the neighbouring village
of St Combs, a mile and a half along the coast, a remarkable
series of annual celebrations—the Temperance Walks, held on
Christmas Day (for Inverallochy), New Year's Day (for
Cairnbulg) and 2 January (for St Combs). They are community marches led by fife bands, usually about forty strong,
and followed by every able-bodied inhabitant. They muster in
the village halls, march through the home community, and
then through each of the neighbouring villages in turn. The
religious origin of these festivals is remembered in the evangelistic hymns played by the fife bands, though popular secular
airs are not taboo. They originated in a widespread and
emotional revival which swept through the fishing communities in the 1850s.

For common purposes the twin villages call themselves
Invercairn, and when St Combs has to be counted in—as
sometimes happens when there is a shortage of stars for the
local football team—the tongue-twisting formula Inversaint-
cairn is resorted to.

West of Fraserburgh the character of the country changes.
The trunk road A98 sweeps inland in a wide curve through
rural Buchan in rather featureless country displaying all the
hallmarks of the 'landscape of improvement' on its way via
Tyrie and New Pitsligo to Banff. The coast road, B9031, is
more interesting. Emerging from the north-western corner of
Fraserburgh and passing the Clubbie Craig, a prominent rock,
one comes in sight of a long, deeply-curving bay, by the verge
of which the road along the coast hugs the Phingask Shore.
Across this bay with its sands and occasional low dark fangs
of rock, one sees, beyond the turbulence of breakers racing to
the beach, the projecting line of the village of Sandhaven. At

this point Sandhaven's twin, the older village of Pittulie, is not visible and the effect is of a modern township, reinforced by new local authority housing stretching inland to the extent of eighty modern homes and a modern school. But a closer inspection alters the impression.

On the outskirts of the village is an old meal mill and opposite it is the great empty expanse of Sandhaven harbour, now quite deserted except in summer when it is used by pleasure craft. It is a harbour that was dreamed about for centuries before it was actually built in 1830 by Sir John Forbes of Pitsligo and the Fishery Board at a cost of £4,206, and has seen many busy days before falling upon its present neglect.

This is a scene which one will see duplicated over and over along the length of the Moray Firth. It is just one of the multiplicity of derelict harbours consequent on the centralization of fish marketing and the change in the nature of fishing vessels. But it does not mean that the fishermen themselves have gone. As one passes through the village and turns the corner beyond the school, the church and the hall into Pittulie one is transported into another era by the genuinely antique.

Here are the old-time fisher cottages with their low tiled roofs, rubble-built walls and gable ends facing the street. The long history of the fishing community is present here in stone and lime. These little houses were built to endure the buffetings of centuries, presenting the least surface to the winds from the sea which, in the Great Gale of 1953, were so severe that fish were blown out of the water and landed up in the school playground.

That could scarcely happen now, for the new school was designed to profit from the wisdom of the old vernacular building of the village. The main frontage facing north is a stout, blank-faced barrier to these formidable winds. It conceals rather than reveals the windowed splendour that lies behind. This is centred by a tall octagonal general purposes room which forms the centre-piece of the design, a spacious assembly area which also serves as dining hall, music room and gymnasium, off which classroom suites and flanking wings form protection for sheltered play areas. To add to the illusion that the school has really grown out of its environment, the sheltered areas have been 'planted' with smooth-stoned rocky 'outcrops', just like the rocks that litter the Sandhaven foreshore, while the G.P. room has been given a mural depicting the fishing, farming and shipbuilding which are the planks of the local economy.

Unless one keeps one's eyes skinned one can pass right through the twin villages without noticing the boat-building yard—a century-old institution which has never been more vital than it is at present.

Except when a boat is to be launched the work here is all under cover and it is a surprising experience to pass out of the empty street into the two great sheds where every inch of space seems occupied by craft under construction. On one visit I found eight vessels being built by the forty-eight skilled craftsmen at work in this famous yard. Three of them were 42-foot cabin cruisers of the Kemrock class hailed at the Earl's Court Boat Show as a "dream boat". The Sandhaven boat-builders have been able to turn from the old staple of fishing-boat building to this luxury line with success. But on my next visit I found a Pittulie fisherman watching a 58-foot dual purpose stern trawler being built for him here. Like many another fisherman in the village he will fish out of Fraserburgh, where the market is, but will consider his craft, with justification, as a Sandhaven boat. Sandhaven has a population now of around 800 but its 'equal partnership' with the much smaller Pittulie is an unquestioned fact of local life.

Pittulie first appears on record in the year 1408 when Sir William Fraser of Philorth took over the lands of 'Over and Nether Pettouly' from his father. Pittulie Castle, on high ground about a mile south-west of the village, probably dates from 1595 when another Fraser, Alexander, married Margaret, daughter of the seventh Lord Saltoun, though the date 1657 is carved on the skew stone of the last gable of the main building which consists of a long, low block with a square tower (from which a cylindrical stair turret projects) at the north-west corner.

The castle and lands of Pittulie passed in 1670 to Sir William Cumine of Auchry and it was probably the Cumines, a strongly Jacobite family, who founded the village. In 1787 the castle, by then falling into ruin, was sold to Sir William

Forbes, the banker friend of James Boswell and founder of New Pitsligo village.

Barely a mile due west on the same 100 foot contour is the ruin of the castle of Pitsligo which looks down today on the old burgh of Rosehearty which its overlord conjured into being at the end of the seventeenth century.The Forbeses of Pitsligo arrived on the scene when Sir William Forbes, son of Sir John Forbes of Druminnor in Strathbogie, married the only daughter of Sir William Fraser of Philorth mentioned above. In 1424 he built the tower house of Pitsligo, the oldest part of the existing ruin, a massive rectangular keep 114 feet high divided into three storeys and with walls 9 feet thick.

The whole house consisted of three rooms one on top of the other. In the basement was the vaulted kitchen, 12 feet high, above it the banqueting hall also vaulted and 25 feet high, and above that again "the sleeping apartment for the whole family, which had in it 24 beds". What more natural than that the Forbes lairds of Pitsligo should stimulate industry within their domain. They improved the shelter for the fishermen's boats, which they provided free on condition that they received a fifth part of all the fish caught. Sir Alexander Forbes, afterwards the first Lord Forbes of Pitsligo, secured the creation of the parish of Pitsligo, by an act of the Scottish Parliament on 18 June 1633. He it was who built the old parish church and the Forbes aisle on a site higher up the slope behind the castle and gave the old kirk a fine belfry of Dutch design. It is said that when the carved stones arrived from Holland he was lying ill and had them conveyed into his bedroom in the castle for his inspection.

The belfry can be seen today on the ruined gable of the old church which was abandoned in 1890 when a new church was built alongside it. The Pitsligo Aisle was moved bodily into the new church where it forms the south transept and contains one of the best extant examples of Jacobean Scottish carved woodwork—probably executed under the guidance of Dutch carvers. From the nave of the church the aisle is completely partitioned off by the massive decorated front of the Pitsligo pew, surmounted by a spectacular canopy. The front of the pew is composed of six panels all containing elaborate carvings with monograms and coats of arms.

The second Lord Forbes of Pitsligo was empowered to

establish the burgh of barony of Rosehearty by a royal charter dated 13 July 1681, given at Windsor Castle. The actual charter of feu contract, half in Latin and half in Scots, a precious sheepskin held by the town council, is dated 18 October 1684. The burgh seal was a rose and heart with the motto CORDE ET MANU. Modern Rosehearty still retains much characterful old building, both in the 'New Town' and the 'Sea Town' where in the 1880s as many as 100 boats were using the port.

The fourth and last Lord Forbes of Pitsligo—always known simply as Lord Pitsligo—was born in 1678 and educated in France where he became the friend of Fenelon. His father died in 1690 and he took his seat in the Scottish Parliament of 1700. He protested against the Act of Union between Scotland and England and retired to his castle of Pitsligo. He became a lifelong Jacobite and joined his first cousin the Earl of Mar in the 1715 Rising. He fled to the continent when it failed, but his name not having appeared in the list of attainders he returned to Scotland in 1720 and lived quietly. When Bonnie Prince Charlie landed and the 1745 Rebellion opened he was sixty-seven and had no hopes that the rebellion could succeed, but he had never renounced his old loyalty to the House of Stuart. As the best-loved landowner in the north he formed a band of volunteer cavalry of the gentlemen of Aberdeenshire and Banffshire and rode into Aberdeen on 5 October 1745.

When the troop was mustered for departure to Edinburgh he moved to the front, lifted his hat and said: "Oh Lord, Thou knowest our cause is just. Gentlemen, march!" He took part in the whole campaign, riding most of the way, and was described by Murray of Broughton as "deservedly the most popular man in the country". He escaped from the rout at Culloden, hid himself in Mr William King's house of Greyfriars in Elgin, and, a week later, reached his ancestral lands and visited Pitsligo Castle, where he obtained a disguise from his wife. For the next four years he lived an extraordinary hunted, wandering life, sometimes hidden in the houses of his tenants, sometimes sheltering in caves or under bridges.

Once, disguised as a beggar, he was given a shilling by the soldiers searching for him, and held a lantern for them while they searched his cave. The hunt was dropped for some years, but as late as ten years after Culloden, when he was nearly eighty years of age, he narrowly escaped capture in his son's house at Auchiries in the parish of Rathen. They hid him in a recess behind the bed of a woman visitor, who coughed loudly all the time the redcoats were searching her room to cover up the asthmatic breathing of the old man in his hiding place. As soon as the soldiers had left the room Lord Pitsligo emerged and told a servant to see that his pursuers got some breakfast and a drink of warm ale "for this is a cold morning; they are only doing their duty and cannot bear me any ill will". The old man died aged eighty-four on 21 December, 1762 and was buried in the family vault in the kirk of Pitsligo.

Rosehearty today has some claim to be a popular holiday resort. Many years ago its inner harbour was converted into an open-air swimming pool and the local guidebook claims that "the breathtaking scene as the setting sun sinks into the Moray Firth at Rosehearty is a grander sight than anything to be experienced on the Norwegian fiords".

As we move west from Rosehearty we enter the parish of Aberdour and a strongly contrasted type of landscape. Hitherto the coast of the Firth has alternated between low sandy bays and shallow platforms of mica-schist rock. Now we come into the realm of Old Red Sandstone conglomerates where the cliffs are high, friable and honeycombed with caves, one of the first of which, to the east of Quarry Head, is Lord Pitsligo's Cave. For a mile west of Quarry Head the cliff sequence is superb and terminates in the promontory on which stands Dundarg, the Red Fort, an Iron Age stronghold which became in turn the site of a Dark Age monastic settlement, a medieval castle, a Renaissance coastal fortification, and ultimately an early twentieth-century castellated mansion.

There is unfortunately no coastal road along the top of these cliffs and some of the country immediately west of Rosehearty is used by the RAF as a practice bombing range, but Dundarg itself can be approached from the landward side by farm service roads leading seaward from B9031, the road from Rosehearty to New Aberdour and Pennan.

The unique Dark Age manuscript the Book of Deer, which contains marginal notes in old Scottish Gaelic, tells how St Drostan set sail from Caithness and crossed the Moray Firth to "Aberdober" i.e. Aberdour, accompanied by his two disciples Medan and Fergus (earlier mentioned as the patron saint of Wick) and how a certain mormaer "Bede the Pict" granted him a site there. Two sets of excavations at Dundarg, the latter conducted by Dr W. Douglas Simpson, confirmed the presence of the Iron Age fort on the spine of the long narrow headland at Dundarg and ultimately uncovered the foundations of a chapel which may well have been Drostan's settlement. In the early Middle Ages a castle was established on the rock. Destroyed by King Robert the Bruce in the Harrying of Buchan, it was restored by the English knight Henry de Beaumont in the time of Edward III and destroyed again after a siege by the resurgent Scots in 1334.

Two centuries later the inner gatehouse of this ruined castle was again rebuilt and provided with gunloops—this time as Scottish coastal defence against English attack by sea by forces of Henry VIII during the War of the Rough Wooing in Mary Queen of Scots' minority. Finally a modern castle was built at the base of the promontory with stones from the former free church in New Aberdour in the year 1938.

Inland from Dundarg there is rich and fertile farming country. About a mile east-south-east of Dundarg on the south side of the B9031 road stands Aberdour House, the old mansion of the parish, a Category A listed building in the national buildings record. Built by S. Forbes of Skellater in 1740—the date and the initials of Forbes and his wife appear on the centre chimney gable on the north front—Aberdour House is the most ambitious of several mansions of the period in Buchan. It has a main block of three storeys and a seven-window south front completed by quadrant links to two-storey wings on each side. With crow-stepped gables and imposing central pediment the whole effect is stately, almost palatial. The mansion and estate were sold in 1750 to Alexander Gordon the wealthy factor of the Earl of Aberdeen, and it was his successor, William Gordon, who founded the village of New Aberdour in 1797. Like many another planned village of the period it now seems to have no clear economic role and most of its working folk commute to Fraserburgh. Its oldest surviving building is the original inn of 1798. The village was laid out on a T-plan with the new church of the parish (designed by John Smith of Aberdeen and built in 1818) on the main axis, through which runs the B9031 road on its way to the west. Far more interesting and picturesque must have been the old Kirkton of the parish which lay in the vale of the Dour Burn on a side road leading north and seaward from B9031 a little west of the modern village. Here still stands the ruins of the St Drostan's Kirk, the medieval parish church. The surviving structure dates from the early sixteenth century, with a south aisle rebuilt about 1760. The kirkyard within a pentagonal rubble-walled enclosure, has grave slabs of 1593 onwards. Both church and manse are within sight of the Broad Shore of Aberdour to which the road now leads alongside the burn in its deeply etched den, characteristic of this Red Sandstone country where all the watercourses have deep, narrow vales carved out of the soft rock.

The Broad Shore, a delightful sandy bay punctuated by dark fangs of rock and sheltered by massive cliffs on either side, is a favourite lido for bathers and picnic parties. Midway along it is St Drostan's Well, now encased in a modern metal and concrete covering with a memorial plaque. But its water still flows cold, clear and abundant as it must have done in the days of the saint himself. At the eastern end of the bay there are spectacular rock arches and caverns at the base of the cliffs. Along the coast the cliffs towards the west now rise in height to around 400 feet at Strahangles Point and there is a further sequence riddled with caves.

We now return to B9031 which snakes its way up hill and down dale, reaching a summit of 518 feet in lush farming country before it descends towards Pennan, without doubt the most spectacular cliff-foot village on the entire Moray Firth coast. Sheltered on the east by the great bluff of Pennan Head and isolated from the outside world by a continuous cliff wall, it is approached by a very steep twisting road from the green plateau above; the houses stand, mostly gable ends to the sea, on a narrow shelf between the foot of the cliffs and the foreshore. There has been a fishing community here at least since the seventeenth century.

The entire village of over fifty houses has been scheduled as a group (Category B) in the Secretary of State for Scotland's list of buildings of architectural or historic importance. In explanation of this the Scottish Development Department state that it is "an outstandingly picturesque fishing village mainly of early nineteenth century date nestling at the base of cliffs and still very complete and unspoilt with only two houses seriously altered out of fifty-odd". It is gratifying that in fact only seven of the houses are holiday homes. All the rest are occupied throughout the year by a cross-section of people including bus-drivers, fishermen, professional men and women, teachers and social workers. Its conservation has been a settled policy of the laird Mr David S. Watt who has laid it down that no building development will be allowed to affect the superb cliff slopes behind the village. He has however planted 200 trees to discover to what extent they will grow on the sea-facing slopes.

Pennan's trim little harbour, first built of red sandstone ashlar in the mid-nineteenth century, was given a new concrete pier in 1904 and a modern sea wall improves coast protection and replaces the old open beach. Besides the pleasure craft which are increasingly using it, four or five local boats still go fishing for lobsters, mackerel and whelks in the summer. With every year that passes Pennan is more visited and enjoyed as a place of resort. The single seafront street is thronged with cars at weekends. The Pennan Inn, opened as a high-quality hotel a few years ago, hires out sea-angling craft. The harbour has been kept in perfect repair, not by subsidy but by the people of Pennan themselves.

Separated from Pennan on the west by a rocky bluff lies the Bay of Cullykan into which run the waters of a little stream called the Tore Burn which forms the boundary between the parishes of Aberdour and Gamrie and also between Aberdeenshire and Banffshire. The deep den which it has carved in the Old Red Sandstone, known as the Tore of Troup, was once well wooded but has now lost many of its fine old trees. At the western end of the bay on a promontory called the Castle Point of Troup a series of excavations recently unearthed a remarkable series of prehistoric settlements dating back to the transition period between the Bronze and Iron Ages. A great Iron Age fort two acres in extent sealed off the neck of the peninsula. Within it around 1260 was built a medieval castle which gave Castle Point its name and which had a finely patterned paved courtyard.

Castle Point, an extensive grass-topped headland, besides commanding the entrance both to Cullykan Bay and Pennan Bay, is almost cut off from the mainland on its landward side and so makes an ideal defensive position. It is this strategic advantage which has given it its history of fortification extending over 2,000 years. Strangely enough, with millennia of human activity going on far above on the top of the cliffs, Castle Point is breached at the base by a subterranean passage under the living rock called the Needle's E'e which leads to an enormous cave known as the Devil's Diningroom. On the west side of Castle Point there projects into the sea another promontory fronted by beetling cliffs, the Lion's Head, and this in turn is breached by a huge fissure—Hell's Lum, 50 feet deep. There is a subterranean gallery 100 yards long driven from the seashore and connecting with this outlet.

"It is," wrote one observer, "a ghastly spot, full of weird gurglings made by the waters pent in their narrow gorge. With a stiff breeze from the north-west, spindrift is blown through the landward outlet, giving the illusion from a distance of a smoking chimney which may be seen as far away as Windyheads Hill, the peak of the moorland uplands to the south in the parish of Aberdour." Windyheads Hill has an altitude of over 700 feet.

How long did the castle survive as a going concern? Was it deliberately 'slighted'—knocked down in the Harrying of Buchan by King Robert I when he overthrew his mighty enemies the Comyns? That would seem very probable and certainly there is evidence that the walls were made to fall outwards. We know that the lands of Troup were bestowed by James I on the Keiths, Earls Marischal, and that they remained in their possession until 1653 when they were acquired by Major Alexander Garden, the first Garden laird.

But the story of Castle Point as a stronghold was by no means over. Very possibly a part of the old keep was still standing when, around 1690, the Government of William and Mary, fearing that the French, in support of James VII and II, might attempt a pro-Jacobite landing in the north of Scotland, sent a certain Captain Fiddes into Buchan to see to coastal defences. Alexander Garden, the second of Troup, besides being an ardent agricultural improver, was, as befits a soldier's son, an ardent supporter of William of Orange and he welcomed Captain Fiddes, entertaining him at the modest two-storey house of large clay bricks which his father had built on the banks of the Burn of Troup. The Captain, no doubt with the assistance of the military, proceeded to throw up near the tip of Castle Point an earthwork fortification known as Fort Fiddes. It may be that stones from the old castle were used in its construction. Either at this time or later the laird of Troup laid down a bowling green on the Point near the fort. Captain Fiddes left a portrait of himself behind at Troup House which shows "a little snub-nosed assertive soldier".

The threat of invasion faded, but it revived again a century later during the Napoleonic Wars and Castle Point acquired new defensive armament in the shape of two heavy 'tween-decks naval cannon. Gun emplacements were made for them on the tip of Castle Point on a flat, grassy platform which soon became known as the Battery Green. Today only one of the big guns remains in its proper position.

The geology of this area is highly complicated. Metamorphic rock replaces Old Red Sandstone in the massive promontory of Troup Head but the Old Red returns in Gamrie Bay on its westward flank where the next coastal village is the small but highly picturesque Crovie.

Gamrie Bay, a shallow inlet about a mile and a half broad, is the only substantial break in the line of high cliffs extending some nine miles along the coast from Pennan and Cullykan to Macduff and the mouth of the Deveron. Two headlands, Crovie Head on the east and More Head on the west, enclose it and steep 'sea braes' overlook it on the landward side. These braes are occupied about the centre of the bay by the large village of Gardenstown (pop. 900) which takes its name from the Garden lairds of Troup, and the smaller village of Crovie (pop. 80) forms a single row of houses under the cliff at the eastern end. As the New Statistical Account puts it, Crovie's cottages lie with one gable end to the sea and the other to the land "like a brood of young seafowl nestling with their heads under their dam". It is linked to Gardenstown by a footpath along the shore and to the outer world by a single steep narrow road from the plateau above.

In this respect it is just like Pennan, but unlike Pennan it has recently undergone a major change of character. The single street is numbered from 1 to 65 and the oldest resident can recall when the population was over 200 and there were twelve skiffs, each with a crew of six, fishing from the little harbour. After the Great Gale of 1953 it looked as though

Crovie was doomed. The footpath to Gardenstown was washed away, a large section of the sea wall was undermined; some houses were completely destroyed, others heavily damaged, and wheeled traffic could no longer get to the foot of the road leading to the village. All this has been rectified. The road has been restored; the footpath to Gardenstown has been rebuilt and now ends in a large and crowded car park. Today the whole village is humming with activity as houses are modernized, rebuilt and redecorated as holiday cottages.

Gardenstown on the other hand retains its original character to a remarkable degree, despite very considerable expansion. It is 133 years since Alexander Whyte the parochial schoolmaster of Gamrie described Gardenstown, but as nobody has ever done it better I can only quote:

At the bottom of the bay, the rocks which are steep and rugged on either side retire a little, leaving room for the village of Gardenstown *and no more* and then they rise with just as much bend from the perpendicular as allows mould to lie upon them, which is closely covered with green grass, except here and there a winding footpath like a staircase, on which few can venture without fear and trembling except the natives. From the tops of these braes as they are called one could almost fancy he could peep down the chimneys of the houses, and so abrupt is the rising of the ground in some places that one house of three storeys has them all ground floors, one entrance being at the front, another at the back and the third at an end.

It has to be admitted that modern road engineering has made the village more accessible and the old snake-like footpaths have become reliable paved steps and stairs. But Mr Whyte's description still holds good for the old ruined church which overlooks the village from the west. "On the west side," he says, "stands the old church and churchyard on a ledge of the hill's brow—which one would think in equal danger of being smothered by the hill hanging over it, and of being undermined by the sea below."

> Hast seen the old lone churchyard,
>   The churchyard by the sea,
> High on the edge of a windswept ledge,
>   And it looks o'er Gamerie?

This is the former parish church of Gamrie, the church of St John the Evangelist, whose western gable bears the date 1004. Its existence in this unlikely situation is attributed to an invasion that failed. Sir William Geddes's melodramatic verses tell the tale:

> Over brine, over faem,
> Thorough flood, thorough flame
> The ravenous hordes of the Norsemen came
> To ravage our fatherland . . .
> The war I ween had a speedy close
> And the 'Bloody Pits' to this day can tell
> How the ravens were glutted with gore,
> And the church was garnished with trophies fell
> Three grim skulls of three Norse Kings
> Grinning a grin of despair;
> Each looking out from his stony cell—
> They stared with a stony stare.

According to a traditional account the Norsemen were remnants of an invading army who had already been defeated by the Scots at Aberlemno. They had intended to sail to Moray where their kinsmen were already in occupation but were driven to the Buchan coast by a tempest.

Spurred on by famine owing to the failure of their provisions, 500 of them resolved to land and either to die bravely or find food and shelter. To begin with all went well. They found and drove before them large herds of cattle. But the Scots were watching from the nearby Castle Hill of Findon and lit beacons to summon reinforcements. The Scots were led by the Mormaer of Buchan who vowed that if St John would give him the victory he would build him a church on the very spot on the slopes of Gamrie Mohr where the invaders were encamped. By a wide outflanking movement the Mormaer's men gained the top of the hill and dislodged the Norsemen by rolling down upon them an avalanche of stones. But the battle was not yet over. The invaders, aided by fresh waves of their compatriots who had landed at the Old Haven of Cullen four miles to the westward, rallied and drove the Scots back to the Castle Hill. But in face of increasing arrivals of Scottish reinforcements they could not hold their gains. The Scots, pouring in from all quarters, forced them to a last stand on the hill and, after they had been surrounded, rushed in upon them sword in hand and cut them to pieces to a man. The three Norse kings mentioned by Geddes in his poem were found among the slain. And wrote an observer: "I have seen their skulls, grinning horrid and hollow in the wall where they had been fixed inside the church, directly east of the pulpit, where they had remained in their prisonhouse 800 years." After the church was abandoned they were pilfered bit by bit by some of the numerous visitors to the site, although one was recovered and placed in Banff Museum. Kirk and kirkyard were allowed to fall into a sorely neglected condition. Geddes's poem was a call to repair time's ravages:

> Rouse thee, village of Gamerie, rouse thee,
> Fishermen, husbandmen, villagers all;
> Swear to protect every slate, every stone—
> Sweeter ye'll sleep neath her sheltering wall.
> Let her sit like a queen by her rock-girdled bay,
> Prouder the place than a baron's hall.

That was over a century ago. The old fabric was restored again in the early 1960s and someone had inscribed on the new cement inside a plaque on the wall "Built 1004, Repaired 1961". It is of course pretty certain that none of the church of 1004 actually remains, but the shell that still stands must be very ancient. Its oldest monument commemorates "an honourable man, Patrick Barclay, laird of Tolly, and Janet Ogilvy, his spouse, who died January 6, 1547".

Gardenstown, founded by Peter Garden, third of Troup (1685-1740), in 1720, has continued to be inhabited by the same fishing families for over a century. In 1835 it was reported that most of the inhabitants bore the name of Watt or Wiseman. In 1922 it was found that in the village there were 68 Watts, 19 Wisemans and 17 Nicols. All these families still abound today, and although all the Gardenstown-owned fishing vessels of any size operate from Macduff, Fraserburgh and other ports, it is often claimed that Gardenstown is the richest fishing village in Scotland. In the harbour itself, occupied only by small craft, I counted eight full-time lobster fishermen, three or four part-timers, a salmon cobble, one hand line fishing boat and many pleasure craft. It is one of the safest harbours on the Moray Firth coast; its population in 1971 was 892. It is difficult to get an exact estimate of the fishing fleet owned by the Gardenstown fishing families, but I was told that it includes ten to fifteen larger vessels of over 70 feet of keel (the modern value of which is around £300,000) and up to 100 lesser boats.

The high cliff wall and deeply etched arable plateau of Gamrie parish continues west of Gardenstown, traversed by the coast road B9031 until about a mile east of Macduff it links with the inland trunk road A98 which has pursued a wide arc through quiet farming country on its way from Fraserburgh to Banff and the descent begins to Banff Bay and the mouth of the River Deveron.

Banff has its past and Macduff has its future. But I would not subscribe for a moment to the suggestion that everything of historic interest at the mouth of the Deveron lies on the west bank. Although its history under its present name is comparatively brief, Macduff, like its much more ancient sister burgh, has had time to acquire the patina of age, and it lies on the eastern Bay of Doune, in the shadow of its impressive parish church, like a jewel waiting to catch the glow of the Moray Firth sunsets. It has one of the most pleasing water-fronts, all the more attractive because it is not merely picturesque but bustling with life and activity.

The town is built on land rising sharply from the shore and many of the streets and lanes are very steep, but the A98 road hugs the low shore and enters the harbour area via Palmer Cove. Over it the spray breaks when the tide is up and the wind onshore. The harbour, deepened and improved a decade ago, is the largest between Fraserburgh and Buckie and claims to be the safest in the Firth. It is sheltered from all the winds that blow except those from the north-west, and in consequence its fishing craft lose only four weeks in a year through adverse weather conditions, whereas the fishermen of some other ports may lose as much as two or three months.

Banff Bay and the mouth of the Deveron as well as Macduff itself are dominated by the Hill of Doune crowned by the Regency parish kirk with its curious domed tower and fronted by the Macduff Cross which bears the inscription: "Rebuilt by the Earl of Fife in 1783 upon the erection of the

Burgh by George III. May it flourish and increase in numbers and opulence." The cross incorporates in its centre a portion of the ancient Macduff Cross of Newburgh, Fife. This was a pillar which stood at an opening of the Ochil Hills some miles from Newburgh and took its legendary origin from the place of sanctuary granted to Macduff, Thane of Fife, during his persecution by Macbeth. For centuries the neighbouring territory was afterwards recognized as affording immunity to any fugitive giving proof that he belonged to the Clan Macduff.

All this however can be regarded as part of the effort made by the second Earl of Fife, originally Lord Macduff, along with his factor, William Ross, the first Provost of Macduff, to equip the 'new town' which they had created with a traditional background to offset the superior antiquity of its near neighbour across the Deveron, the royal burgh of Banff. There had been a small and insignificant burgh of barony of Doune on the site since 1528, but the Earl of Fife really exerted himself to build a viable harbour and establish the place on a thriving basis. Ultimately the deterioration of Banff harbour gave the new town its chance. By 1851 there was a population of 2,527 and by 1871 the total had risen to 3,410. Ever since then Macduff and Banff have run neck and neck in numbers and the figures for 1971 were: Macduff 3,709, Banff 3,723. Before the reorganization of local government eliminated them both, the town councils of the sister burghs were working very co-operatively together in complementary roles. In education too, Macduff's fine new high school developed as a transition centre preparing primary pupils from a wide area for entry to senior secondary schooling in Banff Academy—an experimental concept unique in the educational system in the region.

By 1970 Macduff had a fleet of thirty-three seine-net boats and the value of fish landings at the port exceeded £300,000 a year. At the west side of the harbour there is considerable activity in the shipyard of the Macduff Boat Building and Engineering Company which has the capacity to build three craft, usually 70-foot seine and trawl vessels, at one time, and much fitting out and repair work is also done here.

Although Macduff has grown away from the small, tight rows of fisher cottages that form the oldest part of the town, it has kept the essentially compact character of a fishing village. For such a small town it has a surprising number of listed buildings of "architectural or historic interest" in the schedules compiled by the Scottish Development Department—123 in all, mainly among the fisher cottages in High Shore and Low Shore at the east end of the harbour. With few gap sites in its built-up area of over 1,400 houses (766 of them local authority), one of Macduff's last acts as a burgh was to have its boundaries extended by 127 acres, including a large part of the Hill of Doune which will be reserved for recreational purposes. The other great open-air 'lung' of Macduff is the fine golf course to the east, and beyond it the famous Howe of Tarlair with its open-air swimming pool in a rocky cove. Long before the construction of the swimming pool, Tarlair was a place of summer pilgrimage and a picnic spot for the whole countryside around.

The approach from Macduff to Banff sweeps round the base of the Hill of Doune along the shore of Banff Bay, the wide funnel-like estuary of the Deveron, to Smeaton's graceful seven-arched bridge across the river. The "Bonnie Brig o' Banff" as it is called, which makes a gracious point of entry into the royal and ancient burgh, is in process of being replaced—for heavy traffic—by a modern bridge lower down the Deveron, but it will not be demolished—its preservation has been assured.

From this point one gets the best view of another landmark on the Hill of Doune. On its 200-foot summit is a graceful circular Grecian temple, the Temple of Venus, with a domed roof. It was erected by the fourth Earl of Fife, it is said in tribute to his wife, and formerly contained a statue of Venus which has long disappeared. Among its many cares for the environment Banff Preservation Society took up the cudgels on behalf of this beautiful little structure when it became precarious and in need of restoration.

> O Bonnie Banff, where waters meet,
> 'Tween leafy wood and flowing wave,
> You proudly stand, while round your feet
> The rushing tides of Deveron lave.

These lines by John S. Rae written in the 1880s suggest the

benefit which Banff has derived from its superb situation on a series of terraces overlooking the Deveron estuary. A new bypass road completed in 1962 sweeps round to the west from Smeaton's bridge cutting through what was formerly the country park of the Earl of Fife's palatial mansion Duff House, to arrive at the western end of the High Street, overlooked from above by the classical façade of Banff Academy dating from 1838. This gives a stately approach that was quite unknown to the burghers in historic times when the older heart of the town was directly reached by Old Market Place, Bridge Street, and Low Street, which runs parallel to High Street on another terrace at a lower level, and yet stands one terrace above the lowest level, originally known as Low Shore and now as Deveronside.

Banff's oldest extant royal charter was granted by King Robert II of Scotland in 1372 but it is known to have been a privileged trading town at least as early as 1124 when it belonged to the group of burghs known as the Northern Hanse. Its castle, first built perhaps to defend the coast from Viking invasion, was already a royal residence early in the twelfth century and it was from this that David I granted his charter to the monks of Urquhart. Its great curtain walls, 114 feet long on the north side, guarded the now vanished medieval stronghold on its plateau overlooking the sea, on a site where the eighteenth-century 'castle', now in use as a community centre, stands today. The little town grew up below it in the area now occupied by Low Street, Bridge Street, Carmelite Street, High Shore, and Deveronside.

When one considers that 40,000 of the Banffers of old lie buried in the old churchyard between High Shore and Church Street and bears in mind that even today the population does not exceed 4,000, one begins to realize how long the corporate life of the burgh continued without a break. But the real significance of Banff does not merely lie in its undoubted antiquity but in the extent to which its architecture, particularly from the seventeenth and eighteenth centuries, has survived unaltered, and in many cases lovingly and finely restored, to the present day.

When in 1965 a picturesque old block in the High Street was demolished to make room for a modern store there was a shocked reaction from people who realized what was at stake and the Banff Preservation Society was born. By example and by publicity it brought about an astonishing transformation. The first step was to acquire for the princely sum of £12 an old two-storey three-window eighteenth-century cottage in Deveronside. On being restored this was sold to Mr John Player who extended the property by an extension forming a courtyard at the back and providing a boathouse for pleasure craft which nevertheless left the simple Deveronside frontage quite unaltered. An identical cottage alongside was then restored for another client and the 'decayed' street began to become one of the most desirable residential areas in the town.

Private developers began to restore the characterful old houses of Banff with similar results. A guidebook to the vernacular and public architecture of Banff was then produced by the Society with the assistance of the National Trust for Scotland. More ambitious schemes for the restoration of historic buildings were embarked on with aid from the Historic Buildings Council, the Pilgrim Trust, the local authority and the National Trust for Scotland. It is only possible here to mention a few of Banff's architectural and historic gems and as the new approach to the town is the one universally used by the car tourist it is best to begin with the wonderful western vista which looks up the Deveron valley into the historic domain of the Earls of Fife. Here on the left is the Duff House royal golf course across which can be glimpsed the towers of Duff House, now an ancient monument in the care of the Department of the Environment.

Duff House, the most baroque of all Scottish Georgian houses, was begun by William Duff of Braco, afterwards Lord Braco and first Earl of Fife, in 1735, to designs by William Adam, father of the Adam brothers, but only the central block was completed at a cost of £70,000 when a crack appeared in the fabric and the earl went to law with the architect. Adam's design was a compressed version of his Hopetoun House with the addition of corner towers. The superb carved details were shipped from Leith in packing cases. After World War II when it had housed prisoners of war, and was bombed by the Nazis, the mansion became a problem to successive owners until it was taken over by the Department of the Environment who, after partial restoration, opened a suite of rooms as an exhibition centre in which the story of the house down the centuries is told by a series of exhibits.

On the opposite side of the new artery leading to High Street is Collie Lodge, an admirable small-scale Greek Doric essay of 1836 with details suggestive of the hand of William Robertson, who also designed Banff Academy, which crowns the hill in front. It is an Ionic version of academy design like that of the Royal High School of Edinburgh. Leading up to the Academy from the corner of High Street is Institution Terrace, a fine group of eighteenth-century artisan Georgian houses, nicely stepped in shape to conform to the steep slope. At the corner of High Street is St Mary's Church built in 1789-90. Its fine Gibbsian steeple, designed by Thomas Mackenzie in 1849, tones in with the prevailing Georgian character of Banff. Incidentally when this steeple was being built an ingenious form of scaffolding was set up leading from Banff Academy high on its hill and overtopping some of the intervening buildings so that a gentle slope was formed for the workmen to roll their barrels to the tower.

Opposite the church and forming Nos 1-5 High Street are three typical eighteenth-century Banff 'town houses', each of three storeys and attics. No. 1, with architrave and pulvinated frieze on the doorpiece, is dated 1764, while the large house, No. 5, with five-window front, was the town house of Lord Banff. Farther along, on the same side of the street, is a characterful group of early eighteenth-century houses, low, with small windows, some of them moulded, and one with two tiny swept dormers on the roof and interesting chimney-heads. Beyond this, still on the north side of the street, is a handsome block built by the Shoemaker Incorporation of Banff in 1787 with a central gable and niched centre door. This block is one of the latest to be restored by the Banff Preservation Society at a cost of around £53,000, work which included reroofing with graduated slates.

Near here, but now, alas, demolished, stood the town house of the family of Duff of Hatton, closely linked with the Gordons of Gight and so with the poet Byron. It is said that it was in this house that Byron as a child met Mary Duff, for whom he conceived a childhood passion. There are many Byronic associations in Banff. During holidays Mrs Byron and the little boy visited Banff relations including his great-grandmother, the Lady Gight, who lived in a house called Little Fillicap which stood on the site of the Sheriff Courthouse in Low Street. At the same period his mother's kinsman, the Rev. Abercromby Gordon, was parish minister of Banff and young Byron frequently spent a day at the Old Manse, at the corner of Water Path and High Shore. He fell from a pear tree in the manse garden and when a doctor was summoned and threatened to bleed him he swore he would bite off the physician's nose if he did. In 1816 at Brussels Byron met the minister's brother, Major Pryse Gordon, and described to him his childhood visits to Banff.

Opposite the site of the Old Manse is Ingleneuk. This very old building is built round a square courtyard. Part of it is seventeenth century with crow-stepped gables, but the pend arch is semi-elliptical with the thin margin and single key typical of the Banff area of around 1760-80.

Five short, steep streets or lanes lead down from the High Street to Low Street, at the north end of which is the paved area known as the Plainstones fronting the Banff municipal buildings, a severe classic structure built in 1796 at the south end of which is the earlier town steeple with a hexagonal spire and oval openings designed by James Adam.

There is a fine council chamber on the first floor of the Town House with some good portraits and interesting relics. On the Plainstones stands the old Mercat Cross of Banff. Its sixteenth-century crucifix finial survived the Reformation and got a new shaft in 1627. The carving represents the Crucifixion on one side and on the other the Virgin and Child, with the motto of Banff, "Omne bonum, Dei donum". Moving south along Low Street the building adjoining the Town House has several carved stones including a Virgin and Child dated 1628 and a Royal Arms of 1634. Next door to this and standing back from the street in a small garden is Carmelite House. It occupies a part of the site of the Carmelite monastery and dates from 1753. Its stately five-window front is in neatly squared whinstone and it has a basement with a railed area and a Vanbrugh-inspired doorpiece.

Farther south is the Clydesdale Bank building designed by Archibald Simpson of Aberdeen in 1836, then there are several eighteenth-century buildings including No. 15 dated 1745 and built by a Mr Robinson. In 1771 this gentleman unwisely remonstrated with some of the military who were "occupied in fair dalliance with some of the nursery maids" in the court of the Black Bull Inn across the street. A scuffle ensued and an officer drew his sword and ran Mr Robinson through. The inn, where Dr Johnson stayed in 1773, served as the principal hostelry of Banff for 110 years and was replaced in 1843 by the Fife Arms Hotel, built by the Earl of Fife in a handsome late Georgian Classic style with a large decorative pend arch leading to the stabling behind.

From the north end of Low Street, terminated by the fine New Market Arch dated 1831, Carmelite Street leads east towards the sea front and the Old Market Place where the Crown Hotel, Castle Panton and the *Banffshire Journal* offices, formerly the grammar school of Banff, are notable buildings. On the left-hand side of the street, High Shore fronting the Old Kirkyard and leading on to Deveronside along the base of the castle plateau has some of the oldest surviving houses in the town. No. 1 and No. 3 High Shore, both finely restored by the Preservation Society, date from 1675 and 1740 respectively. No. 1 with its angle turret, probably designed as a lookout for the merchant magnate who built the house, has a courtyard at the back and a tall projecting stair tower. It has been described as a 'little castle in the heart of the town'. No. 5 High Shore, the Market Inn, is dated 1585 on a lunette stone with a grotesque head at the rear, and is certainly the oldest building in continuous occupation in Banff. The old kirkyard opposite contains an outstanding collection of monumental sculpture, although of the original parish church of St Mary only the sixteenth-century vaulted Banff Aisle with canted gable and gridiron tracery remains. On the wall near the main gate of the cemetery are the arms of Provost Alexander Douglas, Sheriff of Banff, who was murdered in Low Street in Covenanting times. In the kirkyard itself Douglas's grave was embellished with the effigy of a knight which disappeared in the eighteenth century and there is a theory that it was removed by James, second Earl of Fife, to a mausoleum in the woods of the Duff House estate, south of the town, which he erected about 1789.

To return to Banff's High Street for a moment, mention should be made of another remarkable building, this time on the south side. This is St Brandon's, a large Georgian mansion built by Sir George Abercromby of Glassaugh in 1780, with a baronial tower added in 1867. Sir George on one occasion entertained in this building the celebrated Jane Maxwell, Duchess of Gordon, a leader of London society and the founding heroine of the Gordon Highlanders regiment. St Brandon's has been restored and converted into luxury flats served by a lift installed in the baronial tower. A charming housing scheme, called St Brandon's Close, has been formed at the back of the mansion out of the former kitchen wing and stables and coachhouse, while the large garden sloping down behind the house affords a fine view over the rooftops of the town and the riverside below.

One more highlight of Banff's vernacular building traditions is in Boyndie Street, the former main exit from the town on the west, at the north end of the High Street. Here Boyndie House with its fanciful gable top has been restored for a private owner. It dates from 1740. Next door is the stately but simple Town and County Club, formerly the home of provost George Robinson. One of the very largest provincial town houses of the eighteenth century in Scotland, it has a grand Venetian feature at the back wing.

Castle Street runs north from the Boyndie Street-High Street intersection to the Seatown. It was laid out in 1750 by Lord Deskford and takes its name from the modern Banff Castle built in the same year—a severe three-storey, five-window block with tallish piend roof and symmetrical wings. A gracious feature on the west side of Castle Street is Trinity and Alvah Church (1843) in an Ionian mode with portico and cupola. Farther on the Town Hall (1852) and Seafield House, also in the Italian manner, were the work of Thomas Mackenzie of Elgin. The Seatown, to which Castle Street leads, was before 1750 a completely separate village entirely populated by the fishing community, but its cottage rows have a character of their own. Banff harbour lies to the west of the mouth of the Deveron at the north end of a small rocky promontory which separates Banff Bay from Boyndie Bay to the west.

In Deveronside, where so much restoration has taken place, there stands gable-end to the street and marked by a plaque the house of Thomas Edward (1814-86), the Banff naturalist whose life story was the subject of a book by Samuel Smiles.

In its heyday as a commercial port Banff had a fleet of twenty sailing ships. Today it is almost entirely deserted by industry but its holiday attractions are multiplying. To the south of the town there are delectable reaches of the River Deveron to be explored, quite secluded and remote from main traffic arteries. Only two miles upstream is a spectacular landscape feature called the Craigs of Alvah where the river, turning westwards, enters romantic narrows between the Hill of Alvah and the Hill of Montcoffer and presses through a precipitous chasm spanned by a bridge built by the second Earl of Fife in 1772. It may be approached by a footpath through the Fife estate from the outskirts of Banff.

To the south of Banff also lies sixteenth-century Inchdrewer Castle recently restored by the English Richmond Herald, Mr Robin Mirrlees, a descendant of the Ogilvys of Banff. Until this restoration the castle had not been inhabited since the fatal night of 13 January 1713 when George, third Lord Banff, was murdered in his bedchamber above the great hall and the castle was consigned to the flames to conceal the dreadful deed. He was a man of "very evil life" but, as Mr Mirrlees says, "it is too much for a man to be murdered because of this". Why were the murderers never brought to book? Thereby hangs a most dramatic tale. The 'bad' Lord Banff had been in Edinburgh for many months in connection with his son's wedding and when he returned unexpectedly on the night of Friday the 13th only his housekeeper, Elizabeth Porter, was at home to receive him.

After a hearty meal, he retired to his chamber above the hall. In the small hours smoke and flames were seen pouring from the windows and chimneys of the castle. The housekeeper escaped but all attempts to reach Lord Banff failed, and he was burned to ashes. His son, the Master of Banff came north to investigate and soon formed the conviction that his father had been murdered—not a matter of great surprise in view of his intense unpopularity. He brought charges which led to the indictment of three young men, Stewart, Milne, and Brodie, two of them sons of local farmers. But the prosecution failed, because their one and only witness, the housekeeper, did not appear. She had fled to Ireland. Her story was that about midnight she heard cries of "Porter! Porter! Porter!" followed by "Murder! Murder! Murder!" She found the door of the chamber locked, and two men within, said to be Stewart and Milne, refused to open it. The presumption is that they had murdered the earl and afterwards fired the castle to cover up their traces. So ended the drama of the burning of Inchdrewer which continued to be haunted down to the period of the restoration.

From the Battery Green of Banff, a public open space which was appropriated "for the exercise and health of the inhabitants" as far back as 1781, a wonderful cliff walk leads westwards along the Sea Braes and eventually links up with the trunk road A98 on its way to Elgin and Inverness. It gives a superb view over Boyndie Bay, the great spread of sandy beach curving westwards towards Whitehills and backed by a fine golf course. On a clear day the hills of Caithness can be seen forty miles across the Moray Firth. Banff Links, as this stretch of coast is also called, extend to the Burn of Boyndie. Two big hotels, one down on the shore and one high above the main road, testify to the popularity of this breezy lung of the burgh of Banff on the west. Beyond the mouth of the burn at Inverboyndie lies the great hump of Knock Head sheltering the fishing village of Whitehills from the east, a distance of exactly three miles from Banff.

For at least 360 years there has been a fishing village of Whitehills. In August 1624 the Kirk Session of Boyndie reported to the Presbytery "anent the keeping of the Saboth by the fischares". The fishermen, they said, were in the way of reformation "for the better performing quhairof every Skipper is obleegit to be bound for his brethren". We know that Whitehills was considered a 'town' as early as 1727 for an elaborate handbell bearing this date and the legend "The Town of Whitehills" is preserved in Trinity church in the village. It was the town crier's bell. By 1797 there was a population of 460 and the parish minister reported: "The town of Whitehills is chiefly inhabited by fishermen. There are seven boats engaged in the fishing and they are generally very successful." By about 1840 the figure had risen to 623 and the parish minister recorded: "The fishermen form a society quite distinct from the agricultural labourers . . . intermarrying almost exclusively among themselves or occasionally with neighbouring seafaring communities. Hence they may be distinguished by their personal appearance, their complexion being clear and their females possessing superior comliness."

He had something to say, too, about the fisher wives who ruled the roost. "The wife", he wrote,

> occupies a far more important position in the family than in other walks of life, while in addition to the ordinary domestic duties she is subjected to the daily labour of baiting the lines and preparing the fish for sale. To her belongs the formidable task of carrying the fish to market, often a distance of many miles. But the prosperity of the family depending upon the success with which the last duty is discharged, she adopts a tone, and is allowed an influence which in another condition of life would appear little consistent either with feminine propriety or domestic order. The introduction of the herring fishing, indeed, has in some degree lessened her pretensions . . . but she still usually claims the disposal of the entire proceeds of the white fishery, prosecuted throughout ten months of the year as her exclusive prerogative.

The extraordinary continuity of the native stock in White-hills can be seen from the fact that in 1842 there were in the 'town' 117 Watsons, 47 Lovies, 35 Adamsons, 25 Findlays and 23 Ritchies. The roll of male voters in 1922 showed that there were 19 Watsons and 18 Lovies, while in 1962 I was assured that in one street alone there were seven Watsons in a row.

Since the beginning of the present century the population of Whitehills has remained stable at about 900 and all who visit it are impressed by the efficiency of the harbour with its twenty-two seine-net fishing vessels and modern fish market. If you ask why Whitehills has so steadfastly maintained its independence as a fishing port despite its close proximity to the much bigger fishing centre of Macduff, you will be reminded that the harbour at Whitehills really belongs to the fishermen. Unlike so many other harbours which belong to the local authorities it has a degree of intimate care and control which makes it certain self-help will triumph in the end.

Two long streets stretch out southward from the harbour area of Whitehills to link it with the A98 highway, in one of which is Trinity Church which was acquired to serve the village, transported from Seafield Street, Banff, and rebuilt stone by stone, being lengthened at the same time. It has a lofty raftered roof and a recent addition was a stained-glass window designed by a monk at Pluscarden Abbey to commemorate a local fisherman lost at sea in 1968. The kind of do-it-yourself enterprise typical of the village is the seashore pleasure park, east of the harbour, with a small basin for pleasure craft, a pavilion formed out of the now closed Ladysbridge railway station, and a concrete boat for the children to play on, appropriately named Bairns' Pride, and equipped with a mast and wheelhouse from an old Macduff fishing vessel.

Still farther east in the shelter of Knock Head, and utilizing clay from the lee of that headland, are the Blackpots Brick and Tile Works, a minor industry over 130 years old. To the west of the harbour Whitehills has a picturesque rocky foreshore, much haunted by artists, with a few cottages on the grassy bents behind. Beyond this the land rises up to the headland of Stake Ness, which in 1969 was selected as the site of an £85,000,000 nuclear generating station. Owing to the needs of the North Sea oil boom at Peterhead, however, this project was put into cold storage in favour of another power station at Boddam which will serve immediate needs.

The cliffed coast continues to the west past Whyntie Head to Boyne Bay where the Burn of the Boyne reaches the sea. In the Middle Ages the burn was overlooked at this point by a stronghold called the Castle of the Craig of Boyne built in the fifteenth century by the Ogilvys of Deskford and Findlater, lords of the Thanage of the Boyne. In 1568, after her marriage to Alexander Ogilvy of Findlater, there came to this castle a famous figure in Scottish history, Mary Bethune or Beaton, one of Mary Queen of Scots' four 'Maries'. She has, strangely enough, no actual connection with the familiar ballad:

> Yestreen the Queen had four Maries,
>   The day she'll hae but three;
> There was Mary Beaton and Mary Seaton
>   And Mary Carmichael and me.

Virtually no trace of this ancient stronghold remains, but a short distance upstream overlooking the burn is a most spectacular ruin the 'new' Castle of the Boyne. Nine years after

Mary's marriage the thanage of the Boyne was transferred to the Ogilvys of Dunlugas and it was they who built this grandiose structure. The site they chose was picturesque to a degree. It was beautifully situated on the margin of a rocky mount, projecting into a deep glen protected on the north-west by a lofty, well-wooded hill and by the burn which nearly encircles the knoll on which the castle is placed. All very fine, but as military men will know, castles which aim to be impregnable should not be overlooked by lofty hills.

Although to all appearances an ancient fortress on the courtyard plan, Boyne Castle is really, as Dr W. Douglas Simpson put it, "a castellated mansion equipped for a certain amount of defence by firearms, but otherwise a sham castle, an architectural atavism, of which other examples from this period are known in Scotland". It is oblong in plan, and at each of the four corners in a sturdy round tower. In front of the castle is a great fosse or ditch, and the entrance to the south front is approached over the fosse by a raised and walled causeway defended by two drum towers. The south front was four storeys high. But today this imposing stronghold is rapidly tumbling to bits, due, it seems, to inferior mortar used in its construction.

About a mile and a half west of Boyne Castle the coast road, B9139, reaches the burgh of Portsoy (pop. 1,667) and rejoins the A98 which has taken a wide sweep inland towards Tillynaught passing Ladysbridge, a large mental hospital, the Kirkton of Boyndie and the former Boyndie aerodrome, now a kart-racing circuit, on the way. A decade ago the visitor tended to feel sorry for Portsoy. It seemed to be a place with a past but no future—or a future which seemed to make nonsense of its past. In the fifteen years from 1930 to 1945 only one private house was built. Council housing schemes were all on the west and south of the burgh, at the opposite side from the seedy decay between Seafield Street and the sea front. From its peak of population (2,091) in 1881 the number of residents declined steadily to 1,651 in 1931. There was a post-war improvement to 1,788 in 1951, but that was a flash in the pan and the decline continued. The time was coming when the now half-derelict but historic area round the Old Harbour must either be restored or demolished. The all-important first step was the restoration of five blocks of houses fronting the Old Harbour from Low Street and Shorehead which earned a grant from the Historic Buildings Council and the special commendation of the Saltire Society.

This award was made in 1968, but it was only the beginning. In the years since then the policy has been extended. The old Star Inn in North High Street, a large L-plan building of three storeys bearing the date 1727 on the north gable, was restored to provide characterful homes for more council tenants. Soy House, in Church Street, dating from the seventeenth century and believed to be the oldest domestic building in the town, was the next to be rescued from dereliction. This two-storey rubble-built mansion with crow-stepped gables facing the street in a pleasant pair was internally reconstructed to provide charming little homes for three more local authority tenants. In the course of the reconstruction a hugh arched ingleneuk, built up with cunningly selected stone slabs, came to light. Another of these big old Portsoy fireplaces was revealed when properties at 11 and 13 Low Street were being restored—also for the town council. One of these houses turned out to have a fine wood-panelled living room, now particularly treasured by the joiner who did the reconstruction work.

The bringing back to life of historic buildings, especially if they stand in groups, has a sort of cumulative force. Once a few crumbling semi-ruins have been shown to have great potential charm if wisely restored, the movement gains momentum and private developers are eager to take a hand in recreating the picturesque past. This, just as at Banff, is what has happened at Portsoy. The restoration of the entire range of old structures facing the Old Harbour was completed by the restoration of Nos 6, 8 and 10 Shorehead and of the Corff House, the great four-storey warehouse which dominates the end of the harbour. No. 6 and the Corff House were taken in hand by Mr Tom Burnett-Stuart of Ardmeallie who revived the historic craft of polishing Portsoy marble, a kind of serpentine, while Nos 8 and 10 were converted into flats by another private developer.

The old warehouse, the name of which suggests that it was a salmon-curing factory, has long vaulted cellarage in the basement, a stone-floored first floor, and two timber-floored storeys above that, the topmost under elaborate rafters supporting the sloping roof. It appears to date back to the late seventeenth century, the golden age of Portsoy, when Patrick Ogilvy, later Lord Boyne, built the Old Harbour for the export of Portsoy marble some of which was sent to France and was used in the furnishing of the Palace of Versailles.

In 1967 Portsoy town council offered the then crumbling and desolate Corff House to the Ministry of Works, but its fate has been far more fortunate. The first floor has been converted into a pottery, the walls of which are lined with a full range of decorative domestic stoneware, tall Chinese vases, coffee mugs, casserole dishes, teapots, plates and saucers. Brian Shand, the potter, creates designs that are highly spontaneous, patterned with rich brush strokes and conveying that warm human feeling which proclaims the individual work of art that contrasts so strongly with the factory-made article. Meanwhile serpentine from the West Beach of Portsoy is being used to fashion a wide range of Portsoy marble souvenirs and works of art in the workshop behind the Corff House.

On the landward side of the town a long-standing eyesore has been converted into a civic asset. Loch Soy, which lies between the centre of the town and the now disused railway station, was once a large and pleasing sheet of water. But the building of the coast railway last century displaced it from its original location and there was a change in the drainage system which had disastrous results on its appearance. It was drained by the Seafield Trustees because of the danger of flooding. Its former bed, with a slimy and sluggish trickle of water running through it, soon become overgrown with weeds and reeds and a noisome morass. For over half a century its ugliness was a recurrent subject of futile local debate. Finally the town council, profiting from the Government's grants for "tidying up the environment", culverted part of the Loch, removed silt from its bed, and converted the remainder of the water into a pleasure boating pond surrounded by a public park with paths, seats, trees and shrubs.

Tourists now enjoy the amenities of Loch Soy as well as the fine beaches on the east and west of the old and new harbours. There is an attractive open-air swimming pool and a large tourist caravan site. The dominating feature of the landscape on the southern horizon here is Durn Hill (652 feet) with its prehistoric fort, about three miles south-west of Portsoy. On the western side of the hill lies the old-world village of Fordyce, a designated conservation area.

Away from main roads, bereft of its last regular bus service, it is a village for real connoisseurs, a village with a remarkable history, many fascinating old buildings and an intimate charm of its own. It is not lacking in fame, neither is it lacking in enterprise. Its fame stems from a celebrated academy which for over a century drew some of its pupils from the far corners of the earth. The academy was founded through the remarkable will of George Smith, a native of the parish, who died in February 1790 aboard the East Indiaman *Winterton* while returning to this country with the fortune he had made in Bombay. He stipulated that £40 per annum was to be paid to a schoolmaster well skilled in English and the modern commercial languages such as French and Dutch, who should dwell in Fordyce for the purpose of teaching as many boys of the name of Smith as the residue of his estate could maintain. Preference was to be given to those who could prove a relationship to himself—down to the fourth generation of his sisters' or brothers' descendants. These unusual provisions were carried out to the letter, so that in the 1870s four of the nine Smith's Bursars at Fordyce Academy were Swedes, all des- cendants, in the fourth generation, of George Smith's sister Jean.

An academic reputation that was the envy of most other schools in the north of Scotland began to accrue to Fordyce Academy in the days of William Cruickshank, the first headmaster to benefit from the terms of the Smith Bequest. Among his pupils were Sir James Clark, Queen Victoria's physician, and Sir John Forbes, an equally famous medico. But the days of academic glory for Fordyce are over. The Academy closed in 1964, owing to the impossibility of something 'small but good' continuing in the age of big centralized secondary schooling.

The village (pop. 200) takes roughly the shape of a triangle with a square in front of the castle at one angle, Church Street forming one side, the School Road another and the most modern street in the place a third. It is called St Tarquin's Place, after the patron saint who was the earliest of the famous men of Fordyce.

The church of Fordyce is first mentioned in 1272 when

Alexander III appointed one Andrew de Garentuly to it. The church stood where the ruins in the old kirkyard still stand today, though it was of course often rebuilt and repaired in the next 500 years. The tall belfry that survives dates from 1661. East of it are the West Loft and the Durn Aisle, and on the north the Glassaugh Aisle (1679). Nearby is Sir James Ogilvy's tomb (1509). This has an elaborately sculptured canopy surmounted by a shield charged with the Ogilvy and Sinclair arms and in the recess lies a sculptured figure of a knight in full armour with a dog at his feet.

The castle of Fordyce was built in 1592 by Sir Thomas Menzies of Durn, who also founded the first school in the village. It is a four-storey L-plan tower with crow-stepped gables, angel turrets and a tall circular stair turret supported on a long cone of corbelling in the re-entrant angle. A handsome two-storey crow-stepped wing with dormer windows was added in the eighteenth century. A start has been made in restoring the characterful old domestic dwellings in the village, notably in Academy Lane, facing the castle, and part of the academy buildings are used for the village's primary school. The present-day church of Fordyce was built in 1804.

The burn of Fordyce running almost due north of the village is crossed by the A98 highway two miles west of Portsoy and reaches the sea at Sandend Bay. Here, west of Redhythe Point, a broad tongue of blue water enters deeply into the throat of the land and forms one of the most beautiful havens in Banffshire. The low, grass-topped cliffs on either side taper to terminate in a semi-circular sweep of sand through which the burn flows. On the grassy plateau above the eastern angle of the bay stands the massive bulk of Glenglassaugh Distillery.

Just over the boundary wall of the distillery grounds is an intriguing landmark, visible from far and wide, called the Cup and Saucer. It looks like a well-preserved broch, as tall as the Broch of Mousa, but is in fact the lower part of an ancient windmill. The guardian heights of the western arm of the bay run north and south from Garron Point for almost a mile inland, and sheltered by these extends the now quite long and straggling village of Sandend, called locally 'San-eyn'.

When the first fishery settled here is uncertain, but in 1692 there were three boats and eighteen fishermen. In 1929 there were eighteen boats and twenty-six fishing families called Smith with a sprinkling of McKays, Sutherlands and Hays among the fishing skippers. Although today only three or four lobster and small line fishing boats remain, there are four thriving fish merchants' processing and retailing firms, two of them operated by Smiths. But a new element has entered into the local economy with craft workers who find this a most congenial base.

Sandend had no harbour until 1883. Reidhaven on the other side of bay had at one time a quay from which lime was shipped for the construction of the Caledonian Canal at the beginning of the nineteenth century. But the main centre of population was at Sandend and a series of fund-raising efforts by the fishermen themselves was supported by the Earl of Seafield and the Fishery Board. The actual building work which went on continuously from March to October 1883 was supervised by William Bennet, engineer of the Seafield Estates, and consisted of rock excavation and the building of a north quay and a south jetty. Unfortunately Mr Bennet did not live to see the work completed. He was standing on the quay one day when a bucket suspended from a crane swung round and knocked him into the harbour. He died a few days later.

There is obviously a future for Sandend as a holiday resort, and this will have been aided by volunteers from the Conservation Corps who completed a path from the village along the cliffs to the ruins of Findlater Castle, about two miles to the west. Of this superb ruin it was said a century ago: "The outer walls of several parts of the building are so founded on the cliffs as to correspond with the face of the precipice, so that the principal tower seems to hang over the sea, and from the windows of several apartments a pebble may be dropped into the waves."

The royal licence to build Findlater Castle was issued by James II to Sir Walter Ogilvy of Deskford in 1455. All around the rock on which the castle was built the cliffs are exceedingly steep, reaching heights of 90 feet, while the summit of the castle rock itself is about 50 feet below the level of the mainland cliffs from which it is reached by a rapid, irregular descent. In two places the rock has been cut across, each gap

Fort George – like a dagger pointing into the Firth.

Ardersier, an old-world fishing village.

Culloden battlefield: Old Leanach Cottage and (*right*) the National Trust for Scotland Visitor Centre.

The Z-plan Castle of Kinkell overlooking Conon Bridge. It was finely restored by the sculptor Gerald Laing.

The ancient cathedral of Ross at Fortrose on the Black Isle.

Cromarty: the historic old Fishertown on its peninsula jutting out into the Cromarty Firth.

Dingwall, the county town of Ross, seen from the Mitchell Hill.

Foulis Castle, Evanton, ancestral home of the chiefs of the Clan Munro. At the gateway are Mrs E. Gascoigne, mother of the present chief, and her sister, Lady Wells.

The Invergordon smelter. Note the long overhead conveyor for ore from a jetty deep in the Cromarty Firth.

The historic Tolbooth Tower at Tain.

Portmahomack –
the old fishing
haven looks north
across the Dornoch
Firth to the hills
of Sutherland.

Kildonan: Panning
for gold in the
Suisgill Burn are
two holiday
prospectors from
the north of
England.

Dornoch: a part of Castle Street with the castle (now a hotel) farthest right and the Old Jail (latterly a craft centre) on the left.

Visitors on the terrace at Dunrobin Castle.

Once a very typical sight – a thatched croft house on the edge of the Caithness moors.

Dunbeath Castle on its clifftop, scene of a notable siege and counter-siege in 1650.

having been spanned by a bridge. As no carriages could reach the castle, a forecourt was formed on the mainland. From there visitors had to go on foot.

The main castle building is on the palace plan and is built against the west side of the rock and so carried up from a lower floor that the main floor is level with the summit of the rock and raised above two tiers of vaulted substructures.

The castle had a chequered history. Shortly before 1560 the barony of Findlater passed from the Ogilvys to Sir John Gordon, third son of the Earl of Huntly, because the last Ogilvy owner, having quarrelled with his son, disinherited him and made over the castle to Sir John. There followed a fierce struggle but Sir John remained in possession and during the Gordon rebellion in 1562 he held the castle against Mary Queen of Scots and her half-brother James Stewart, Earl of Moray. After the Battle of Corrichie in that year he was captured and executed on the Heading Hill of Aberdeen; Findlater Castle surrendered and was reoccupied by the Ogilvys. By the middle of the seventeenth century, the Ogilvys having moved to their new home at Cullen House, it was abandoned and empty.

# CHAPTER V

# THE MORAY DISTRICT

> Since Vikings were your Summer Visitors
> And beached their longships on your shining shores,
> Since Bruce, in pious memory of his Queen
> Pronounced you Royal, a multitude of keen
> Admirers have enjoyed your ozoned air;
> And still they come in summer flocks to share
> Long lazy days with you, Cullen the Fair.

FROM SANDEND the trunk road runs through pleasant woods to the old Royal Burgh of Cullen. On the whole of the Banffshire coast there is surely no more favoured spot than this. Banff alone vies with it in antiquity, and it has never attempted to rival Banff as a centre of administration, but its natural beauties of situation and amenity are without peer.

To the holidaymaker it is a paradise: the smiling bay with its "singing sands" sheltered on the west by Scarnose; the wooded policies of Cullen House, with the Bin and the Little Bin, two distinctive hills, rising up behind; the sleepy little harbour; the spectacular railway viaduct; the rocky inlets stretching away in a succession of coves to the east—all these plus the 18-hole golf course, the caravan site at Logie, the gaily painted cottages of the Seatown, and the dignity of the modern burgh laid out by George MacWilliam in the 1820s give it character.

The visitors who flock there in the eight to twelve weeks of high summer may or may not become aware that for the permanent residents there are problems. The little town has a population of 1,207. At least a quarter of this total are old-age pensioners. Because Cullen has little industry it cannot keep its young people, and the ranks of the elderly are swollen by those who choose it as a place of retirement.

This made things difficult for the burgh council in the last years of its existence before local government reorganization swept it away altogether. Nevertheless, it built around 100 council houses, fought coastal erosion, redeveloped the disused railway station, and equipped a holiday caravan site for 100 vans. And in these years a small-scale industrial revival was brought about by the Seafield Estates who gave work to between 320 and 350 people in the Cullen area. Forestry and a tree nursery enterprise account for a large part of the estate manpower and today trees from Cullen, and the expertise in landscape gardening that goes along with them, are being exported all over the country.

The A98 road enters Cullen from the south and debouches upon the Square in the centre of George MacWilliam's carefully planned 'new town' laid out on a grid-iron plan. Seafield Street leads west to the long tree-lined avenue to Cullen House and to Old Cullen and the ancient parish church where the history of the community really begins. The oldest relic of man's handiwork in the vicinity is at the Castle Hill, a vitrified fort on a knoll approached by a path leading off on the right from the avenue to Cullen House. The steep hillock is guarded by a deep ditch on three sides and on the flat top a rustic enclosure was built in comparatively modern times and carved stones from Old Cullen (demolished in 1820-30) were placed there. They include the Royal Arms of Scotland, the Baird arms (a boar passant) the quartered arms of Ogilvy and Sinclair, and a stone with the initials M. P. O. and the date 1688. It refers to Patrick Ogilvy, son of the Earl of Findlater. Cullen's ancient mercat cross stood here for a time after the demolition of Old Cullen before it was re-erected in the centre of the modern town.

But let us now press on to Cullen Old Church on the site of Old Cullen itself. Its oldest feature, a round-headed arch, originally a doorway, indicates a building of the period 1180-1280. We know that the church existed in 1236 and that it remained unchanged until, in 1536, the present south transept was built by Elena Hay, mother of John Duff of Maldavit, and ancestor of the earls and dukes of Fife and dedicated to St Anne. It has been known as St Anne's Aisle to this day. In 1543 the church of Cullen was elevated to the status of a collegiate church, the second last of the thirty-eight such churches erected in Scotland between 1342 and 1545. The chancel of the church was lengthened to its present extent and it was staffed by a 'college' consisting of a provost, six prebendaries and two singing boys, to ensure that Masses should be sung every day.

Only twenty years were to elapse before the Reformation was to sweep away these Catholic usages but in these years the church was embellished with two treasures which have survived. One is the beautiful Sacrament House in the north wall. This with its sculptured angels upholding a monstrance survived intact hidden behind a huge marble monument to the Chancellor Earl of Findlater and was only rediscovered when this was moved in 1877. The other is the ornate baroque monument to Alexander Ogilvy of that Ilk, one of the founders of the collegiate church, who died in 1554. The tomb and effigy of John Duff dating from 1539 was carried off by the second Earl of Fife to Duff House in 1792, but restored to its proper place in 1965. The effigy rests on a sculptured slab, on which, in facing panels, are two charming miniature figures of knights, fully caparisoned, with an inscription in the space between.

One other feature which cannot escape notice is the massive two-tiered Seafield Loft extending virtually the whole length of the south wall of the chancel. The date 1602 on the front panel of the loft tells us the year of the erection of this overwhelmingly imposing laird's gallery. It was in 1600 that work began on the building of Cullen House itself and Findlater Castle was abandoned by the Ogilvy family. No doubt an earlier building stood on the site. The tradition is that the earliest part dates from the Middle Ages and consists of a series of monks' cells forming part of a monastic school. When these come to be incorporated into the chief residence of the Ogilvys of Deskford and Findlater they were converted into wine cellars.

Founded on a rock over 60 feet above the channel of the Burn of Cullen, which winds picturesquely in a flowery den called the Punchbowl far below, the house began as an L-plan tower, the wings of which were gradually extended to the south-west and the north-west, while an extensive court of servants' quarters, extending north-eastwards, was added to the north-west tip of the L-shape.

The main entrances to the house are on either side of the north wing, in the east and west courts, but close to the re-entrant angle of the L, in the west court, is the sculptured surround of the original doorway, now filled in and supplied with a window. The treasures with which the house came to be filled told in their own way the story of the two great dynasties, the Ogilvys and the Grants, united in the person of the fifth Earl of Seafield, Sir Lewis Alexander Ogilvy Grant, in 1811. A great many of these treasures were sold by auction in September 1975 when the present Lord Seafield, after moving to a smaller house in the grounds disposed of the "remaining contents". The house, which had been open to the public, was then closed.

Before the sale Moray District Council and the Scottish Civic Trust intervened to point out that as the house was a listed building certain precious fixtures, including six fine marble fireplaces, and a historic carved door could not be legally disposed of and they were withdrawn from the auction. Never intended to be auctioned was the most famous item of all, the unique seventeenth-century painted ceiling in the timber vault of the King Charles Salon depicting in flamboyant colour the gods of Olympus, the Siege of Troy and a boar hunt. The state entrance to the Cullen House grounds from the south is an imposing Ionic triumphal arch with fluted pillars designed by James Adam.

Early in the nineteenth century the decay in the linen industry hit Old Cullen badly and as fishing was booming the Earl of Seafield decided to 'remove' the old town from the immediate vicinity of Cullen House and build a new town nearer the sea. It was based on the axis of Seafield Street, intersected by the Square, and with Grant Street, Deskford Street and Castle Street also intersecting. This has now been designated a conservation area. So too has the contrasting Seatown, down on the foreshore, with its regimented rows of fisher cottages, and a third conservation area to the north-west includes Victoria Street and Campbell Street.

At the heart of it all is the handsome complex of combined public buildings and inn—the Seafield Arms in Seafield Street and the Town Hall in the Square. When built in 1822 the Seafield Arms was called the Cullen Hotel. Writing about 1840, the parish minister of Cullen said:

The only modern building deserving of notice is the Cullen Hotel, attached to which, and under the same roof are three public rooms, viz. an elegant ballroom 43 ft. in length, a commodious Court Room in which are held the sheriff and justice-of-peace courts, and Council Room of the burgh, a handsome apartment of a circular form.... The entire building was erected at the expense of the Earl of Seafield and cost £3000.

The Town Hall was destroyed by fire in 1941 and reopened in 1955 after being rebuilt. What was the Court Room is now the Memorial Hall and the ballroom above it still has the same dimensions. As for the Council Chamber, it is still a "handsome apartment of a circular form", its walls lined with portraits of civic dignitaries of the days that are gone.

Cullen has been a seaport for well over 500 years. In 1881 there were ninty-three boats and by 1929 there were still forty-two but today the small harbour is used almost exclusively for pleasure craft. The spectacular railway viaduct which produces a sharp division between the New Town and the Seatown twice crosses the main road to the north and its tall arches have been under threat of demolition for some time. Beyond the closely clustered fisher cottages and the defile where the Burn of Cullen crosses the foreshore lie dazzling white sands stretching in a wide arc backed by the golf course and punctuated by three isolated rocks, the Three Kings Cullen, and farther along towards Portknockie by the Bow Fiddle, Boar Crag and Red Craig.

The small burgh of Portknockie (pop. 1,210) slopes down to the cliff-tops just west of Scarnose. At one end is the harbour with its paddling pool and scenic rocks, at the other a grassy peninsula with a superb view over Cullen Bay. It was colonized by Cullen fishermen in the year 1677. The event is recorded by George Donaldson, parish minister of Rathven, in the Old Statistical Account of 1793. He wrote: "About 20 years ago died Katie Slater aged 96. She recollected that she was as old as the House of Farskane, as her father had often told her that he built the first house in Portknockie in the same year in which the House of Farskane was built, and that she was brought from Cullen to it and rocked in a fisher's scull instead of a cradle."

The Gordons who built the House of Farskane have long

left it, but the Slaters, the Mairs and the Woods, who came to Portknockie at the Gordon laird's behest, are still the predominant stock, and are present in such numbers that, as they freely admit, "we couldn't manage without tee-names". On a recent voters' roll there were 220 Mairs, 134 Woods and 74 Slaters. One of the last provosts of the burgh, Mrs H. J. Geddes, whose maiden name was Slater, explained what 'tee-names' are thus: "When I was at school I was never called Nelly Slater, always Nelly Mash, to avoid confusion with the three other Nelly Slaters in my class." As late as 1929 Portknockie had a fleet of fifty-eight steam drifters belonging to the 555 fishermen. Today the harbour is empty but many fishermen still live here.

While the neat, brightly painted terraces of Portknockie, laid out on a regular plan, are impressive, it must yield in picturesqueness of arrangement to Findochty (pop. 1,203) a mile and a half to the west along a coastline of jagged cliffs with isolated reefs and fangs of fragmented rock. Findochty lies in a semi-circular inlet bounded on the east by an old church on a grassy knoll and on the west by a cliff surmounted by an obelisk. As the visitor admires the sprinkling of small boats in the otherwise deserted harbour, his eye will fall on the statue of a seated fisherman gazing out over the waters. On the pedestal is the inscription: "They see the works of the Lord and his wonders in the deep". The sculptor was a local girl, Coreena Cowie.

Although a charter of 1568 mentioned "port, customs and fishing grounds" at Findochty, the village was founded in 1716 when thirteen men and four boys, their names being Flett, Campbell and Smith, came here under a kind of contract from Fraserburgh to homes built for them at the Broad Hythe by John Ord of Findochty Castle, and later worked for the Earl of Findlater. The present village, however, owed its layout to a deliberate act of town planning when George MacWilliam laid it out as a Seafield Estate township in 1833. The fifty years from 1861 to 1911 were the years of expansion. In that period the population rose from 383 to 1,785. The four and a half acres harbour, built in 1883, is now entered in the valuation roll at £10, but, if no gold mine today, the charm and character of the burgh still depend upon it. Most of the houses in the old fisher-town are scheduled for conservation.

Findochty Castle, a rectangular tower house with a small oblong tower attached to the north front, dates from 1568 but is now a sorry ruin. The real beauty of the inland horizon is in the gorse-covered slopes of the Bin Hill from which a superb view opens up of the sweep of the coast westward to Spey Bay, with, beyond the much favoured Strathlene golf-course, the three-mile-long ribbon of housing that embraces the havens of Portessie, Gordonsburgh, Ianstown, Seatown and Buckpool and comprises modern Buckie (pop. 7,919).

One need not be mesmerized by figures but the last census showed that Buckie had fully recovered from the painful post war depression which at one time caused much anxiety. For a century it has been the largest town in Banffshire, drawing to itself the lion's share of the fishing industry, but there was a period after World War II when unemployment was high and diversification of the economy was the aim.

After the establishment of an electrical components factory and other light engineering ventures this was achieved and land-based industry and the fish trade in Buckie are now almost in equilibrium, with about 900 employed in each vocation—though it must be remembered that the sea jobs are for men and the land industry needs large numbers of women. It is not for nothing that the burgh motto of Buckie is "Mare Mater"—"Our Mother Sea". When fishing is prosperous Buckie booms and is most itself, with annual fish landings in excess of £1 million in value and an active fleet of over 100 fishing vessels. Shipbuilding in the three local yards is of the highest importance in building up a reservoir of skilled craftsmanship.

When Robert Burns visited Buckie in 1787 Nether and Easter Buckie had between them 165 houses and 700 inhabitants. Most of the houses were thatched but and bens, as was Lucky Onlie's alehouse—

> Lady Onlie, honest Lucky,
> 　　Brews guid ale at Shore o'Bucky;
> I wish her sale for her good ale,
> 　　The best on a' the shore o'Bucky.

There followed what has been called the fairy tale of Banffshire fishing development, through the modification of boat types from undecked Skaffies to Fifies and Zulus, with yacht-like lines, and eventually to wooden steam drifters, all of which have now gone to be succeeded by the motor-driven dual-purpose boats of today. It was John Gordon of Cluny who in 1872 by building the Cluny Harbour raised Buckie to its pre-eminence as the greatest line fishing port in Scotland, and soon after, in the heyday of the herring, to the role of busiest fishing district in the country. At that time Buckie had a population of close on 9,000. There has been decline since then, but the town has shown a capacity to adjust to the fluctuations inseparable from fishing.

Dominating the centre of Buckie, the crown tower of the North church is a symbol of the powerful religious life of the burgh. The outstanding architectural feature at the west end of Buckie is St Peter's Roman Catholic Church, built in 1857. Its twin spires and cathedral-like proportions are a fitting reminder of the long history of Catholicism in the Enzie, as the western corner of Banffshire is called. In 1617 it is recorded that there were over one thousand Catholics in Banffshire and only fifty in the city of Glasgow!

Although it has been almost forgotten now, the hinterland of Buckie was very much Gordon country which explains the persistence of Catholicism. Apart from the Gordons of Buckie there was another branch of the family, the Gordons of Letterfourie, and Letterfourie House is one of the oldest structures in the area. The road leading to it at Craigmin boasts a strange architectural freak, a sort of aqueduct over the defile of the Buckie Burn which consists of one bridge built on top of another, with a quaint chamber in the parapet of the upper storey. It dates from the eighteenth century and owes its existence to the fact that the original bridge, low down over the stream, while adequate for the pack horses of an early period, could not be negotiated by carriages and had to be raised by the addition of the second tier.

Beyond Buckpool, which united with Easter Buckie to form the police burgh of Buckie in 1888, a short stretch of open country leads to Portgordon, a planned village or 'new town' laid out by the fourth Duke of Gordon in 1797 to serve as a grain-exporting port for the farmlands of the Enzie. Its now deserted harbour remained the responsibility of the Dukes of Gordon and their inheritors the Dukes of Richmond

and Gordon right down to the break-up of the Richmond
and Gordon estates in 1938 and is today owned by their
inheritors, the Commissioners of Crown Lands. It was rebuilt
in 1874 and enlarged in 1909. Older residents can recall when
it was packed with the smaller class of fishing boats so thickly
that you could walk dryshod from deck to deck across the
basin. In 1880 there were as many as ninty-nine fishing craft
registered at Portgordon. But in the gale of 1953 the harbour
was so damaged that it now dries out at low tide. There is still
a salmon fishing station here, with the fishers operating on the
tidal reaches of the Spey, and two small lobster boats still use
it. But streets once occupied by fishermen from end to end are
now largely peopled by incoming settlers and it is reckoned
that of the total population of a little over 900 around 200 are
now retired couples.

To arrest decline the local authority has carried out a 'face
lift'. Derelict houses have been demolished and an attractive
amenity area created on the steep grassy slopes between the
upper and lower levels of the village. The sea wall has been
renewed and some economic revival has been brought about
by the introduction of a fish-processing plant deriving its
supplies from Buckie.

Efforts are being made to bring Portgordon and its rural
hinterland together by the parish minister who is also the
minister of the Enzie with its rolling farmlands to the south,
but the original grain-exporting function of the "port" is now
part of a forgotten past.

Between Portgordon and the mouth of the Spey a small
stream called the Tynet formed the old boundary between
Banffshire and Moray. In 1687 those faithful to the old
religion built at Chapelford on the Tynet, where there had
been a pre-Reformation chapel of St Ninian, the first Catholic
church since the great upheaval of the previous century.
Today the site is marked by a cross in memory of Bishop
Nicholson, the first Vicar Apostolic in post-Reformation
Scotland. After another small Catholic church at Bridge of
Tynet had been burned down following the 1745 rebellion,
the laird of Tynet in 1755 offered the use of an old cottage
that had been converted into a sheepcot and this humble
structure, long, low and white-washed, distinguished only by
a ball of stone on the western gable, still survives and is

cherished as the 'Banffshire Bethlehem' of the Catholics. In due course they were able to build a much more elaborate church at nearby Presshome.

Among the farms in the vicinity of Portgordon is Nether Dallachy, given a certain fame of its own by the poet J. M. Caie in verses beginning:

> Doon at Nether Dallachy
> There's neither watch nor knock,
> But denner time and supper time
> And aye, Yoke! Yoke!

The call to 'yoke' was of course the summons to restart work. These and other Enzie poems by Caie underline the fact that a unitary rural culture, using the same dialect of Scots, prevails throughout what is now the Grampian Region from easternmost Buchan to the Spey. From the vicinity of Buckie the A98 trunk road, keeping some distance from the coast, sweeps south-westwards to Fochabers through big Forestry Commission plantations and joins the A96 trunk road from Aberdeen before crossing the Spey on the way to Elgin.

Fochabers is the perfect introduction to the special character of Moray. Nowadays it has a mini-climate of its own owing to the sheltering effect of its surrounding necklace of woodlands, the Forest of Speymouth. It is just 200 years old, the first house in the modern village having been built in 1776. It has a population of 1,054 while its rural hinterland adds only 696 to make up a total of 1,750 for the parish of Bellie as a whole. The Dukes of Richmond and Gordon, the Commissioners of Crown Lands who took over from them, and the Forestry Commission who took over from the Crown Lands have all contributed to Speymouth Forest. Since the end of World War II it has grown from 4,000 to 10,500 acres and then, with the acquisition of additional land from the Seafield estates and Sir Brian Mountain, to 13,500 acres all under management from Fochabers.

Standing back, a little from the east bank of the Spey about five miles from its mouth, Fochabers is a fine example of Georgian town planning. It was laid out by John Baxter, mason to William Adam, for Alexander, fourth Duke of Gordon, when he found it necessary to demolish the original village which stood in the way of the extension of Gordon Castle. Baxter designed it in the form of a rectangle bisected lengthways from east to west by the main road. On this major axis is a large market square with the parish church of Bellie (1798) in the middle of its south side. From the square, Duke Street ran north in a direct line to Gordon Castle, but in 1852 this vista was closed by the erection of an Episcopal chapel balancing the church at the other end of the street. The plan is completed by another cross street (Westmoreland Street) and by a series of lanes.

Bellie Church, with pillared portico and spire, gains in effect by symmetrical flanking blocks, one of which houses the offices of the Crown Lands Commissioners who have administered most of the former Richmond and Gordon lands since 1938. East Street and West Street bound the 'new town' at either end and the other streets retain names which link them with the family of the founder.

It was George, second Earl of Huntly, who founded Gordon Castle towards the end of the fifteenth century. But the stronghold itself had its beginnings before the Gordons came upon the scene. The lowest portion of the old tower, the first fourteen feet, dates from the twelfth century. This was the "pillbox in a bog" from which everything else followed. It was long known as Bog o' Gight, the windy bog, and its successive Gordon lairds, the heads of the whole Gordon tribe, were called Gudeman o' the Bog. The second earl heightened the old tower to six storeys and it remains today for all to see as a 'stark strength' crowned by its battlements and ameliorated as a living place by the insertion of larger windows in the upper portion. A rambling and inconvenient castle was added on to the tower but this was swept away and replaced by the ducal palace which the fourth duke commissioned Baxter to build on his marriage to Jane Maxwell in 1767.

The "world of a house" which he designed was based on a central block of four storeys incorporating the ancient six-storey tower, with capacious wings on either side connected to the main building by galleries or arcades of two lower storeys, while beyond the wings were extended pavilions of one floor and an attic storey—forming altogether a front of 568 feet faced with Elgin Freestone and finished with a rich cornice and with battlements.

One may regret the disappearance of the older house. It must have had its charms, inspiring the attachment evident in the old ballad:

> If I were amang the hills of Foudland
>  Where hunting I have been
> I would gang to bonnie Castle Gordon
>  Without either stockings or sheen.

But the new Gordon Castle with its great formal gardens, its islanded lake and opulent interiors was a fitting setting for the gay and brilliant Duchess Jane who dazzled high society for several decades. With a kiss and a shilling for recruits she played a notable part in raising the Gordon Highlanders regiment in 1794. When the regiment set out with her son, the Marquess of Huntly, as its colonel on the Den Helder expedition of 1799, Mrs Grant of Laggan penned the famous air "Highland Laddie" which contained the stanza:

> Suppose, ah! suppose that some cruel cruel wound
> Should pierce your Highland Laddie and all your hopes
>  confound!
> The pipes would play a cheering march, the banners round
>  him fly,
> The spirit of a Highland chief would lighten in his eye.

And it so happened that the Highland Laddie did receive a wound. In the fight at Bergen op Zoom he was knocked over by a bullet in the shoulder. He came home to Gordon Castle. All the countryside turned out to greet him and an ox was roasted in the Square of Fochabers. The "Highland Laddie" in due course succeeded as the fifth and last Duke of Gordon. On his death Gordon Castle passed to the fifth Duke of Richmond, and a second creation of the dukedom of Gordon was later made in favour of that family. Appropriately the present laird, a grandson of the seventh Duke of Richmond and Gordon, is not only Colonel of the Gordon Highlanders but has, since 1951, recreated the ancestral home, after it had passed through rather sad vicissitudes.

The castle passed with the Richmond and Gordon estates to the Commissioners of Crown Lands in 1938. In World War II it was used by the Army, but when vacated by them it suffered calamitous deterioration by water damage. Lt. General Sir George Gordon Lennox then acquired it from the Crown Commissioners, but by this time the central block and the west wing were so badly affected that there was no alternative to their demolition. This was carried out in 1953. There remained the old tower and the east wing, both of which have been preserved and rehabilitated, the tower being linked to low farm buildings and the wing, internally modified, has regained its status as a stately home.

Towards the east end of the main street of Fochabers stands the elaborate neo-Tudor pile of Milne's High School with its turrets, battlements and pinnacles designed by the Elgin architect Thomas Mackenzie in 1846.

Alexander Milne was born at Fochabers in 1742. As a youth on the household staff at Gordon Castle he wore his hair in a queue and resented the order of the fourth duke that all servants' hair must be cut short. He then emigrated to America and built up a thriving business in New Orleans, bequeathing on his death 100,000 dollars to his native place "to be employed in establishing a free school". Owing to a legal argument only resolved by the U.S. Supreme Court, it was not till 1845 that the money was handed over and the school built. It has since had a distinguished academic record.

West of Fochabers the A96 sweeps past the imposing gateway to Gordon Castle and crosses the Spey by a modern bridge beyond which is the Baxter food factory. They have heard of Fochabers in Addis Ababa and Honolulu, among the capitals of seventy-eight countries where the Gordon tartan decorates containers of the "fresh food from Scotland" exported from here by the enterprise founded in 1868 by a retired gardener to the Duke of Richmond and Gordon, whose wife was a genius at making jam.

The River Spey, second river of Scotland, 98 miles long and draining a basin of 1,153 square miles, retains its Highland character almost to its mouth in the middle of Spey Bay. Here at Fochabers it debouches into the Laich amid picturesque scenery diversified by earth pillars formed by erosion. It is flanked by red sandstone cliffs and shingle beds; looking south there is a breathtaking view of the wall of hills which marks the great divide between the Laich of Moray and the mountains of the hinterland. The A96 slices through the parish of Speymouth by Mosstodlach, once a small hamlet but now a long ribbon development which has gained importance by the proximity of food and saw-milling industries. On the right is the road by the riverside to the villages of Garmouth and Kingston, on the left is the 816 foot summit of Findlay's Seat, from which, according to tradition, Findlay could survey the hill passes through which invading reivers and caterans from the Highlands could be seen afar off as they approached the low country in search of plunder.

Such a view would be rather impeded today, for since 1925 Findlay's Seat has been the centre of the Teindland Experimental Reserve of the Forestry Commission. Teindland, which forms the southern tip of the parish of St Andrews-Lhanbryde, is an area of barren hill land where, tradition says, the people's cattle were formerly herded so that the bishop's officer of the diocese of Moray might select the bishop's tithe or teind, to which he was entitled as church dues. Today Teindland has bleak, thin soil full of glacial detritus that burnishes the ploughshare to silver. There is point in the story of the farmer's boy who was being questioned by the parish minister on the Shorter Catechism and what it said about Works of Creation. To press home their excellence the minister asked the boy whether there was anything which the Creator had made which was not very good. "Ay," said the boy, "for my faither was ploughing the Teindland last week and he said it was surely made o' the leavin's."

These leavings of creation have been the subject of research now for fifty years. In 1924 the Forestry Commission acquired 3,000 acres of the Teindland and set up the Teindland Forest. At Findlay's Seat a special natural laboratory was established. First experiments were started in 1925 when it was recognized from the evidence of 115-year-old planted Scots pine scrub that the ground was unplantable by normal methods. It was found that while surface roots could develop, the lower roots were unable to take a hold because underneath the surface lay an almost unbroken undulating iron pan. Frustrated by this obstacle, trees could not root sufficiently to withstand winter gales.

A succession of ploughing techniques was used but the full answer did not come until 1969 when deep tine ploughs mounted on tractors achieved soil disturbance up to 94 centimeters. The battle to break up the soil had been won with results which can be seen in the impressive forest rides at Findlay's Seat today.

Trees have played a leading part in the story of the Spey valley for centuries. At the mouth of the Spey is the village of Kingston, approached by the B9015 road from Mosstodlach. It was here in 1784 that a settlement was created by two Yorkshiremen, Ralph Dodsworth and William Osbourne, and named after Kingston-upon-Hull. They had bought the timber of the forest of Glenmore on the threshold of the Cairngorms and were floating it down the Spey. At first they merely shipped it away in log form, but in 1786 they established the first of Kingston's shipyards. During the first ten years they built twenty-five vessels and by 1815 nearly fifty. In their day Kingston was merely a collection of temporary shacks, but in the second quarter of the nineteenth century the present handsome village was laid out on a regular plan and a total of around 300 vessels were built till the demise of the industry in the 1890s.

The countryside at the mouth of the Spey, on the left bank of the river, is both beautiful and strange. To the west the long rounded shoulder of the Binn Hill falls rapidly to below the 50-foot contour. Kingston faces the sea behind a long lagoon between great banks of shingle and the more ancient village of Garmouth, three-quarters of a mile to the south, overlooks the maze of shallow waterways forming the river delta.

It must have been on one of these little creeks that Charles II reached Garmouth from Holland on 23 June 1650, to be carried ashore pick-a-back by 'King' Milne when the boats which had taken him from his ship at the river mouth grounded in shallow water. The Garmouth which he saw then could not have been so very different from the village described in an early guidebook: "The streets are nearly as sinuous as the houses, which, as regards size and position are nearly as irregular as it is possible to make them."

The great day of the year in Garmouth (pop. 352) is 24 June, the day of Maggie Fair, said to have taken its name from the Lady of Innes who received King Charles. Until World War I this famous fair was manned by travelling fair folk from Keith, who went from fair to fair throughout the country. But when they ceased to pursue this practice the women of Garmouth had the happy inspiration of reviving Maggie Fair as a local charity bazaar in aid of good causes.

The oldest structure in the two villages is Dunfermline House, also known as the Old Red Corff House. In its lower portion it dates from the Middle Ages and was erected by the monks from Dunfermline Abbey who manned the nearby Priory of Urquhart, and used as a changing house or hospice. About 1780 an upper storey was added by a Garmouth ship-builder, John Duncan, whose shipyard lay in front of the house. In the ship-builder's loft of the house is still to be seen the drawing of a pilot cutter built here for the Clyde Pilotage Authority in the year 1833. Here too Duncan had his office from which he would have paid up to 200 men employed in his yard. Today the old house looks out over a peaceful scene of great beauty stretching beyond Tugnet to the Banffshire coast.

One more relic of a faded past in the area is the long railway bridge and viaduct on the former coastal railway linking Garmouth and Spey Bay across the river's delta. It cost about £100,000 to build and the great steel tracery of the central span proved such a magnet to athletic small boys from Garmouth that trains frequently had to be halted while they were cleared off the line. There are now plans to convert it into a scenic walkway.

Before we push on to the west a thought must be spared for the little-known lower reaches of the Spey. The best way to approach the western Cairngorms is surely via Strathspey from the Moray Firth. Above Fochabers the Spey winds through the pleasant Haugh of Dipple before the hills close in on either side at Boat o' Brig, where the Aberdeen–Elgin railway crosses it above the woods of Delfur, one of the finest salmon stretches of the river. With great curving meanders the river descends here from the lovely Vale of Rothes, where the woods of Arndilly and Aikenway (the way of the oaks) clothe the western flanks of Ben Aigan (1544 feet) whose shapely cone dominates a sylvan landscape. Rothes itself, on the haughland under the very fragmentary remains of its castle, is a whisky town, living by its five distilleries and the ingenious 'Purie' or purification works which convert distillery effluent into animal feeding stuffs.

Three miles upriver is Craigellachie, which also has a distillery but is more famous for its rock, the great landmark signalling the lower limit of the Grant lands of Strathspey, a beetling cliff under which the road from Elgin used to run to Telford's delicate bridge of cast iron tracery anchored at each bank by picturesque battlemented turrets. "Stand Fast, Craigellachie!", the battle cry of the Clan Grant, refers to the two Craigellachies. This is the lower Craigellachie, the upper one being the craggy hill behind Aviemore. A new road bridge slashes across the river valley just below the Rock, but Telford's fairy-like span remains to decorate one of the most beautiful bends in Spey's course.

Between Kingston and Lossiemouth, along five miles of curving coastline, stretches the Lossie Forest by Milltown airfield, while inland from Garmouth a quiet road slants through the farming parish of Urquhart to Lhanbryde on the A96 highway to Elgin. No trace remains of the ancient priory of Urquhart save a Celtic cross built into the fabric of the parish church and a carefully preserved piece of moulding. The two most remarkable houses in this stretch of country are Innes House (about a mile and a half north-north-west of the village of Urquhart) and Coxton Tower (about a mile south-west of Lhanbryde).

Of Coxton Tower, Dr Douglas Simpson wrote: "No building in Scotland more startlingly exemplifies the long and stubborn native devotion to the tower house as a suitable plan for a small laird's residence. Although entirely medieval in conception it was actually completed in 1644—an anachronism in stone, equipped to withstand any sort of attack short of a barrage of artillery." Basically it consists of four rooms one on top of another, all of them vaulted and communicating with each other by means of hatches in the floors, though there is a mural staircase between the great hall on the first floor and the rooms above it. The uppermost vault is of a high pointed form, so as to carry the stone-slabbed roof, which lies between the usual crow-stepped gables, each crowned with a chimney stack with moulded cope. At two corners are fat round turrets with conical stone helmets ending in ornate pinnacles and at a third corner is a square turret, open, embattled and machiolated.

In the same period, between 1640 and 1653, Sir Robert

Innes of that Ilk was building Innes House, a small Renaissance masterpiece. It follows the traditional L-plan with three full storeys and a top storey partly in the roof of the two wings of the L, but it is no old-style tower house but a gracious mansion with windows and ornaments which proclaim a love of the arts and of gracious living. Large and pleasing additions, forming a courtyard to the north of the original building, were made by the Tennants, the present owning family, early in the present century.

Lhanbryde, centred by a tree-shaded churchyard on a high knoll overlooking the main road, has been expanded from a sleepy hamlet of 525 folk at the 1961 census to a booming dormitory suburb of Elgin which is only three miles away, with a population of 1,500 and the prospect of being doubled in size to reach an optimum of 3,000 in the next few years.

The road to Lossiemouth passes through Calcots where there was a station on the now closed railway to Garmouth and the Moray Firth coast. About a mile to the north-west, on the west side of the Lossie, is Pitgaveny House, an imposing mansion built in 1776 for James Brander, who by his marriage with Helen Dunbar of Duffus founded a local dynasty which for long held the superiority of Lossiemouth. Most renowned of all the lairds of Pitgaveny was James Brander-Dunbar, nicknamed 'the Lairdie', who died in 1969 at the age of ninety-four after a life that had become a legend. Captain Brander-Dunbar decorated the walls of the hall, the staircase and of his own sitting-room with trophies of the chase, including 230 heads, showing sixty kinds of deer and antelope, with lion, giraffe, rhinoceros, hippopotamus and buffalo, and skins of lion, tiger and African cheetah.

Most famous of the trophies is the stag's head he acquired as the result of a bet that it was possible to poach in an intensely guarded forest, while under the head is a facsimile of the cheque used to pay the bet. In the library is an autographed copy of John Buchan's novel *John Macnab* which celebrates this poaching exploit, inscribed "From John Buchan to John Macnab". The head of a lion shot in 1896, preserved with 'the Lairdie's' bonnet and dog leads, is a memento of survey work in Somaliland for the Royal Geographical Society.

A further mile and a half to the north-west lies the Loch

of Spynie, relic of a mighty sheet of water five miles long and over a mile wide which once occupied 2,500 acres of the Laich of Moray. Before AD 1100 in fact it was a great arm of the open sea extending from Burghead Bay to Spey Bay, sheltered on the north by two islands, one embracing the parish of Duffus and extending from Burghead to Covesea and the other extending from the fort of Kinneddar to Stotfield Head at Lossiemouth.

Four stages of land emergence can be traced since this state of inundation inherited from the flooding that followed the last Ice Age. At the second of these stages, which gave rise to 25-foot beaches, the Burghead and Duffus island was joined to the mainland by a neck of land at Roseisle on which shingle bars had formed. This closed the western outlet of the Loch of Spynie to the sea, but the eastern end of the loch remained connected with it long enough for the creation of a thriving Bishop's Port on the loch two miles north of Elgin. Medieval records tell us that boats sailed up the Lossie to this port until the fifteenth century.

For a mere ten to fifteen years the church of the Holy Trinity at Spynie was the cathedral of Moray. In 1224 the cathedral was moved to Elgin, but the bishops of Moray continued to live at Spynie in their castle there, above the shores of the loch. By the end of the fourteenth century Spynie was "a town and harbour inhabited by fishermen who sailed from Spynie to the sea, and boats and nets were kept by Bishop Bar in the lake for catching salmon, grilse and other fish". In 1451 it was erected into a burgh of barony. In the following year the burgh took one step up by being declared a regality "with right of harbour and passages".

By that time at least a part of Spynie Palace had been built. The credit for this belongs to Bishop John de Winchester who held the see of Moray from 1437 to 1458. He was a personal friend of King James I and King James II and the second of these monarchs gave him the supervision of building work at Linlithgow Palace and the castles of Inverness and Urquhart. It was probably he who planned the great courtyard on a rectangular plan enclosed by walls over 5 feet thick and 25 feet high and built the main gate on the east curtain wall over which he placed his coat of arms. It has been suggested that the "superior and exotic style" is due to the presence of skilled master-masons working on the restoration of Elgin Cathedral after its burning by the Wolf of Badenoch in 1390. But when Winchester died the palace was by means complete and its most spectacular feature, the great six-storey keep at the south-west corner, was begun by David Stewart, bishop from 1461 to 1476 and dubbed 'Davie's Tower'.

Over 62 feet long and 44 feet wide, its walls, which are 11 feet thick, rise 75 feet to the parapet walk. It was defended at basement level by enormous gunloops. Above the hall window on the south front are the arms of Bishop David Stuart and Bishop Patrick Hepburn (1535-73) surmounted by the royal arms of Scotland, while near the parapet are the arms of another bishop, William Tulloch (1477-82). For three centuries Spynie Palace played a part in the history of Scotland. King James II visited it at least twice. James IV was there in 1493 and again in 1505. On 17 September 1562 Mary Queen of Scots stayed there on her way south from Inverness before the Battle of Corrichie. Four years later it was the prison of Ruxby, "a fraudulent agent of Queen Elizabeth's malign diplomacy".

For a time Spynie and its palace were bestowed by James VI and I on his favourite Alexander Lindsay, whom he created Lord Spynie, but after fifteen years Lindsay had to hand them back, because the king had decided to restore episcopacy and the palace was wanted once more as the home of the bishops of Moray. Came the Civil War and John Gordon, Bishop of Moray, was deposed and excommunicated by the General Assembly. He retired to Spynie Palace and stocked up with arms and provisions for a long siege. But in July 1640 the Covenanting General George Monro frustrated this design. The bishop and his family were taken to Edinburgh and warded in the Tolbooth there.

A siege did take place in 1645, but with the Covenanters as the besieged and the royalist Marquess Earl of Huntly as the besieger. Although he had an army of 2,000, Huntly failed miserably to crack so tough a nut and had to retire "steeped in disgrace" before General Middleton. After the Restoration the last bishop to dwell in Spynie was Colin Falconer, who died within its walls in 1688. Though now an empty shell, the ruins are carefully preserved by the Department of the Environment.

Meanwhile, by the end of the fifteenth century, the Loch of Spynie, soon to be cut off from the sea on the east, had become so shallow that the old port was useless and efforts had begun to drain the loch. On the advice of David Anderson of Finzeauch, nicknamed "Davie Do A'thing" the River Lossie was diverted out of the loch into a new channel and drains made to carry the waters of the loch into the river. By 1640 this stategy had succeeded, but in 1694 windblown sand caused an obstruction which blocked the exit and widespread flooding occurred. In 1720, Alexander Dunbar of Thunderton devised a system of dykes and imported a windmill to keep the waters of the loch at bay. But this produced only temporary relief and by 1770 the loch had again swollen so that it inundated 2,500 acres. New drains were devised by James and Alexander Brander who had acquired several estates in the area and by this means 1,000 acres of land were reclaimed.

Finally in 1807 the engineering genius of the day, Thomas Telford, was consulted by the lairds of the region. He devised the Spynie Canal, seven miles long, running through the centre of the loch and thence to the sea at Lossiemouth.

By 1820 it was possible to drive a new turnpike road from Elgin to Lossiemouth right through the centre of the now vanished loch at what had been its deepest point, and, though the Muckle Spate of 1829 temporarily undid most of this good work, the situation was fully restored by 1860. Today all that remains of the great Loch of Spynie is a tiny fragment between Spynie Palace and the farm of Scarffbanks, deliberately preserved as a refuge for swans and other wild birds.

Beside Spynie Palace there is a pleasant old mansion house of Spynie on the L-plan with crow-stepped gables, decorative dormers and a round stair tower corbelled out to square in the upper storey. It belonged originally to the Douglases, descendants of Bishop Alexander Douglas, and was eventually acquired by Captain Brander-Dunbar of Pigaveny. In 1736 the old kirk of Spynie was abandoned and the present parish church was built at Quarry Wood on the slopes of Cuttie's Hillock, overlooking the plain to the north. The hamlet which grew up around the church was called New Spynie. The bell of the old kirk, dated 1636, and the belfry (1735) were removed to the new church, together with the cut stones of the two doorways which were built into the south wall. The larger of the two doorways is late Gothic and the smaller seventeenth century. Between the two large windows in the south wall is a charming sundial inscribed: "Johannes Dugall fecit 1740".

There is something anomalous about the parish of Spynie, which one enters as soon as one crosses the Lossie in the heart of Elgin and ascends North Street, traversing the 160-year-old village of Bishopmill. In 1801 when census-taking began, the parish had a total of 843 inhabitants. By 1961 it had a population of 6,001—and well over 4,000 of these had been added since the end of World War II. Acting for the Seafield Estates, Provost Brown of Elgin prepared a plan for the original village of Bishopmill in 1795 and building began in the following year. The plan provided for a row of large houses with gardens of from three to six acres on the south edge of the high escarpment overlooking the Lossie. Behind these houses there was a grid of small streets, built only on the north side, so that every street faced south into the sun.

The original plan was disrupted in 1820 by the making of the Lossiemouth turnpike (now North Street) and a bridge had to be built across it to link the two severed halves of the original High Street. But Bishopmill began to be fashionable in the 1860s when a set of handsome villas arose on the escarpment facing the river. At various times the municipality of Elgin bought up all the land on both sides of the original village, and early in World War II, by a major act of town planning, completed the layout of the new community. Of over 1,000 houses, 800 of them local authority, 350 were later set aside as homes for the permanent staff of the Royal Naval Air Station at Lossiemouth.

In the kirkyard of Spynie under a large flat stone lie the remains of Moray's most famous son, James Ramsay Mac-Donald, first Labour premier of Britain. This was the spot he chose to be the last resting place of his wife Margaret Ethel Gladstone in 1911 and when he died in 1937 his ashes were placed in the same grave and his name added to the stone. Around the stone are inscribed the "Pass to where, beyond those voices, there is peace". The small town to which he brought such fame was initiated by the magistrates of Elgin to replace the 'lost' port of Spynie.

When Spynie's port stood high and dry
    Auld Lossie rose to take its place,
And syne, when Seatown's day won by
    Came Branderburgh to set the pace.
And now, athwart the Coulard Hill,
    And west by Stotfield and Covesea,
Four quarters link to make a whole
    And modern Lossiemouth we see.

King Charles I, about the year 1633, gave a grant to the magistrates of Elgin for a tax on ale within the burgh to enable that town "to erect a commodious harbour at Elgin-head or Lossie-head". But the place was just a tiny hamlet. In 1793 it had a total population of 150 and boasted one small sloop and two small fishing craft. On the other side of the Coulard Hill the fishing havens at Stotfield and Covesea had three boats each.

The big leap forward came in 1819 when herring fishing was started with four boats. By 1820 the number of boats had risen to ten. The little harbour became too small for the growing boom and a company was formed to build a new harbour at Stotfield Point. It was quarried out of solid rock and completed in 1839. As this was taking place a 'new town' was laid out on the northern slope of Coulard Hill called Branderburgh after the Laird, Col. James Brander of Pitgaveny, with a square in the centre of a regular grid of streets. By 1881, when the Zulu boats, the first of which, *Nonesuch*, had been designed by a Lossiemouth fisherman in 1879, were making history, the port had 149 boats, employing 395 fishermen.

It was during this exciting period, on 12 October 1866, that the future prime minister was born at 1 Gregory Place in the old Seatown. This two-roomed but-and-ben cottage, then thatched, and backing on to the railway, not far from the Market Cross, has since been marked for identification by a plaque of dressed Clasach sandstone from Hopeman.

The MacDonald links remain in Lossiemouth. The Hillocks, a house in Moray Street which the premier originally built for his mother and which became his own home, is still owned by the family, and his daughter Ishbel, Mrs Peterkin, made her home in nearby Macduff Street. In Lossiemouth

High School, on the Coulard Hill, the Ramsay MacDonald Trust Awards which he endowed are much cherished. The log of the school records that on 12 January 1929 "in honour of the Prime Minister's homecoming the school did not meet today".

When the police burgh of Lossiemouth and Branderburgh was formed in 1890 the town had a population of 3,486. Today the figure is 5,678 and fishing has remained at the heart of its economy. From Zulu sailing craft, local men soon turned to steam drifters, but after World War I these became too costly for small capitalists to operate and in 1921 Lossiemouth first adapted the Danish seine net for use in this country, an example which was soon followed all along the Firth. In 1961 William Thomson in the *Kittywake* pioneered a new type of seine net which brought about another small revolution.

When the Royal Naval Station (HMS *Fulmar*) closed down a few years ago it was replaced by RAF Lossiemouth so that the Services element in the local economy was not greatly affected. At the same time more emphasis was placed on tourism. What Ramsay MacDonald called "our Bay of Naples", the magnificent sweep of sands from Stotfield to Covesea, terminating in the Covesea Lighthouse, was increasingly exploited.

Though now a quarter of hotels and boarding houses, Stotfield has very old fishing traditions. The Stotfield Disaster Memorial records how on Christmas Day 1806 "three boats containing the whole seamen of Stotfield, 21 in number, went to sea, and, a sudden storm arising, all perished". The memorial tells how "by this terrible calamity 17 widows, 47 children and eight aged parents were left destitute, but so successful was the appeal to public sympathy, that a fund of £1152 2s 3d was collected for their relief". Disaster funds of this kind are no novelty in the Moray Firth. Vessels lost without trace are still not infrequent and funds raised for the dependants are always generously supported.

Beyond Lossiemouth and its airfield lies the parish of Duffus. Mention has already been made (in Chapter II) of Duffus Castle on its mound dominating the level Laich. North of it is the estate of Gordonstoun and its school where the Duke of Edinburgh, the Prince of Wales, and now Prince Andrew have been pupils. The school, founded by Kurt Hahn, has, besides pioneering the kind of education aimed at developing the 'whole man', cherished and preserved its inheritance of an ancient territorial estate round which colourful and historical associations cling.

Though cut off on the south by the Loch of Spynie and by the boggy land to the west of it where once the sea had flowed in from Burghead Bay, the major part of the parish of Duffus shared the fertility of the great Moray plain. As late as 1795 the minister of Duffus was describing it as "one continuous arable plain capable of producing everything that will grow anywhere in Scotland". In that he was but following the eulogy of Robert Gordon of Straloch 150 years earlier: "Nothing grows anywhere in the whole kingdom which does not thrive here luxuriantly ... The earth pours forth the crops from a wonderful and never-failing horn of plenty."

In this little paradise Gordonstoun had its beginnings as Bog o' Plewlands, acquired in 1616 by the first Marquess of Huntly who before 1636 had built the oldest surviving parts of Gordonstoun House—the wings with their pleasant little angle turrets. In 1638 the second marquess sold Plewlands to his cousin Sir Robert Gordon who envisaged it as an island of peace amid the turmoil of the Civil War. In 1640 he had the estate reorganized as the Barony of Gordonstoun, the name it has held ever since. His son Sir Ludovick, laird from 1656 to 1688, drained the ancient 'Bog' of Plewlands into a single long pond—the Gordonstoun Lake of today, which lies to the south of the house and has proved a splendid sporting amenity to the school. His heir, Sir Robert, third baronet, known as the Wizard of Gordonstoun, reigned over the estate for only sixteen years (1688-1704), yet he is the hero or villain of its most colourful legends. He was an intellectual and has been much misunderstood. Far be it from me to spoil a good story by disbelieving his compact with the Devil, or discounting his potent spells, but his greatest piece of magic was the wonderful Round Square.

As H. L. Brereton has put it: "bringing to his aid his extensive study of necromancy and the inventive originality which he shared with contemporaries like Robert Boyle and the Gregorys of Aberdeen, Sir Robert contrived his stables as a circle of magic proportions, a scientific sanctuary for his soul". Though probably not architect-designed and thus 'amateur' from the start, it is a unique example of Scottish good taste in building and it has been finely restored and converted into a collegiate court for Gordonstoun School.

Sir Robert built four dovecotes, two of which can still be seen near Gordonstoun House. Each housed about 1,000 pigeons which it is estimated consumed 120 bushels of corn a year, for which his farming tenants had no redress. People put about a story that the laird was trying to get rid of his wife with whom he had quarrelled permanently, it being a common belief at the time that the building of a dovecote would by followed by a death in the family. The fact was that at the end of the long northern winter pigeons were often the only source of fresh meat and only landed proprietors and parish ministers had a legal right to build dovecotes and keep pigeons.

From the furnace where the peasantry imagined the Wizard Laird to be colloguing with the Devil, he produced some of the finest contemporary examples of the blacksmith's art. When he died in 1704, his widow, his second wife Elizabeth Dunbar of Hempriggs, built Michael Kirk (often described as the latest known example of old Scottish Gothic) to his memory. This lovely old church has since been twice altered, first in 1900 when glass was put in the windows and furnishings added, and again in 1959 when it was reroofed and a dark elaborate reredos at the east end taken out. At this time also the statue of St Michael was moved with the altar to the west end. Gordonstoun School holds a commemorative service in Michael Kirk in the first week of each January term.

The centre and north face of Gordonstoun House were reconstructed by the Wizard laird's son, known as "the Ill Sir Robert", in 1729. Gordonstoun School took over the old building in 1934. The presence in the school of the Duke of Edinburgh and of the Prince of Wales brought upon it the spotlight of world interest, but for the most part its work goes on as little observed by the outside world as that of any other school, except when innovations like the admission of girls to its select roll create a flutter of attention.

Around Michael Kirk volunteers from Gordonstoun have been uncovering on weatherworn slabs of stone the domestic annals of a parish that ceased to exist over three centuries ago. This was the graveyard of the ancient parish of Ogstoun, annexed to the neighbouring parish of Kinneddar in 1669. Among the sculptured emblems on these old stones is a windlass and anchor commemorating a local skipper. Seafaring traditions are very notable in this part of Moray, but it was only in 1805 that the first houses were built in Duffus's surviving port, Hopeman, a 'new town' laid out by William Young of Inverugie. The harbour was the creation of Admiral Duff of Drummuir in 1837 and of his successor Major Lachlan Duff Gordon-Duff at a later date. Only small craft can still use the harbour, entering at high tide, but Hopeman is extremely popular as a holiday place. Like so many sea-towns on the Moray Firth, the fishing folk are still faithful to their old homes here and twenty-four seine net vessels are locally owned. The harbour separates the East and West Beaches, both attractive to tourists. The village has a population of around 1,200.

One factor which has spread the fame of Hopeman is the mellow golden-coloured stone from its quarries at Greenbrae and Clasach. The Greenbrae quarry was worked by one family, the Andersons, for 150 years and when they passed from the scene it was acquired by Halls of Aberdeen who expanded its production and reopened the older workings at Clasach. The Hopeman freestone has been much used for hydro-electric power stations in the Highlands.

Inland there has been much modern building at Duffus village, where the church of St Peter is now an ancient monument. Well preserved is the porch in the outer doorway, built by Alexander Sutherland, rector of the church, in 1524. In front of it is the kirkyard cross over 14 feet high.

Barely three miles west of Hopeman on the coast road B1092, passing the village of Cummingstown (a settlement made at the time of the Highland Clearances), we reach Burghead (pop. 1,282) on its long promontory pointing west and separating the rocky coastline to the east from the great sandy crescent of Burghead Bay, which sweeps uninterruptedly to the mouth of the Findhorn. Burghead was one of the most ancient settlements in Moray with a great Iron Age vitrified fort on its strategic headland. For many years the Burghead fort was thought to be Roman and was identified as the Ptoroton of Ptolemy and the Torffness of the Orkneyinga Saga. Now after extensive excavation it is thought rather to

have been a Pictish stronghold, a conclusion which fits in well
with the discovery of the Burghead Bulls, Pictish sculptured
stones of which the most notable original is now in the British
Museum. There are vivid plaster casts in a small harbour
museum.

Burghead turns its best face to the sea. This is because the
headland on which it is built rises in gradual ascent from the
sandy plain on the landward side to a rocky sandstone
precipice over 80 feet high surrounded on three sides by the
Firth. It has a useful little harbour which ships of up to 1,000
tons burthen can enter at one tide, unloading 500 tons of
cargo with the aid of its crane grabs and leaving on the next
tide. Sixteen standards of timber can be unloaded here in a day
and an average of eight vessels use the port every month. It
imports coal from Poland and timber from Finland and the
White Sea. It handles lime for the farms of the Laich of
Moray and exports their grain. The plan of the town and
most of its buildings date from an 'improvement' in the early
nineteenth century, the most impressive feature of which is the
line of tall warehouses on the main quay.

Herring and white fishing from Burghead reached a peak
about 1850 but today the locally owned boats go seine-netting
on the west coast or prawn-fishing nearer home, and do not
use Burghead harbour. On Clarkly Hill to the east of the
town is the BBC transmitter for a large area of northern
Scotland, while the Moray Sea School, with its graceful
training schooner *Prince Louis II*, for many years drew to
Burghead boys from all over Britain and overseas to receive
training in seacraft and in climbing skills.

One of the chief worries of the amenity-conscious inhabitants was the poor impression given to visitors by the almost
derelict branch railway line from Alves and its abandoned
passenger station, but this has been mitigated by the use of the
line by a large malting establishment recently opened up by
the Distillers' Company to supply the many distilleries in the
interior.

On Doorie Hill, a grassy mound on the promontory plateau, stands the Doorie Pillar, rather like a smoke-blackened
miniature broch. In itself it is comparatively recent, having
been built last century, but around it every Auld Eel (Old
Yule) on 11 January is celebrated Burghead's immemorial

ritual, the Burning of the Clavie. The Clavie is an outsize flaming torch which is deposited here to burn itself out after ceremonial kindling. Over three centuries ago it was carried from boat to boat—to the sorrow and anger of the local clergy who considered it a pagan superstition. On 20 January 1689, the young lads of Burghead were rebuked by the church courts for "having made a burning clavie, paying it superstitious worship, and blessing the boats after the old heathen custom".

Burghead has one more mysterious antiquity. No one knows who built the remarkable underground well, traditionally called the Roman Well, which was discovered in 1809. It had long lain under the rubbish of ages until water supplies were being prospected for the town 'improvements' of the nineteenth century. An old fisherman recalled a tradition that a well existed in the vicinity. Digging was commenced and a stair appeared excavated in the solid rock. It led down to a large chamber 11 feet high with a well or cistern about 11 feet across and 4 feet deep cut into the floor. Surrounding the cistern is a stone ledge 4 feet wide with a raised seat or altar at one corner. The entire cavity is cut out of rock and the present roof, a lofty 'Roman' arch, was built in 1910 to replace a vaulted ceiling carved in the rock.

The 'improver' in this case was William Young who acquired the superiority of Burghead at this period. His work at Burghead and Hopeman so impressed the Countess–Duchess of Sutherland, Lady Stafford, that he was invited to mastermind the transformation of the Sutherland estates which led to the notorious Clearances there.

Before we pass on via Alves to Forres, we must spare a glance at the very beautiful country south of Elgin. To the south-east the A941 road strikes through the suburb of New Elgin to Longmorn with its distillery and so by the defile of the Glen of Rothes to the Spey valley at Rothes and Craigellachie. Separated from this defile by Hart Hill to the west lies the vale of the River Lossie which flows by Dallas and Kellas to Birnie with its very ancient church, once the cathedral of Moray.

People come from far and near to see Birnie Kirk on its knoll above the Lossie and during the summer it is open all day so that one can slip in and savour the simple beauty of

this historic building dating from 1140 with its fine Norman
arch. It claims to be the oldest church in continuous use in the
north of Scotland.

It is quite a small and simple structure built of the squared
ashlar typical of Norman work. The west gable was reconstructed in 1734 and the belfry is dated accordingly, while the
windows in the south wall of the nave were enlarged in the
early nineteenth century. Otherwise it is very much as it left
the hand of its builder and the chancel arch is most impressive
in its absolute simplicity. The 'Holy Hillock' on which the
church stands was the site of a stone circle dating from 1500
BC and at the gate to the minister's glebe is a Pictish sculptured
stone, dating from about AD 800 and bearing the conventional
X-rod symbol surmounted by a large bird. Nearby at the
village of Tomshill is the Glenlossie Distillery and alongside it
a huge central bonded store consisting of six warehouses each
100 yards long and 100 feet wide. Here are stored whisky
stocks from distilleries as far west as Nairn, as far east as Banff
and as far south as Grantown.

Three miles to the north-west on the other side of the
Lossie is another great distillery at Miltonduff and here we are
on the road up the vale of the Black Burn, a tributary of the
Lossie, which leads to Pluscarden and its abbey.

In theen centuries since the priory of Pluscarden was
established by the foundation grant of King Alexander II in
1230 it has given a special identity to this lovely neck of the
woods. Everywhere the place-names of the locality derie from
the presence of the monks. The great wooded hill immeetely
north of the abbey is Heldon Hill—that is, the Holy Hill—and
the hill itself is part of Monaughty Forest which in its Gaelic
derivation means 'the monk's place'. Until a year or two ago
the water supply of the abbey came from St Margaret's Well,
so named after St Margaret of Scotland. Today the abbey is
one of the outstanding show places of Moray, a fact which
was recognized when the Moray District Council recently
gave a small grant of £1,000 to help the monks rehouse their
library.

The present establishment of Pluscarden is one of twenty-
five Benedictine monks and it is probably true that never in
all its history has the number been so large, although in
historic times the prior of Pluscarden regularly occupied a

place in the Scottish parliaments. The original grant in 1230 was made to the Valliscaulians, a little-known order founded in France at Val des Choux in Burgundy only thirty years earlier. They wore white gowns and in deference to this tradition the Benedictines, normally dressed in black, wore white when they came to settle anew at Pluscarden in 1948 following the gift in 1943 of the ruined priory and its lands by Lord Calum Crichton-Stuart to the Benedictine community at Prinknash.

The great achievement since the recolonization of Pluscarden has been the restoration of a large part of the buildings and their embellishment with modern stained glass. In 1955 the central tower had been roofed and the bells of Pluscarden once more rang out across the valley. The long block of the domestic buildings was roofed in 1960. The windows in the gable of the north transept are the work of Sadie McLellan, a Glasgow artist who conceived them "as a single flower, the stem rising from the lowest light, with the movement of the thorns, up through the long central panel, and the movement of the doves through to the Woman and her Child throned on high". The theme of the huge rose window which surmounts the whole composition is from Revelation XII—"A Woman clothed with the Sun, the moon at her feet and on her head a crown of twelve stars".

Apart from this all the stained glass in restored Pluscarden is the work of Dom Ninian, one of the monks. His studio in the abbey has won world-wide renown and has supplied churches up and down the country of all denominations as well as secular institutions, and he has now been joined by a second expert Fr Basil Heath-Robinson, originally a stone-cutter who is now carrying out stained-glass commissions.

Today the material economy of the abbey (recently elevated to that status from its original priory rating) is on a relatively small scale. The total land held by the monks is 23 acres, only nine of which are cultivated, mainly for the growing of soft fruit. To provide manure for the fruit-growing there is a herd of thirty pigs with breeding sows, and a flock of thirty geese provide the monks with their breakfast eggs, while bee-keeping is an additional enterprise. But the peace of the religious and contemplative life and the artistic work of the craftsmen attract very large numbers of visitors.

Small groups of visitors arrive by car throughout the day during the summer. Coach tour parties are frequent. Students come in considerable numbers. Long-staying guests who come with more serious purpose for fortnight-long retreats stay in two hostels, one for men and one for women, and there is a range of small guest-houses along the west side of the cloister garth. There is also a scheme whereby young men who feel they have a vocation for the religious life may spend a month or more at Pluscarden sharing in the life and discipline of the order.

"How far is't called to Forres?" The distance from Elgin is twelve miles by road and the A96 passes at first through the deep shade of the Quarry Wood with occasional glimpses of a tower-crowned hill rising above the glades of fine trees on the left. This conical wooded height rising only 335 feet out of the Laich of Moray is—

> The fam'd Knock of Alves,
> Where fairies and spirits repair
> To revel and dance in the moonbeams
> And trip it o'er meadows of air.

The tower on the summit, an octagonal structure of three storeys finished off with battlements, is the York Tower, built in 1827 by Alexander Forteath, the Laird of Newton, in memory of the Grand Old Duke of York. It is, if you like, a rival to the better-known Nelson Tower which crowns the Cluny Hills at Forres, but whereas the Forres landmark is much more familiar and can be more clearly seen from a great way off, the York Tower and the hill which it crowns have an elusive quality which is only fitting for such a 'fey' site.

The village of Alves—anciently Crook of Alves—which one meets a mile and a half farther west has been trebled in size in the past twenty years. The old parish church of Alves, built in 1769, is a long, narrow, plain building but with fine round-headed windows. The present church, handsome and broad, with a fine bell-tower, was the former free kirk of the parish.

Alves is as good a place as any for taking stock of the patchwork of woodland and arable country which is the favoured Laich of Moray. From the top of the York Tower, despite its modest elevation, there is a magnificent view across the shelf of low country extending to Burghead, behind which on the other side of what now seems quite a narrow stretch of Firth—though this impression is deceptive—rises the tumbled profile of the hills of Sutherland.

Many miles before you reach it, the Nelson Tower on top of the rounded pyramid of the easternmost of the Cluny Hills signals the outskirts of Forres across the farmlands of the Laich, and just as you approach the base of the hills, at the junction of the A96 road and B9011, which branches off on the right to Kinloss and Findhorn, stands the largest sculptured stone in Scotland, the Sueno Stone, a mighty pillar of grey sandstone hewn from Covesea quarry, which holds the secret of some terrible Armageddon of the Dark Ages. It towers 23 feet above the ground and is thought to penetrate 12 feet under it. Its south side tells the serial story of a battle in five vivid pictorial instalments like a strip cartoon. On top is a council of war, below that an army on the march, led by cavalry at the gallop and followed by infantry with spears and shields in their hands. Below that again is the actual battle in progress, with single combats, a general mêlée, piles of headless bodies, heaps of severed heads, and something that looks like a Pictish broch or a cenotaph. In a fourth division a row of warriors with unsheathed swords are shouting victory above a row of bound and naked captives, some apparently women, while below that again are "warriors from the field returning". This remarkable antiquity was called Sueno's Stone on the assumption that it recorded a battle between the Scots and the Danes in which Sueno, father of Canute, took part. But in fact it was carved long before Sueno (better known now as Svend Forkbeard of Denmark) was born, and dates from the ninth or early tenth century.

There is no evidence that Macbeth had any real connection with Forres. It was a trio of his predecessors in the previous century, Donald II (889-900), Malcolm I (934-54) and Duff (962-67) who all died in the vicinity. Duff has a connection with the Witches' Stone, another monolith which is pointed out at the foot of the Cluny Hills. He had to contest his throne with a rival who enlisted the aid of the "weird sisters" and, says an old chronicle, was subjected to the "craft of wychis of which gret nowmer was in Forres". Three particular

witches were blamed and it was these three beldames who
were rolled in spiked casks down the slopes of the Cluny Hills
and burned at the site now marked by the Witches' Stone.
But poor Duff could not escape the malice of his enemies. He
was murdered in the Castle of Forres with the connivance of
the Governor, Donewald, who buried his body under the
bridge at the burn of Kinloss.

Two centuries later another episode in the life of a king
made legendary fame for Forres. It was in the vicinity that
David I, while on a hunting expedition from the castle of
Duffus, found himself lost in a wood. When he could find no
way out he said a prayer and was answered by the apparition
of a white dove which led him to an open spot where two
shepherds were tending their flocks. They gave him shelter for
the night and while he slept the Virgin appeared to him and
directed him to build a chapel on the spot where he emerged
from the wood. Before he left in the morning he marked out
the line of the building with his sword. On 20 June 1150 the
foundations of the abbey of Kinloss were laid.

For four centuries the Cistercian monastery which thus
became Forres's near neighbour flourished, but after the
Reformation it was despoiled, and in the seventeenth century
the laird of Lethen turned it into a quarry and sold the stones
to Cromwell's men to build the Citadel of Inverness. Today
immediately in front of the ruined abbey is a double row of
the simple headstones of the men of Kinloss RAF Station who
gave their lives for their country. The only parts of the ancient
buildings now remaining are one of the walls of the cloisters
in the west, two fine Saxon arches on the south and a fragment of a two-storey structure with a groined roof—the
priest's lodging—on the east.

If one looks at the Ordnance Survey map one sees a great
white triangle of land bounded on the west by Findhorn Bay,
on the south by the railway and the Kinloss Burn and on the
north and north-east by the wide sweep of Burghead Bay.
Almost on the western border runs B9011, the road to
Findhorn. East of this is the great blank containing the simple
legend KINLOSS AIRPORT. But Kinloss is not really a secret
enclave. It has a door which is guarded for security reasons,
but not closed. Before 1939 there were seven farms and the
mansions of Kinloss House, Langcot House and Sea Park in

this area. In place of the farms 1,700 servicemen are at work
in an enterprise which never halts. Including the wives and
families of the RAF personnel the community that now
subsists in this corner of Moray is equivalent to a town of
4,000. In fact the two air stations in Moray, Kinloss and
Lossiemouth, account for 20 per cent of the county rates.
Three squadrons of Nimrod planes here form a vital part of
the protection of Britain's northern approaches. Over 2,000
families are housed on the station, the others outside it. Life
on such a station demands catering arrangements on a vast
scale. The sergeants' mess is like a 160-bed hotel. The ratings'
mess provides 2,000 meals a day, while the officers' mess caters
for 120. Relations with the civilian community of nearby
Forres are of a quality that has no parallel anywhere on the
Services map. The Service families go out to meet their civilian
neighbours and those neighbours come to see the station and
very often to share in its fine facilities for recreation and
entertainment.

The civil parish of Kinloss, created as a sequel to the
demolition of the abbey, dates from 1657. The present parish
church was built in 1765 but its mullioned windows, which
have a true cross for their central partitions, may actually have
come from the abbey, and the beautiful old bell in the tower
bears the inscription "Kinglosse 1667".

Two more miles along B9011 from the Kirk of Kinloss, at
the end of the long sandy promontory which almost cuts off
Findhorn Bay from the open sea and causes it to take the form
of a wide, almost circular lagoon, is the village of Findhorn
(pop. 650), now famous as a yachting centre and holiday
resort but once the principal seaport of Moray. It had its
beginnings on the estate of Muirton, part of the Kinloss Abbey
lands broken up at the Reformation, and developed in the
seventeenth century as a port from which many Moray lairds
engaged in trade, importing from the continent wines, silk,
tapestry and other luxuries and exporting beef, hides, salmon,
grain and malt; but there was one hazard which could not be
controlled—the shifting mouth of the Findhorn. Twice the
village had to be rebuilt on a new site. The third and present
village, dating from 1701, replaced one a mile north-west of
its present position and now at the bottom of the sea. The
*Survey of the Province of Moray* (1798) tells us: "The irruption,

though completed in one night and by one tide, had long been apprehended and the inhabitants had gradually withdrawn."

At one period in the last century there were eighteen Findhorn boats taking part in the herring fishing. Today it is still a salmon fishing station and as a sailing and water-skiing centre it is the gem of the Moray coast. At high tide Findhorn Bay is alive with yachts and sailing dinghies and long processions of cars and lines of spectators throng its grassy seafront along the western promenade. It has a fine architectural heritage from the eighteenth century centred by Findhorn House (1775), now the clubhouse of the Royal Findhorn Yacht Club, formed in 1931. In a large caravan site halfway along the road to Kinloss is the Findhorn Community, one of the most successful communes in Britain, founded by Peter and Eileen Caddy on religious and mystical tenets.

Forres is an ancient town with modern amenities on a lavish scale, in part due to its two great benefactors Sir Alexander Grant and Lord Strathcona. Its character is dominated by its wonderful parklands, from the magnificent Grant Park along the skirts of the Cluny Hills on the east to the Burn Green on the west, where a fine piece of landscaping involving the creation of a new duck pond recently earned a grant from the British Wildfowl Trust. This proliferation of amenity areas has made it a Mecca for retired folk with the result that of the total population of around 7,000 at least 2,000 are old-age pensioners. Another attractive feature is that the outlines of the medieval town plan of the royal burgh remain virtually unaltered. The burgh was laid out on a level spur projecting westwards from the Cluny Hills and circled on the south, west and north by the Altyre or Mossat Burn. At the western extremity of the spur is the site of the royal castle, beneath the protection of which the burgh originated and developed.

From the castle, now represented merely by a lofty grassy knoll, High Street stretches eastward, widening slightly at the middle of its length to form a market square and a site for the tolbooth and the cross. As at Elgin, the High Street is paralleled on either side by a North Road and a South Street marking the outer limits of the original settlers' strip-holdings or 'rigs', and between these rigs a series of narrow 'wynds' (among them Batchen's Wynd, Milne's Wynd, Tolbooth Wynd and Urquhart's Wynd) provided outlets from High Street to the north and south. So faithfully has this ancient town plan been adhered to that it occasionally raises startling problems for unwary incomers to the town. In one case a prominent official took a house at the corner of a High Street wynd and ordered carpets for the rooms on the assumption that they would all be strictly rectangular. When they came to be fitted it was found that at one end the carpet was short of the wall and at the other it disconcertingly climbed up a foot of the wall surface. This was because the wynd struck off from the High Street at a slight slant and the corners of the rooms were not true right-angles!

Of the traditional town many old houses survive to give the aspect of an ancient burgh. These are usually harled with steep-pitched roofs covered with slates or stone slabs and with crow-stepped gables often set towards the street. The dates of the building of each house and the initials of the owner and his wife are often to be found on the skewputt—the lowest stone of the gable—or over the lintel of the main door. Examples can be found at the west end of High Street, where No. 160 has crow-stepped gables and is dated 1668 and No. 164 has the initials IA.EH and the date 1784 on a skewputt. Farther east No. 30 High Street, a two-storeyed house with its gable towards the street, has a chimney with a carved panel inscribed JOHN YOUNG.MARY ELDER. 1778.

The distinctive Town House steeple has been Forres's 'signature tune' for 137 years. Built in 1839 on the site of the previous tolbooth dating from 1700, it is a square tower with bartizan "on which is raised another of octagonal shape surmounted by a dome and vane". The tolbooth itself, as described over a century ago in a famous guidebook called *Morayshire Described,* has "Prison Cells three in number which are generally empty as all prisoners condemned to any lengthened period of confinement are sent to Elgin prison". These cells, for a long time white elephants, have now proved to have a most valuable quality. They are ideal for the storage of muniments—and in them will be stored the historical documents of all the royal and ancient burghs in the Moray district, who have appointed an archivist to sift, catalogue and translate their treasures and record them on microfilm. Forres's own records extend backwards in time to 1515 with a volume of the burgh court records for that year.

Among the treasures of a more solid and physical kind in this building is a decorative snuff box, the top of which takes the form of a carved head of Admiral Lord Nelson dating from the year after Trafalgar. This snuff box was passed round for the last time at the closing meeting of Forres Town Council in May 1975 where it had had a ritual function for over a century. It was passed round the council table for every councillor to take a sniff to mark the official opening of each session of municipal business. Forres's oldest surviving charter, which hangs on the wall of the council chamber, dates from 1594. The Mercat Cross (1848) is an elaborate neo-Gothic structure. The Nelson Tower, a battlemented octagonal structure 70 feet high on top of the most prominent of the Cluny Hills, also dates from the year after Trafalgar. Completed in 1806, it was the first national monument to the Admiral and was raised by public subscription. From it one can obtain a fine view of the town and a wide swathe of the surrounding country.

The town kirk of Forres, the ancient parish church of St Laurence, survived until 1775. The present building, standing on the identical site, dates from 1906. It has been greatly enhanced by a set of stained-glass windows in the south wall, the work of Douglas Strachan, and a gift of Sir Alexander Grant, the donor of the Grant Park. For centuries the burgh of Forres owned extensive lands outside the burgh bounds, mostly farms and woodlands. With the reorganization of local government and the consequent demise of the burgh, the local council decided to realize these assets and expend the proceeds on further amenities. These included the modern youth and community centre, Forres House, in High Street, costing £220,000, which is open to visitors, a community swimming pool attached to Forres Academy at Roysvale, and a novel paved garden with fountains and flower beds between High Street and the Grant Park.

The wide arc of the parish of Rafford lying south of the A96 and extending from the Findhorn Bridge a mile and a half west of Forres to Glenburgie Distillery, five miles east, cuts a swathe through some of the most attractive rural country in Moray. Its total population is little over 800 and the hamlet of Rafford itself is barely three miles south of the town, yet there is no sense of being on the outskirts of a substantial burgh.

Everything seems to go in threes in Rafford. Its three great estates are Altyre, Burgie and Blervie. It has also three outstanding hills—Burgie Hill on the east where it marches with the parish of Alves, Romach Hill rising to 1,000 feet on the extreme south, and Craigroy in Altyre, on the west. Three streams carry its drainage system: the Burn of Altyre, which eventually flows through Forres to the Bay of Findhorn; the Lochty Burn, rising on Romach Hill which flows eastwards to become the Black Water, tributary of the Lossie, and a lesser stream on the borders of Alves which flows into Burghead Bay. It has also three main roads—the Forres–Grantown road, A940, which follows the right bank of the Findhorn to Dunphail then crosses the Moor of Dava to Strathspey; the Forres–Dallas road, B9010, which sweeps south-eastward through the heart of the parish, and, of course, A96 which runs along the northern fringe.

Near the centre of the parish a little north of B9010 is the ruined Tower of Blervie, originally part of a Z-plan castle dating from the sixteenth century, while farther to the east is Burgie Castle, a ruined tower of similar date. In 1800 the central part of the present Burgie House was built largely of stone from the old castle, but much later in the century it was acquired by Alexander Thomson and entirely recast. He restored and refurnished the old tower and superimposed a modern leaded roof on the old stone one.

The ruins of the old church of Altyre dating from pre-Reformation times survive alongside a fine Pictish sculptured stone. The present parish church of Rafford was built in 1826 to designs by Gillespie Graham. It is said that Lady Gordon-Cumming, wife of the second baronet of Altyre, the principal heritor, made a model of the sort of church she wanted out of orange peel and the architect worked on that to create the magnificent Gothic edifice of today. This still beautifully cared-for church is bordered by a fine floral display.

At the eastern tip of the parish is its only industrial enterprise, Glenburgie–Glenlivet Distillery, the oldest in Moray. It was started in the year 1810 by William Paul, son of Dr Lister Paul a well-known physician, and to begin with dealt with 16 bushels of malt per week. Today the intake is 5,250 bushels.

Just across the River Findhorn, which here, near the end of its 62-mile course, flows majestically between broad shingle beds, begins the parish of Dyke and Moy, a quiet stretch of country which the passing motorist may traverse in a few minutes without being aware of any cause for wonder. But on either side of the rather featureless road to Nairn are marvels in plenty.

The shape of the parish is triangular with the base lying along the coast of the Moray Firth and extending from the western shores of the Bay of Findhorn to Maviston, on the county boundary of Nairn, a distance of four miles. Inland the parish extends in a sharp-pointed salient for nine miles with the Findhorn as its eastern boundary. Along the coast for its whole length lies the Forest of Culbin. In the inland apex is the Forest of Darnaway, once a royal chace, while close to the western side of the triangle is the domain of Brodie Castle, also richly wooded. With wood and water on either side, the heart of the parish is fertile farming land divided by the sinuous course of the Muckle Burn.

In the matter of land use it would be difficult to find a parish anywhere in Scotland with such a story to tell. When the Rev. John Dunbar wrote the Old Statistical Account of Dyke and Moy in 1793 he described it as extending to 21 square miles containing 2,697 Scots acres of cornfield, only 1,191 acres of planted wood, and the rest in pasture, heath and exhausted mosses, with a sandy desert all along the shore, "which desert", said he, "is fully half the whole contents". A hundred years later this sandy desert of Culbin covered 9,500 acres, with the sand over 100 feet deep in places.

The conquest of the Culbin Sands—the Morayshire Sahara—was begun by Major Chadwick at Binsness, taken up by the Forestry Commission in 1921, and carried through stage by stage until the whole operation was completed about 1955 and they had 7,700 acres under timber which reached down to the high-water mark along the entire coast. Culbin today is one of the most impressive forests in Britain. The yield, beginning with 150,000 cubic feet a year, will rise over the next decade until it reaches a maximum of 500,000 cubic feet per annum. The ecology of the area has been transformed.

The sea birds which haunted the sandhills and the shore in the days of the 'desert' have taken their leave. In their place have come the capercaillie, accompanied by foxes, badgers, roe deer and red squirrels.

The greatest threat to the achievement of Culbin is no longer the creeping smother of the sand and the winds and the waves but the danger of fire. From the treetops of Hill 99 the platform of the fire-precaution tower looks out over a vast planted area and when the watchers lift their eyes from the wood beneath they can see Ben Klibreck, the Duke of Sutherland statue at Golspie, and Morven and Scaraben in Caithness far across the Moray Firth. An elaborate mobile radio system keeps the watchers in touch with headquarters and assures instant action in the case of emergency.

In times past Culbin was not always a desert. In the Kirk of Dyke there is a stone with this quaint inscription:

> Valter Kinnaird: Elizabeth Innes
> The builders of this bed of stone
> Are laird and lady of Coubine.
> Quhilk twa and thairs, when
> Breath is gane, please God
> Vil sleip this bed within.
>                 1613

There were not to be many more lairds of the Barony of Culbin. Walter's great-great-grandson, Alexander, on 17 July 1695 petitioned the Scots Parliament to be exempted from paying cess "because his estate which 20 years before was one of the most considerable in Moray was nearly all covered with sand, and the mansion-house and orchard destroyed".

For hundreds of years the tragedy of Culbin had been in the making. Sand carried down by the Findhorn built up into sandhills at Maviston. Their stability was undermined by the pulling of marram grass by the folk of the parish for the thatching of cottages. In the autumn of 1694 a succession of gales set the sand in motion and it swept eastwards burying everything in its path and blocking the mouth of the Findhorn so that it was forced to cut a new exit to the sea several miles to the east. The situation continued to deteriorate until the end of the eighteenth century, but by then a great campaign of tree-planting had begun in other parts of the parish.

The first stages in reclamation began at Binsness, at the eastern tip, in 1870, and for forty years work was continued by the laird, Major Chadwick. In 1921 the Forestry Commission commenced the piecemeal acquisition of land and began systematic replanting. They used from 36 to 40 tons of brushwood per acre to thatch the naked sand, prevent it from moving, and provide in course of time humus to feed the young trees planted. Planting was completed in 1955 largely with Corsican pine. The northern third of the parish is administered by Moray Estates (Development) Ltd who own between 7,000 and 8,000 acres, of which 5,000 are devoted to forestry, 1,000 to directly controlled farms and the remainder to let farms. In the heart of this salient is historic Darnaway Castle, the ancestral home of the earls of Moray.

Of Darnaway it has been said that, except for royal residences, no other place has been so much associated with kings and queens and princes of the royal blood. William the Lion, Alexander I and Alexander II came there to hunt. After the Battle of Bannockburn, Robert the Bruce created his nephew, Thomas Randolph, Earl of Moray in 1314 and Randolph built a hunting lodge on the site of the present castle. But the documentary evidence is that Randolph's Hall, the only part of the original castle to survive, was built in 1450. In 1810 the present castle was raised in front of the ancient hall and connected with it so that the hall forms part of the existing mansion. The magnificent oaken roof, without a peer in Scotland except that of Parliament House in Edinburgh, remains. It belongs to the latter half of the fifteenth century. One of the treasures of Randolph's Hall today is the remarkable posthumous portrait of the "Bonnie Earl of Moray" with the wounds inflicted by his murderers fresh upon his naked body. To understand the background to this dramatic work of art it is necessary to go back to the first years of Mary Queen of Scots' reign, when the leader of the Protestant nobility of Scotland was Lord James Stewart, the Queen's half-brother, whose arch-enemy was the Catholic Earl of Huntly. It was in Darnaway Castle, where she danced in Randolph's Hall, in the course of a progress in the north, that Mary bestowed on Lord James the earldom of Moray. To

the Gordons, of whom Huntly was the head, this was gall and
wormwood. The earl, soon in a state of open defiance of royal
authority, met his death in the Battle of Corrichie (1562).
Time passed and Lord James's eldest daughter, the Lady
Elizabeth, married Sir James Stewart of Doune who, on the
death of his father-in-law, succeeded to the earldom of
Moray. He it is whom history knows as "The Bonnie Earl".

The deepest hostility still subsisted between the Gordons
and the Stewarts and between the earls of Huntly and of
Moray. So when in 1592 the "Bonnie Earl" was suspected of
having sheltered the Earl of Bothwell, who had plotted against
James VI, that monarch was induced to give Huntly a commission to arrest him. Forty Gordons under the Earl of
Huntly then went to Donibristle Castle in Fife where the
"Bonnie Earl" was in residence, set it on fire and murdered the
earl. The countess carried his corpse to Edinburgh and laid it
with the dagger thrusts exposed in the kirk of Leith, crying for
justice. Popular indignation was intense, as the ballad suggests:

> Ye Highlands and ye Lowlands,
>   Oh, where hae ye been?
> They hae slain the Earl o' Moray
>   And laid him on the green.
>
> Now, wae be to thee, Huntly,
>   And wherefore did ye so?
> I bade you bring him wi' you
>   But forbade you him to slay.
>
> He was a braw gallant,
>   And he rid at the ring,
> And the Bonnie Earl o' Moray,
>   Oh! he might hae been a king.

So today the death-bed portrait of the Bonnie Earl with the
legend "God revenge my caus" hangs in Randolph's Hall in
Darnaway. The story of the great afforestation of western
Moray is linked not only with Darnaway but with Brodie
Castle farther west. From documentary evidence we know
that there have been Brodies at Brodie since 1160. Michael,
Thane of Brodie, had a charter from King Robert the Bruce
in 1311. The oldest part of the present castle dates from about

1430 but may have been built round an earlier nucleus. It is on the Z-plan and the parapet of the existing old tower is in the style of the seventeenth century. There is an old doorway dated 1615. The Brodie lairds were of the Covenanting party and the castle was burned by Lord Lewis Gordon's royalist forces in 1645. It is probable that the eastern gabled portion, one storey lower, dates from the rebuilding that followed this event. The northern wing, also built about this time, appears to have been altered from the first-floor level. Considerable additions, designed by William Burn, were made in 1824.

The interiors at Brodie are particularly fine. The dining-room has a ceiling of seventeenth-century plasterwork. A sword is preserved at the castle which had been a gift to Prince Charles Edward. The Old Statistical Account records: "For the first judicious and spirited exertion on a large scale in planting and improving an estate this parish has been much indebted to the example of a lady of most respectable memory, Mary Sleigh, the wife of Alexander Brodie of that Ilk. When she saw the situation of the country she pitied it; she knew the value of people on an estate and studied to make them industrious by contriving work and giving them wages and bread for their services."

Francis, Earl of Moray, soon followed Mrs Brodie's example. Before he died this earl, who built the 'new' castle of Darnaway, had planted 13,000,000 trees.

Above the forest glades of Darnaway the River Findhorn, which rises in the Monadliath Mountains 2,800 feet above sea level and flows through the three counties of Inverness, Nairn and Moray, is probably the most picturesque river in Britain, compassing a variety of scenery ranging from the starkly alpine to the lushly fertile. In Edinkillie, the parish that lies south of Dyke and Moy and Rafford, it is joined by an equally picturesque tributary, the Divie, at Relugas. The most famous spot in the parish—a little above Relugas—is Randolph's Leap, where the river rushes through a gap in the rocks only eight feet wide, now a picnic haunt signposted for the benefit of the sightseeing public.

Some distance above Randolph's Leap is Daltulich (pronounced Dalt-lich) Bridge over a rocky reach of the Findhorn. It was built at the end of the eighteenth century on the initiative of Mrs Brodie of Lethen. On the cape of land at

the confluence of the Divie and the Findhorn is an inscribed
stone erected by Sir Thomas Dick Lauder to mark the limit
of the great Moray floods of August 1829. Below Relugas is
Logie House, a handsome mansion. Its oldest portion was built
in 1655 and one of the ladies of Logie was "Bonnie Lesley",
a beauty immortalized by Robert Burns in a poem which
begins:

> O saw ye Bonnie Lesley
>     As she gaed o'er the Border?
> She's gaen like Alexander
>     To spread her conquests farther.

She went, she saw, she conquered, and after meeting Captain
Robert Cumming at a London ball she returned as the Lady
of Logie.

> Return again, fair Lesley,
>     Return to Caledonie!
> That we may brag we hae a lass
>     There's nane again sae bonnie.

Captain Robert died in 1813 through eating a plateful of
mushrooms that had been "kept warm for him in a copper
skillet".

An idyllic spot in the vale of the Divie is Glenerney, where
in the grounds of the mansion an intimate ballet theatre has
been created from an indoor squash racquets court. Providing
seating for an audience of seventy, the little theatre has held
annual festivals in the summer for a number of years.

The present parish church of Edinkillie was built in 1741
and was extended in 1813. It is long and narrow and still
preserves the old Presbyterian pattern with the pulpit in the
centre of the south wall, but it now faces a large organ
presented by Sir Robert McVitie Grant. The second decade of
the nineteenth century was a stirring time in the parish.
William Henry Playfair, the Edinburgh architect, had been
called in to design the new mansion of Dunphail in his best
classical manner and at the same time he designed a new
Edinkillie manse in the "cottage style". This remarkable
building is modelled on a bird in flight—with two circular

central rooms and long tapering wings on either side. Edinkillie with Dyke and Moy form the western-most parishes of Moray. Across the old county boundary of Nairn we enter what is now the Highland Region.

# CHAPTER VI

# THE NAIRN DISTRICT

FOUR MILES east of Nairn the A96 highway crosses Hardmuir, long identified as the "blasted heath" where Macbeth met the witches, and a mound 161 feet high on the right-hand side of the road is labelled 'Macbeth's Hillock'. Two miles farther on we reach Auldearn, a village famous as the site of one of the Marquess of Montrose's victories over the Covenanters. Auldearn with its lines of low cottages and brightly painted Lyon Inn is a terraced settlement (pop. 550) dominated by two outstanding focal points, the great, plain, barn-like church and the gleaming white dovecote, the Doocot of Boath.

Shaped rather like an elongated beehive or a giant shell standing upright on its base, the Doocot crowns the Castle Hill on the western edge of the township. Since 1947 it has belonged to the National Trust for Scotland to whom it was presented by Brigadier James Muirhead of Boath as a perfect specimen of its kind. The Trust have done it proud, keeping it spotlessly whitewashed and gaily painted by an encircling blue band, and the 'doos' or pigeons are still there, flying out and in through the decoratively spaced out apertures constructed for their convenience.

The Dunbars of Boath built the doocot on its grassy summit over 300 years ago but even then the Castle Hill of Auldearn was a venerable site. On it there stood a castle of the early Scottish kings and here William the Lion was in residence when he signed the second charter of the burgh of Inverness in 1179. Here, too, Montrose mounted his cannon before the battle in 1645. It is, besides, a superb viewpoint. The view was described by the Rev. William Barclay around 1840. "The spectator," he wrote, "has immediately under his eye the tender green of the fields and woods, the herds feeding in the pastures, the Firth, which is here seven miles broad, the bold rocky coast of Ross, its mountains and those of Sutherland

. . . altogether such a scene as cannot be surpassed by any parish in the North of Scotland."

The church of Auldearn also occupies a lofty site. One climbs to it past a pleasant row of old-world cottages. The kirkyard is girdled by a massive outer wall, through which one ascends by a broad flight of steps to the grave-filled plateau. The church, built in 1758, is plain and grim, but age has mellowed it and the ruined walls of its predecessor show traces of fine pre-Reformation work. The school complex on another mound on the eastern edge of the village includes the original parochial school, the Innes Infant School built in 1840 (now the schoolhouse), and the present school, a solid piece of masonry dating from 1895. The mansion house of Boath is a handsome neo-classic structure with tetrastyle Ionic portico designed by Archibald Simpson of Aberdeen in 1827.

It was on 8 May 1645 that the Marquess of Montrose, who had been playing a game of hide-and-seek with two Covenanting armies in the north following his shock triumph at Inverlochy, arrived in Auldearn and pitched his camp on the high ground north of the village. In the darkness of a drizzling night his adversary the Covenanting General Hurry, who had lured him this far west, turned to strike, but his soldiers, finding the powder in their muskets damp, fired them off to clear them, and thus gave notice of their approach. This gave Montrose the time he needed to make his dispositions for battle; on the Castle Hill and along the ridge between it and the village he placed the forces of his intrepid Highland lieutenant Alasdair (Colkitto) Macdonald. The centre of his line was in front of the village itself, but a thin scattering of men were placed along the line of the roads to the House of Boath and to Cawdor, south of the village, behind dykes or walls which still stand there today, and they were ordered to keep up a continuous firing to deceive the enemy. Lord George Gordon's cavalry were concealed in a hollow on the left wing.

The battle began at noon on 9 May and at first it seemed that Colkitto and his Highlanders would be trapped and ground to pieces, but Montrose by a clever ruse misled Lord Gordon into thinking that if he did not attack immediately the Highlanders would win single-handed. The Gordons thus rushed into the fray and in the confusion the Covenanting flank guard wheeled to the left instead of to the right and overrode some of their own infantry. At the same time Montrose unleashed his reserves, hitherto concealed behind the eastern ridge. Four regiments of the Covenant army died gallantly, but the levies on their left rear and the cavalry in reserve fled without striking a blow. The pursuit continued for fourteen miles.

In this way General Hurry's army of 4,000 foot and 400 horse was routed by Montrose with 2,000 foot soldiers and 250 horse. Major Drummond, the commander responsible for the flank-guard's mistake, was court-martialled and shot. Among the many Covenanters buried in Auldearn kirkyard, three are commemorated by a monument in the north porch of the church.

The great mansion in the southern hinterland of Auldearn is the House of Lethen, built in 1758 to replace an older castle of the Brodies, who bought the estate in 1634 and still own it today. It lies some three miles south-east of Auldearn and consists of a three-storey central block with two-storey flanking pavilions. Some two miles to the west of Lethen, on the other side of A939, the Nairn-Grantown road, is the ruined Castle of Rait which by appearance seems half-church, half-castle and is under the care of the Department of the Environment. There is a gory story of the feud between the Cummings of Rait and the Clan Mackintosh. A landmark called Knock-na-Gillan, the Young Men's Hillock, commemorates twelve young Mackintoshes slain by Cummings while passing through Auldearn parish. In revenge, the Mackintoshes, ostensibly arriving as guests at Rait Castle, where two members of the feuding families were being wed, fell upon their hosts and murdered them.

Rait Castle was said to have been destroyed by fire on this occasion. The surviving building is believed to date from the early fifteenth century. It is a simple oblong with a round tower at the south-west angle. It has a series of pointed, mullioned and traceried windows which are quite exceptional and give the structure an ecclesiastical air. The walls are over five feet thick. The arched doorway is on the first floor and has portcullis grooves near the outside, with jambs for a wooden door inside. The workmanship is superior to that of normal castles and its origin is something of a mystery.

South of Auldearn lies the upland parish of Ardclach which reaches south to the middle reaches of the Findhorn via its tributary the Meikle Burn. A hundred years ago there were 1,330 folk to share the work in field and forest here. Today there are only 398. They are scattered over an area of 37,953 acres divided into four widely separated communities: Ferness, Coulmony, Fornighty and Meikle Burn. Fornighty is only five miles from Nairn as the crow flies, on the northern tip of the parish, but it has succeeded in retaining its own school and has its own public hall. Fornighty and Littlemill to the west of it are in the basin of the Meikle Burn and are separated from the Findhorn valley to the south by the long ridge of the Lethen Bar rising to about 750 feet. South of the Bar is Coulmony, while farther up the Findhorn there are fine farms in the Haugh of Logie. Above Logie Bridge on the south side of the river one enters Glenferness, owned by the Earl of Leven and Melville, where the village of Ferness is the centre.

Coulmony House, built by the Roses of Kilravock in 1746, with its balustraded central tower and projecting wings is one of the most charming mansions in the parish. Tenanted at one time by Henry Mackenzie "The Man of Feeling", it was later acquired by the Brodies of Lethen, to whom it still belongs.

The old parish church of Ardclach, built in 1626 in what seems now an incredibly remote and awkward situation on the left bank of a loop of the Findhorn, but which had more real meaning when the population was over four times greater than it is today, is now disused and the former free church at the Crask is utilized in its place. Because of the old kirk's low and secluded situation by the riverside a detached bell-tower was built for it half a mile away on the top of a hill by Alexander Brodie, the first laird of Lethen, in 1655. This historic structure, said to be the highest tower of the kind in Scotland, is a compactly built cube of two storeys with two gables, one of which forms an open granite belfry.

A mile or two farther upstream is Dulsie Bridge, built in 1754 by General Wade's successor, General Caulfeild, as a link in the great military road from Edinburgh to Fort George, and surely the most picturesque of all the Findhorn crossings. It leaps across the river at a steep angle passing above rocks, pools and birches in a den of incomparable wildness.

Having reconnoitred upland Nairnshire, we may cover the

last two miles of A96 from Auldearn to the county town of Nairn and cross the Nairn Bridge into the town. We see, as we cross, a rugged, rough-and-tumble river in a boulder-strewn gorge, in the act of breaking through the glacial deposits dropped at the edge of a great Highland ice-sheet, which in its heyday 12,000 years ago lay 4,000 to 5,000 feet deep, and left a deep sandy covering on a platform cut in Old Red Sandstone.

Its situation on this site has given Nairn, anciently known as Invernairn (Gaelic: The Mouth of the River of Alders), great strategic significance. It is said to have received its first charter from Alexander I, and William the Lion built its royal castle on the site of the present-day Cawdor Estates offices, known as Constabulary Gardens, for the Thanes of Cawdor were the king's constables of the royal burgh. Lying between High Street and the river, the stronghold was the key-point of the old town. Modern Nairn has developed on the other side of High Street with a by-pass road which carries the A96 and from which long, straight boulevards stretch in a grid to the West Beach, with its hotels and boarding houses, claiming somewhat inappropriately to be the "Brighton of the North".

There was nothing of this to be seen when Johnson and Boswell reached Nairn in 1773. The Doctor acidly remarked that "the royal burgh . . . if once it flourished is now in a state of miserable decay; but I know not whether its chief annual magistrate has not still the title of Lord Provost. At Nairn we may fix the verge of the Highlands, for here I first saw peat fires, and first heard the Erse language".

There is an irony here for Nairn did officially have a Lord Provost, at least in the year 1734. It was all an accident in the writ authorizing a parliamentary election, but the town council promptly accepted the accidental honour and made out their commission in favour of "Hugh Rose of Geddes, Esquire, Lord Provost of the Burgh".

The grandiose title was not perhaps so irrational as it may seem, for members of the Rose family, beginning with John Rose of Broadley in 1450, provided forty-two provosts of the burgh in succession down to the year 1764, when the office went to one of the Roses' in-laws, Major James Clephane. When he demitted office in 1768 Roses once more held the provostship down to the year 1782.

While Dr Johnson was mistaken in suggesting that peat fires were peculiar to the Highlands—they were universal throughout Scottish rural areas both Lowland and Highland at this period—he was correct in writing of Nairn's "miserable decay". Twenty years later the parish minister, the Rev. John Morrison, wrote in the Old Statistical Account: "The number of people who want employment in the town and its vicinity is absolutely incredible . . . The poor are extremely numerous and many of them very indigent indeed." Johnson was also correct in his reference to "the verge of the Highlands". Almost two centuries earlier James VI had joked that there was in his kingdom a town with a street so long that the folk at one end of it spoke a different language from the people at the other end, a reference to the ethnographic Highland Line which was said to cross the High Street at Rose Street, dividing the Celts from the Saxons.

Certain of the original inhabitants of Nairn were quite clearly not just Lowlanders but Scandinavians, for the names of the families in the old Fishertown of Nairn, which lies immediately west of the river near its mouth—the Ralphs, the Mains and the Mansons are pure Norse in origin and "undoubtedly derived from Hrolf, Magnus and Magnusson". It is in the Fishertown that one may savour the atmosphere of the old town, the economy of which was really based on crofting and fishing although the harbour today is largely monopolized by pleasure craft. The harbour dates from 1820 when Telford was called in to design a pier which was later rebuilt after damage. In the 1850s there were 105 boats and 410 fishermen. By 1927 there were still 41 boats of which 24 were steam drifters.

The harbour and the two beaches, east and west of it, form the centrepiece of a remarkable stretch of coast where long spits of sand and shingle enclose salt marshes and elongated lagoons. The spit to the east, known as the Bar, is two miles long and is formed by a series of shingle ridges open to the sea at the west end. The spit to the west, similar in form and culminating in Whiteness Head, is a more substantial landform fringing the Carse of Delnies and today has been pressed into service as the protective 'breakwater' within which McDermott (Scotland) Ltd have established a flourishing yard for the fabrication of North Sea oil production platforms and jackets, employing up to 2,000 men. From this remarkable 'green fields' site was launched Oxy, the Piper Field production platform, and immediately this was achieved work on further North Sea structures commenced. Although the county boundary between Nairn and Inverness crosses the Carse of Delnies and bisects the Whiteness Head lagoon, it is Nairn that has provided the housing for the greater part of the large incoming work force.

Nairn had a stirring time in Bonnie Prince Charlie's rebellion. It was occupied by the army of Sir John Cope in 1745 and a baby born to the wife of a Nairn fisherman was given the name of Cope, which has survived in a branch of the Main family to the present day—they are known as the Main Copes or Coups. Then on 14 April 1746 the Hanoverian army clashed with Jacobite forces holding the Bridge of Nairn, but a major battle was averted by the withdrawal of the Jacobites and the Duke of Cumberland entered the town and celebrated his birthday there in lodgings at the Rose of Kilravock town house in High Street. This site is now occupied by Lipton's shop which still bears a lengthy Latin inscription from the old house, which happens to be rather apposite. In translation it reads:

> All terrene things by turns we see
> Become anothers property.
> Mine now, must be anothers soon,
> I know not whose, when I am gone:
> An earthly house is bound to none.

Nairn's Mercat Cross with slim cylindrical shaft and square top was renovated in 1757 and stands outside the Town and County Buildings with clock tower and spire, built in 1818 and much altered in 1870. The old church of Nairn stood in the kirkyard beside the river but was rebuilt in the 1890s in Church Street in an imposing Early Gothic style. It faces across a pleasant open space to Nairn Academy opened in 1830 and much altered since—only to be finally replaced in the 1970s by a new building to the west of the town. The impetus for building a new quarter of the town as a holiday resort came from Dr John Grigor (1814–86) who is commemorated by a lively statue in front of Viewfield, a former Grant mansion now the town library and museum.

As the driest town in Scotland and also one of the sunniest, Nairn's destiny as a holiday place was almost a foregone conclusion, but Grigor helped it on the way and its three fine golf courses, the Nairn Golf Club's championship course, the Dunbar course on the east beach, and the nine-holes Newton course inland, have given the town a special status. Industries include a large laundry, a lemonade factory, wood mills, and quarrying and building and joinery firms, while an energetic campaign for new light industries was under way when the North Sea oil boom brought the platform-construction yard to Whiteness Head and radically altered the employment prospects of the burgh. The population figure shot up from 4,899 in 1961 to 8,037 in 1971, though this latter figure was a freak result due to the temporary presence of a large body of naval personnel in the town. Today the population level is about 6,000.

For fifty years Nairn county had been linked to Moray for many local government purposes. But it was an uneasy partnership and under reorganization it was glad to join the Highland Region and turn its face to the west where it could share in the benefits and promotional activities of the Highlands and Islands Development Board.

West of Nairn the trunk road reaches the county boundary with Inverness in less than three miles, but the two roads, B9090 and B9091, emerging from the west end of High Street follow either bank of the Nairn River into very interesting country. B9090 crosses the river at Howford and passing the Bracla Distillery reaches Cawdor with its village, church and castle, which has been the home of the thanes and earls of Cawdor for six centuries. The name Cawdor is one which, thanks to Shakespeare, is known to virtually every schoolchild throughout the English-speaking world, but despite the evidence of *Macbeth*, it is extremely doubtful whether the office of 'thane' had been introduced into Scotland as early as Macbeth's day.

Thanages were introduced as part of the administration designed to implement the feudal system in the fringe territories between Highlands and Lowlands. In the reign of Alexander III, towards the end of the thirteenth century, Donald Thane of Cawdor appears as hereditary sheriff of the shire of Nairn and constable of the royal castle of Nairn. He is thought to have lived at Old Cawdor, half a mile north of the present castle, which first appears on record in 1398. Donald's successor, Thane William, had a charter from King Robert the Bruce in 1310, and it was his grandson Andrew who built the oldest part of the present castle—the great central keep on the highest point of a chosen site on the steep and rocky bank of the Cawdor Burn.

It is said that this thane dreamed a dream in which he was instructed to place his treasure chest on the back of an ass, set the animal at liberty, and follow whither it led. He did so, and the ass, after strolling from one thistle to another, arrived beneath the branches of a hawthorn tree where, fatigued by the weight on its back, it knelt down to rest. Around that tree the keep of Cawdor was built. It stands today in a vaulted chamber at the base of the tower. For centuries it has been a custom for guests of the family to gather round it and toast "Success to the hawthorn!"

When the tower was built it was cut off from the level ground on the landward side by a dry ditch and engirdled with a curtain wall built on the edge of the rock above the river and close to the ditch on the other side. This wall, which has a vaulted basement, survives today, exposed in parts but mainly forming the ground floor of the great extensions to the castle on the north and west sides of the keep. The drawbridge at Cawdor is a feature not to be seen in such perfect preservation anywhere else in Scotland.

A crisis in the Cawdor fortunes came in 1498 when John, the eighth thane, died without male issue. He left a baby daughter Janet who also died within the year and that might have been the end of the line, had it not been that a second daughter, Muriella was born to his widow, Isabella Rose of Kilravock, some months after his death. Little Muriella automatically became a Ward of the Crown and the king bestowed her wardship upon Archibald, second Earl of Argyll. Relatives of the Cawdor family endeavoured to frustrate this arrangement and attacked Campbell of Innerliver and a party of sixty men who were sent to escort the infant to the Campbell country. But the child was saved from their intervention by a ruse involving a 'dummy' infant in a large inverted camp kettle which the six sons of Campbell defended at the cost of their lives in a bloody ambush. Meanwhile

Muriella reached Argyll safely, grew up and married the earl's third son, Sir John Campbell, and the couple came to make their home at Cawdor in 1524. Muriella died at the ripe old age of seventy-five in 1573 and there have been Campbells at Cawdor ever since.

Cawdor Castle reached its peak of grandeur in 1672 when the north block was raised to its present height and connected to the keep by a central block containing the main stair. The fifth Earl of Cawdor was renowned as a forestry expert and by his enterprise as a cattle breeder.

Barevan Church, the original parish kirk of Cawdor, dating from 1296, survives as a picturesque ruin. The present parish church, built in 1619, owes its existence to a vow by Sir John Campbell, Muriella's great-grandson, on surviving a stormy voyage from the island of Islay, then one of the Campbell possessions.

Several times I have mentioned the family of Rose of Kilravock, so closely linked with the burghal history of Nairn and close neighbours of the Campbells of Cawdor. Kilravock lies about two miles due west of Cawdor on the left bank of the River Nairn, in the parish of Croy, and is approached by the B9091 road. Here on a superbly picturesque site, visitors from all over Britain and abroad, as well as members of the Rose clan, come to savour the atmosphere of a fifteenth-century tower house where continuity has been maintained by a succession of Highland lairds down five centuries. The castle has been developed by the twenty-fifth and present laird, Miss Elizabeth Rose, as a Christian guest house and group and conference centre.

The original—and surviving—tower house, a great square keep, was built in 1460 by Huchone de Rose, seventh laird of Kilravock (pronounced Kilrock) under licence by John, Lord of the Isles and Earl of Ross. The handsome five-storey domestic south wing was added in 1553 by the tenth baron, mainly to accommodate his household of seventeen female dependants, sisters and daughters. A third building phase came in the eighteenth century when the main staircase and corridors and the east and west wings were added. At this time the lovely Queen Anne window in the drawing-room was inserted, the ceiling heightened and the old stone walls in most of the rooms plastered. The building of the main stairway made the old stair turrets available for other uses and powder closets were added to four of the rooms. No further change in the structure took place until 1926 when small additions were made.

Exactly how true in a literal sense the story of Bonnie Prince Charlie's sojourn at Kilravock may be it is impossible to confirm, but the tradition is too pleasing to overlook. On Monday 14 April 1746 while Cumberland was settling down at the Roses' town house in Nairn, Prince Charles halted at Kilravock Castle and was received with "becoming respect". He asked to see the children, kissed each of them and praised their beauty. Spotting a violin, he asked if the laird played and begged a tune, upon which the baron played an Italian minuet. He then walked out with the laird to see the tree-planting operations. "How happy are you, Mr Rose," he said, "who can enjoy these peaceful occupations, when the country is so disturbed." Preserved in the drawing-room is the punch-bowl from which he was served, and the cup from which he drank out of it.

Next day the Duke of Cumberland arrived at Kilravock and remarked: "I believe you have had my cousin here?" When the laird would have apologized on the ground that he had no means of resistance, the Duke stopped him and said that he had done quite right—he could not refuse to receive Charles Edward, and, receiving him, he must treat him as a prince.

What Cosmo Innes the historian wrote of the Roses 150 years ago is still true:

> Anyone must be struck by the family resemblance of the successive lairds. One generation passes after another of these peaceful barons of Kilravock, with scarcely a shade of variety in their individual characters. The revolutions of their country or the Empire little affected them. Through changes of government and of dynasty, amid church schisms and Celtic rebellion, they held the even tenor of their way—keeping aloof from faction, shunning the crowd, yet not merely vegetating nor sunk in stupid indifference. They had felt the charms of music, and solaced themselves with old books, and old friends and old wine. They enjoyed the society of a few neighbours; they did their duty to their people; they had their gardens to tend, the interest of their woods and fields, the sports of the moorland and river.

Close to Kilravock on the north is the little hamlet of Clephanton which takes its name from Elizabeth Clephane, wife of Hugh Rose, the fifteenth laird. The village of Croy, farther west on B9091, at the heart of the twelve miles long parish, is across the county boundary in Inverness-shire and so must feature in our next chapter on the Inverness district.

# CHAPTER VII

# THE INVERNESS DISTRICT

INVERNESS-SHIRE is the largest county in Scotland, but what we are concerned with here is the Inverness district at its north-eastern tip, created by the reorganization of local government, and in particular, the amphitheatre of uplands and mountains overlooking the inner enclave of the Moray Firth, comprising three basins: the Inverness or Inner Moray Firth, the Beauly Firth (its western offshoot), and the north-eastern sector of the Great Glen with Loch Ness, Loch Dochfour and their link with the Moray Firth—the River Ness, the final section of the Caledonian Canal, and the part of the Great Glen Fault in which they lie.

In this natural theatre of hills and ridges overlooking a fertile strip by the waterside, four great human dramas were played out, along with innumerable minor ones. Here prehistoric man gravitated between 3,000 and 2,000 years BC to create a major settlement pattern; here, in all probability, Calgacus took his stand against the Romans. Here St Columba challenged the pagan soothsayers of King Brude, and here after twelve centuries of frontier-like interaction of Celt and Saxon the last great battle on British soil was fought at Culloden.

West of Whiteness Head with its long, shallow inlet where the oil production platforms are now built, a tapering peninsula of the kind which geographers call a cuspate foreland—meaning that two shallow arcs of a circle bisect in a sharp point—juts out into the centre of the Firth and almost meets another cuspate foreland on the opposite side, projecting from the coast of the Black Isle at Fortrose to a headland called Chanonry Point. The two forelands however are not directly opposite one another. The headland on the southern shore, terminating in Fort George, lies a little to the north-east, so it is separated from Chanonry Point by exactly a mile of water. Nevertheless the effect is to provide a narrow strait which forms the eastern gateway of the Inverness Firth and adds to the enclosed nature of that firth and its offshoots.

In the wide sheltered bay on the west side of the Fort George Peninsula lies the village of Campbelltown of Ardersier. Although Ardersier represents a very ancient fishing community, the present long, straggling village, about two miles south of Fort George (which can be approached by the B9092, the B9090 and the B9039 roads debouching on the north of the A96 trunk road), had no existence before the building of Fort George in the twenty years from 1747 to 1767. It was founded for the benefit of the displaced villagers of Blacktown (a site now occupied by the Fort George rifle ranges), and called Campbelltown in honour of the laird, Campbell of Cawdor.

From the beginning it has benefited greatly from its proximity to the fort. This is quite clear from the population statistics. In 1732 the total population of the parish of Ardersier was 300 or less. By 1750 when the building of Fort George had just begun it had risen to 426. By 1792 it was 802 and by 1941—not taking into account the regiments stationed in the Fort—it was 1,447, of which the village alone accounted for 750. Nor was that the whole story, for the village had, by then expanded into the neighbouring parish of Petty and had a total of 958 folk.

Old-world Ardersier with its fishermen's thatched cottages and 200-years-old Ship Inn, which retained its thatch until 1912 when the roofing was replaced by slate, had eleven boats engaging in herring fishing for a great part of the nineteenth century, but by 1927 there were only thirty-three fishermen and ten small boats left, and today nothing remains of the old pier but a few stumps jutting from wet sand. Before the platform yard came to Whiteness Head its working population mostly commuted to work in Inverness.

Meanwhile in April 1964 the Regular Army handed over Fort George to the Ministry of Works, and since then the Department of the Environment has established this wonderful old structure as a major show place. It has swept away many unsightly modern buildings and restored the fort to its classic state as built in 1749. On the extreme tip of the headland, the great polygon with its ramparts, casemates, barracks, ravelin and glacis points like a dagger into the firth. The restoration was acknowledged by a special award of the Scottish Civic Trust.

Experts regard the fort's "incredible survival, undamaged and complete, from the mid-eighteenth century" as something of a miracle. It is part of Britain's story, a direct and fascinating sequel to Culloden. The site of Cromwell's citadel at Inverness was originally chosen by the government for the situation of the fort, but the magistrates of the town, fearing that the presence of a garrison would "tend to corrupt the morals of the people", put such an exorbitant price on the ground that the Duke of Cumberland, in a huff and on the advice of engineers, found the Ardersier site the most eligible. The large farm on which the fort stands was then bought from the Campbells of Cawdor and work began in 1747 under the direction of General William Skinner, Director of Engineers, on the 15-acre site. The result, says H.M. Inspector of Ancient Monuments, "was in every respect a complete textbook example of a self-sufficient garrison fortress".

The seaward apex of the fort is flanked by demi-bastions, flat bastions project from the centre of each long side and there are full bastions at each of the basal angles. Across the base, to confront and halt the landward approach, there is a wide and deep moat. Before it is the ravelin, a triangular work connected to the main fort by a long timber bridge of fourteen pairs of uprights, with a drawbridge at each end.

What observers thought of it 200 years ago is clear from the eighteenth-century *Survey of Moray* which tells us that "the bastions are provided with eighty cannon and well supplied with water. Besides the bombproof apartments under the ramparts, the interior of the citadel consists of handsome squares of barracks, elegant accommodation for the Governor and other officers, a spacious armoury, a secure bombproof magazine, convenient stores and a neat chapel. It is sufficient for the accommodation of 3,000 men".

The building was estimated to cost £120,000, but by the time it was completed by the construction of the beautiful garrison church in 1767, it had taken £40,000 more. King George III is reported to have exclaimed: "By G..! Are the streets of this place being paved with gold?" when he signed the bill.

A veteran who was born in the fort summed up its subsequent career in these words: "To the thousands of soldiers who through two centuries garrisoned the stronghold, there learned the art of war, and marched forth from it to battle for the Empire in every corner of the globe, it has been either 'a grand place to soldier in' or 'a dreary gaol'." This observer, W. S. Robertson, added his personal tribute: "For a child brought up within the ramparts each day overflowed with interest: the boom of the morning cannon, the sweet bugle notes of the long reveille, followed by the skirl of the pipes playing 'Johnnie Cope', duty bugle calls and pipe tunes until 'The Last Post' and 'Soldier lie doon on your wee pickle strae' [more properly 'The Highland Lullaby'] closed eventful days."

In former days a regular ferry plied across the mile-long strait between Ardersier and Chanonry Point. Ardersier would like to see it revived. "And why not a hovercraft ferry?" they ask. "That could mean that air passengers landing at Dalcross, which is really nearer Ardersier than Inverness, could be in Invergordon, the boom town of the Cromarty Firth, in an hour, instead of going the long way round via Beauly." Dalcross (Inverness Airport) is less than two miles south of Ardersier. The B9039 road skirts it on the west, hugging the shore till it passes Castle Stuart, an impressive E-plan towerhouse dating from 1623-25, the builder being James Stuart, third Earl of Moray, son of the "Bonnie Earl". It has remained a possession of the earls of Moray to this day. Castle Stuart has lofty square towers at the south-east and south-west corners, and there are splayed angle turrets corbelled out at the north-east and north-west corners.

The great military road from Edinburgh to Fort George, erroneously called General Wade's on Ordnance Survey maps, though it was actually built in the 1750s runs straight as a die south-east from the fort and has been modernized as B9090 as far as the A96 road. It then crosses it at right angles and proceeds to climb the ridge between the Nairn valley and the coast, reaching the 255 foot contour at Clephanton. En route it passes the head of Loch Flemington, a pleasant sheet of water now lined on the south side by modern houses. Here we are on the exact route taken by the Duke of Cumberland and the Hanoverian army on their way to Culloden. At Clephanton we turn right and proceed along the summit of the ridge westward to Croy, an unpretending village recently doubled in size by local government building. It has a pleasant parish church built in 1767 and a handsome manse with shaped gables of somewhat later date. The road now climbs south-westward as B9006 to Culloden Moor, passing on the way the side road to Dalcross Castle, a splendid L-plan tower-house, built by Simon, sixth Lord Lovat, in 1621. It stands on the summit of the Croy ridge, around 430 feet up, offering a superb view ranging from Mealfourvonie beyond Loch Ness on the south-west to the Ord of Caithness across the Moray Firth on the north, and was constructed of free-stone from Covesea with the stair tower in the re-entrant angle and charming little angle turrets at the corners of wing and main block, with pedimented dormers on the four-storey wallheads.

After various changes of ownership Dalcross was acquired by the MacKintoshes. When Lachlan, the nineteenth chief, died, his body lay in state at the castle for a month. Two thousand armed men attended the funeral and the procession extended for four miles. This fantastic funeral celebration was repeated at even greater length when the twentieth chief died in 1731. This time the body was brought from Moy to Dalcross and lay there in state for two months, while the number of mourners was 4,000. This chief, another Lachlan, had taken a leading part in the 1715 Rebellion and was captured at Preston but reprieved. In the nineteenth century the castle had fallen into ruin but in 1897 it was restored on the original plan. It is now owned by Mrs J. H. Scott, a granddaughter of Alfred Donald MacKintosh of MacKintosh.

Beyond Dalcross Castle the moorland road continues to rise and the stretch of the valley crossed by the spectacular Culloden Viaduct of the Highland Railway comes into view. The viaduct, built between 1893 and 1898, spans the River Nairn by twenty-nine arches 124 feet above the bed of the river.

At Cumberland's Stone on the eastern verge of the battlefield we are at an altitude of 486 feet, but what might be a breathtaking view over the firth is denied by the dense tree cover of the Forestry Commission's Culloden Forest. Only at one point, near the memorial cairn, has the Commission been prevailed upon by the National Trust for Scotland to cut an avenue through the trees so that the firth can be glimpsed at the foot of the slope, two and a half miles to the north. Thus the natural theatre of encircling hills and gleaming water is frustrated of its full effect at a crucial point. On the other hand Culloden today is much more beautiful and solemn than it was on the fatal day of 16 April 1746. It was then a bleak, open and almost treeless moorland, broken by bogs and a few stray patches of cultivation. Today the plantations have given it shelter, the few simple memorials have given it great dignity; the land has been drained and new roads and buildings made. The most prominent building is the National Trust for Scotland Visitor Centre sited on the south side of the road almost opposite the position in the woods to the north where the second line of Cumberland's 9,000-strong army was drawn up at the outset of the battle. Contrary to a widespread misapprehension, the Duke did not watch the action from the Cumberland Stone 700 yards to the east. He positioned himself on horseback between his first and second lines throughout the action, though it is probable enough that he utilized the stone, a massive boulder, to survey the field before the carnage began.

Today the thousands of pilgrims who visit the scene normally pursue on foot a quiet walk along a footpath designed to take them to the principal sights. From the visitor centre they cross a field to Old Leanach Cottage, once the farmhouse of the holding of Leanach, given to the Trust in 1944, by the Gaelic Society of Inverness, and restored and adapted to house a small display. From here the pathway traverses at first the Field of the English where the Hanoverian dead were buried. It is marked by the English Stone which merely states "The English were buried here". The pathway then passes close to the Well of the Dead where the body of the commander of the Clan Chattan regiment, MacGillivray of Dunmaglass, was found and identified. The path now reaches the oval-shaped clearing that is the Culloden holy-of-holies, the Graves of the Clans. Green mounds break the level surface of turf and heather, each identified by simple stones bearing only one word—the name of the clan concerned: Mackintosh, Cameron, Fraser, Stewart, and so on. They were so placed by Duncan Forbes of Culloden, the tenth laird of his line, in 1881, replacing various earlier means of identification. It was this laird, who, in the same year, erected within the oval clearing, where the fiercest part of the battle was fought, the chief battle memorial, the Culloden Cairn, 20 feet high and 18 feet in diameter at base, where each year a commemoration service organized by the Gaelic Society of Inverness is held on the morning of the Saturday nearest to the battle anniversary. A large stone plaque bears the inscription:

> THE BATTLE OF CULLODEN
> WAS FOUGHT ON THIS MOOR
> 16TH APRIL 1746
> THE GRAVES OF THE GALLANT HIGHLANDERS
> WHO FOUGHT FOR
> SCOTLAND AND PRINCE CHARLIE
> ARE MARKED BY THE NAMES OF THEIR CLANS

This inscription is in some degree controversial, for many gallant Highlanders also fought on the other side, and felt that they too were fighting for Scotland's interests, but all criticism is stilled when we remember that the laird who erected the cairn and placed the plaque was a Forbes of Culloden, whose ancestors, and in particular Duncan Forbes, Lord President of the Court of Session, strongly espoused the Hanoverian cause. To him more than to any other was due to the fact that the 'Forty-five Rising was ultimately a failure. Had his advice and his warnings been heeded by the Government it might indeed have been averted and great bloodshed prevented. His pleas for clemency for the vanquished went unheeded, and it was said by his contemporaries that when he died in 1747 it was of a broken heart for his ravaged native country.

Of the battle itself little need be said. It is too well known how the weary and ill-fed Jacobites, led by Prince Charles Edward Stewart in person, were mowed down by Belford's devastating grape shot and outnumbered and overwhelmed by Cumberland's army. Those Highlanders who fought for the Hanoverians, the Campbells of the Argyll Militia and Loudoun's Regiment, were buried where they fell. A little stile over the boundary fence at the roadside leads to the Campbell graves in the forestry plantation south of the road. In the wood to the north of the road, 240 yards north-west of the cairn, is the Keppoch Stone, a large boulder believed to mark the spot where Alasdair MacDonell, sixteenth Chief of

Keppoch, was mortally wounded leading his clansmen in their charge, and near here also are Clan Donald graves.

Half a mile west of the cairn is the Irish Memorial—to the Irish soldiers of the French service, known as 'The Wild Geese', with its Irish Gaelic inscription. In 1966 King's Stables Cottage, a thatched eighteenth-century structure amid trees west of the battlefield, was opened as a Gaelic information centre. Thus at Culloden the Jacobite clans, the Irish allied to them, and their opponents—the English, the Hanoverians and the Campbells—all are remembered by simple tokens in a scene of great beauty. To visit Culloden is an experience that can never be forgotten.

After Culloden it may seem like anticlimax to recommend a visit to the Clava Circles (dealt with in Chapter II) which lie a little over a mile from the battlefield in the wooded low ground on the other side of the River Nairn but this, too, is an experience on no account to be missed. Here at Balnuaran of Clava on summer days a constant stream of visitors enters the tree-shaded enclosure, with its wicket gate and Department of the Environment notice board, and threads its way into the amazing series of passage graves, each of them surrounded by a circle of free-standing monoliths and containing a long passage flanked by densely packed boulders leading to a central space in the heart of what had been a domed chamber tomb.

At Culloden only a belt of sheltering forest separates one from a spectacle of great modern development and expansion. The battlefield is five miles from Inverness and at the Cumberland Stone crossroads one may leave B9006 and turning north down a side road descend through the woods to the open slope above the Inverness Firth where the suburb of Balloch with its spread of modern bungalows extends across the hillside. Between Balloch and its neighbouring suburb of Smithtown, on the 100 foot contour, is modern Culloden House with its palatial classical façade comprising a three-storey central block linked to two-storey pavilions by pillared single-storey corridors. This imposing structure, now a 22-bedroom luxury hotel, dates from 1777-83 and was built by the Forbeses of Culloden after the castle on the same site, which had housed both Bonnie Prince Charlie and the Duke of Cumberland in turn, was destroyed by fire in 1772. Among the mementoes of this earlier period is the Culloden Chest, made in 1742 and now in the foyer of the hotel which has lofty rooms with Adam-style decoration. Vaults of the old castle remain in the cellarage of the new building and here there is a small prison chamber in which seventeen Jacobite officers lay in hiding for three days, in the care of the Forbes's steward, before being discovered and led out to be shot in the woods nearby, on the orders of the 'Butcher' Cumberland.

Here we are less than three miles from the major round-about where the A96 and A9 trunk roads meet on the outskirts of Inverness. The town was described in Chapter III but something must be said of its magnificent hinterland. This may be done by reference to its necklace of engirdling parishes: Inverness and Bona, Daviot, Dores, Boleskine and Abertarff, Glenurquhart and Kirkhill.

The varied and beautiful country between Culloden Moor and the upper reaches of Strathnairn has had a turbulent history as well as being physically a most remarkable tract of territory. The picturesque white-walled church of Daviot with its tall and ornate steeple, divided into five tiers and surmounted by belfry and spire, is a conspicuous landmark on the A9 (Inverness to Perth) highway a little over six miles south of Inverness. This is the centre of the parish of Daviot and Dunlichity, which lies along the axis of the valley of the Nairn and extends for over twenty miles up the strath. There is a tiny village with a hall and school and cluster of houses and there was in historic times a great courtyard castle enclosing an area of 360 yards, with four circular towers, each vaulted and three storeys high, only one of which survives, overlooking the defile of the Nairn a little to the north of the Daviot House of today.

United to Daviot in the year 1618, the parish of Dunlichity in the wild south-western corner of Strathnairn has its own venerable church, the special features of which are set forth in a plaque erected by the Inverness Field Club. On the site of a chapel of St Finan (AD 575), the kirk was reconstructed in 1768 and again in 1826. At the east end are the burial enclosures of the MacGillivrays of Dunmaglass and the Shaws of Tordarroch. An old parish minister of Daviot, James Macphail, remarked that the stones in his parish were "so plentiful as to be an encumbrance", and this can be well understood by anyone who explores Dunlichity, a weird network of lochs amid rock-strewn hillsides. It is part of the rugged Moine schist plateau above the eastern shore of Loch Ness and eventually the Strathnairn road (B851) crosses over a col and links up with A862, the Dores–Fort Augustus road which traverses Stratherrick, the upland shelf or level running parallel to the Great Glen, but separated from it by a narrow range of hills. A862 in fact follows the line of General Wade's highway to Inverness. Two streams, the Farigaig and the Foyers, break through the hill barrier to reach Loch Ness at Inverfarigaig and Foyers by picturesque descents, while Loch Mhor, the long sheet of water into which so much of Stratherrick drains, is now being used by the North of Scotland Hydro-electric Board as the main reservoir of a 98-square-miles catchment area of their Foyers power scheme, which draws upon the basins of the Foyers and Fechlin Rivers. Under this scheme water to drive the turbines is first conveyed to the new power station by pipeline and after use is pumped back from Loch Ness to Loch Mhor to replenish the supply.

Foyers, a remarkable two-tier village, lies rather more than halfway down the 22-mile length of Loch Ness on its south-eastern side and affords, from the upper village, what is probably the finest view of the mighty canyon of the Great Glen. Both sides of the loch, densely tree-clad for the most part, are fronted by lofty heights which on the south-east have an average height of 800 to 1,000 feet and on the north-west of 1,200 to 1,500 feet. The bottom of the loch, the surface of which is 50 feet above sea level, slopes rapidly down to between 40 and 60 fathoms close to the shore and the depth in the centre is from 106 to 130 fathoms. For most of its length the loch is one mile broad. The loch is at its widest opposite Urquhart Bay where there is a break of a mile in the steep mountain wall and an inlet half a mile deep at the entrance to Glenurquhart.

It is at this point that most 'sightings' of the celebrated Loch Ness 'monster' have been made and one must assume that here, six miles from the north-east end of the loch, the creature, however bulky it may be, has ample scope to disport itself. Since 1933 when the monster began to claim sensational credibility with the aid of photographic evidence, increasingly sophisticated techniques ranging from underwater photography to radar scanning and electronic devices have been used in Nessie-hunts. The pursuit continues.

In written record the Loch Ness monster made its first appearance in St Adamnan's life of St Columba, though it appears to have been operating then on the River Ness. When the saint came to a crossing of the river he found the people just burying a man who had been killed by the monster. Undismayed, he asked his companion, Lugne Mocumin, to swim across the river and bring him a boat that lay against the opposite bank. Lugne obeyed, but when halfway across, the monster gave an awful roar and darted after him.

"Then", says Adamnan,

the blessed man raised his holy hand, while all the rest were stupefied with terror, and commanded the monster, saying 'Thou shalt go no further nor touch the man. Go back with all speed!' As Columba made the sign of the Cross in the air, the monster fled more quickly than if it had been pulled back with ropes. And even the barbarian heathens who were present were forced by the greatness of this miracle, which they themselves had seen, to magnify the God of the Christians.

In the eighteenth century Foyers was famed for its waterfall which was acclaimed in verse by Robert Burns:

Among the heathy hills and rugged woods
The foaming Foyers pours his mossy floods

But for seventy-three years the falls suffered through the diminution of their volume when Foyers became the pioneer aluminium processing site in Britain. Part of the waters were drawn off in the British Aluminium Company's intake and were carried by iron pipes through a tunnel half a mile long down an inclined plane to a factory on a little plain by the shores of Loch Ness. When this industry was closed in the sixties of this century it became possible once more to see the falls, and particularly the Lower Fall (80 feet high) in all the splendour which made our ancestors marvel, and the Hydro Board's £11,700,000 combined pumping and generating station scheme, which was brought in to replace the aluminium factory, aimed to leave the falls unaffected.

The upper village of Foyers, a semi-circle of whitewashed cottages with square gabled dormers forming a fine sweep behind a village green centred by a fountain, built by the aluminium company as a model settlement for their workers, became semi-derelict when the great copper bell of the factory tolled its last in 1967, its lifeless windows staring emptily over the tumbling slopes above the river in its deep romantic chasm, but two years later a development company bought it, along with an area of 1,600 acres, as the focal point of a new community based on holiday and tourist activities.

In its heyday the Foyers plant employed 500 workmen and as early as 1908 the company was boasting: "The impoverished crofters and fisherfolk of the Western Highlands acclaim with gladness the advent of this industry into their midst ... It inspires a genuine hope that the devastating tide of emigration may be stayed and that their beautiful but desolate glens may ere long possess a prosperity hitherto unknown." But the experience at Foyers led to a much greater project at Kinlochleven and at Fort William and ultimately to the huge smelter at Invergordon, and the small-scale pioneer works had to be sacrificed.

Above Foyers the south-east shore of Loch Ness is roadless so the way to Fort Augustus leads back through Stratherrick on its plateau. At the southern end of the strath, General Wade's road, now carrying the A862, reaches an altitude of 1,162 feet and descends by Loch Tarff with its wooded islets in the midst of barren sheep-sprinkled uplands. It dips briefly down into the lush hollow of Glen Doe, then climbs once more across the flank of Borlum Hill to reveal suddenly the breath-taking vision of a little town of close on 1,000 folk far below.

Fort Augustus clusters in a corner of the semi-circular sweep of shoreline at the upper end of Loch Ness. It claims to be "the most centrical point in the whole of Scotland". The fort which gives the little town its name was completed in 1742. With the deep waters of the loch in front, the four blocks of buildings stood around a square 100 feet in extent giving accommodation for 300 men. There was a bastion at each angle mounting twelve six-pounder guns and a ditch, covert-way and glacis completed the defences. It was attacked and captured by the Jacobites in 1746, and before they abandoned it they destroyed as much of it as they could, so that when the Duke of Cumberland reached the structure which bore his name it was uninhabitable. After repair it was used until the Crimean War, after which it was sold to the Lord Lovat of the day for £5,000. In 1876 a nephew of Simon, thirteenth Lord Lovat, told him, while on a visit, of the search then being made by the Benedictines of the English Congregation for a monastery site and he offered them the fort and its surrounding land. Building began at once and in August 1880 St Benedict's Abbey of Fort Augustus was solemnly inaugurated. Today in the hospice of the abbey is a model of the old fort made by one of the monks, from drawings lent by the War Office.

The chief architectural glories of the abbey are due to Peter Paul Pugin, who designed the monastery tower with a lovely court of arches underneath leading to the grand staircase. Here and in the cloisters one is conscious of a noble conception. The abbey church on the north as designed by Pugin would have been in Decorated Gothic, but work was discontinued in 1893 and when resumed in 1914 was converted into a Norman conception of moving simplicity to plans by Reginald Fairlie.

Tourism, forestry, hydro-electric development and the Caledonian Canal are the economic planks of Fort Augustus today, along with a little farming, while the village is a favoured residential centre. Halfway along the heavily wooded north-western shore of the loch, between Fort Augustus and Urquhart Bay there is a small hamlet with school, post office and hotel at Invermoriston where the A887 road sets off up the glen towards the west coast.

> In Highland glens 'tis far too oft observed
> That man is chased away and game preserved.
> Glen Urquhart is to me a lovelier glen—
> Where deer and grouse have not supplanted men.

These words were written by John Bright, the Quaker radical reformer, in the visitor's book of the inn at Drumnadrochit on 21 June 1856. The population of the glen has been halved since Bright's day, but it is still relatively high at around 1,000, and the majority of crofts and small farms are owner-occupied. On the south side of the glen however the beautiful birch woods and much of the heather have disappeared and have given way to the solid ranks of conifers, with a new forestry village at Shenval to house the foresters. Meanwhile the three villages of Milton, Drumnadrochit and Lewiston that ring the Bay of Urquhart on Loch Ness have been swelled by residents who actually work in the hydro-electric enterprises and public works many miles away in Cannich, Strathglass and Glenmoriston, for the A831 road through the glen is a convenient access route between the Great Glen and that other great valley contributing to the inner enclave of the Moray Firth—the Glen Affric-Strath Glass river system which feeds the Beauly Firth.

The outside world knows of Glenurquhart largely because of the Drumnadrochit highland games, the numerous Loch Ness monster expeditions, and the dramatic profile of Urquhart Castle where it juts out into Loch Ness. Under the care of the Department of the Environment the castle enjoys a ceaseless influx of visitors during the holiday season and is the highlight of innumerable coach tours and of the Loch Ness excursions of the Caledonian Canal pleasure steamer *Scott II*.

The promontory on which the castle stands was the site of an Iron Age fort similar to that which crowns Craig Phadraig near Inverness. The castle is one of the largest medieval stone castles in Scotland. The earliest fortress here was Caisteal na Sroin, a dun with timber-laced walls upon which a shell keep was superimposed on the motte-like mound. In the thirteenth century a double bailey was added within stone-built enclosure walls, including a donjon tower, and the deep ditch on the landward side, probably part of the prehistoric defences, was enlarged. It was occupied by the English in 1296, liberated by Sir Andrew de Moray, and reoccupied by the English in 1303, being finally recaptured by the Scots in 1308.

The upper parts of the donjon were rebuilt by the Grants of Grant who became lairds of Glenurquhart in 1509 and the surviving wallhead features of the high tower are believed to have been the work of the master mason James Moray in 1627. Castle Urquhart was blown up and left in ruins after Bonnie Dundee's Jacobite rising in 1689.

In 1952 the world water-speed record attempts on Loch Ness by John Cobb ended in the death of the pioneer, who had endeared himself to Glenurquhart folk by refusing to countenance any racing on the loch on Sundays. The local folk, who are strongly Sabbatarian, showed their gratitude by contributing generously to the Cobb memorial cairn which remains one of the landmarks of Urquhart Bay.

For the remaining stretch of Loch Ness to its northern tip, and along the north shore of little Loch Dochfour beyond that, the A82 road, now constantly thronged with traffic as the favoured Road to the Isles, hugs the waterside with its magnificent tree-girt slopes, and crossing the Caledonian Canal enters Inverness to link up with the A9 on its way to Clachnaharry, where it sweeps westward along the southern shore of the Beauly Firth.

At the Burn of Bunchrew the road enters the parish of Kirkhill which extends to the south bank of the River Beauly and includes much rich farming land skirting the south bank of the Beauly Firth. Nestling on the edge of the Beauly Firth and concealed from the main road by trees is Bunchrew House, the oldest part of which was built in 1641. Built for the Frasers of Inverallochy, it was sold to the Forbeses of Culloden in 1667 and was the birthplace of Lord President Forbes in 1685. Its most striking feature is an octagonal tower.

The village of Kirkhill, with the parish church, lies north of the A9 road on the road marked B9164. Behind the village, along a quiet tree-shaded road, we reach the old burial ground of Wardlaw on the hill of Cnoc Moire. The tombstones themselves spell the history of the parish and only the site of the ancient kirk remains. It was abandoned for worship in 1790 when the present village church was built on a less interesting site. But beside the site of the old kirk stands the Wardlaw mausoleum, where the Frasers of Lovat chiefs were buried in vaults down to the year 1815. It dates from 1634.

Rich clay farmlands stretch with long fields between hedgerows towards the narrowing upper end of the Beauly Firth, with the snow-sprinkled, jagged ridge of Ben Wyvis towering up a dozen miles to the north over the gentle slopes and shining water that lie between. Soon we come to Lovat Bridge over the River Beauly, carrying down here the combined waters that have come rolling in from Strath Glass, Glen Strathfarrar and Glen Cannich, deep in the mountainous heart of the Highlands.

The contrast between the panorama of tumbled heights in

the background and the lush, fertile haughlands where the river, twisting in mighty meanders broadens out into the Firth has impressed man from the earliest times. Less than a mile north of the bridge is the village of Beauly with its priory. This little town has a population of 1,386 and it is the point where the current of power flowing from the glens reaches the national grid. The priory of Valliscaulian monks was founded by Sir John Bisset of the Aird in 1230. He or his protégés gave the spot a new name, Bellus Locus, the Beautiful Place, and we cannot wonder that when Queen Mary slept at the Priory of Beauly, she, on hearing its name adopted from the language of her beloved France, exclaimed: "C'est un beau lieu!"

Apart from the priory whose walls seven centuries have not been able to pull down, modern Beauly is largely the product of the past 200 years. Its spacious square, however, is an inheritance from the days when the entire space within it was utilized for four great annual fairs. The priory stands at the north-east corner of the square. The monastic buildings have gone but what survives is the ruined priory church—nave and chancel and south transept, while the north transept, the burial aisle of the Mackenzies of Kintail, was restored in 1901.

It was the War of Independence which brought the family of Fraser to the Aird. Simon, the first Fraser laird of Lovat, died fighting at the battle of Halidon Hill in 1333. Hugh, the fifth laird and first Baron Lovat, could be called the founder of Beauly, for which he obtained marketing privileges. In the square is the Lovat Scouts' monument erected in 1905. The formation was raised in 1900 to provide the answer to the Boer Commandos. The present Lord Lovat, despite his renown as D-day hero and leader of the British Commandos in World War II, prefers to be thought of as "a farmer to trade", and his administration of the 181,000 acres of the Lovat estates, including the cattle-rearing venture in Glen Strathfarrar, has been the lifework nearest his heart.

# CHAPTER VIII

# EASTER ROSS AND THE BLACK ISLE

AT TOMICH, two miles north of Beauly, the A9 crosses the Inverness-shire–Ross and Cromarty boundary and we are in the very large Ross-shire district of the Highland Region. If we count in the Beauly, Inverness, Cromarty and Dornoch Firths, Ross has by far the longest Moray Firth coastline. The eastern half of the district, which crosses Scotland from sea to sea, is broken up by these offshoots of the Moray Firth into two great peninsulas, the Black Isle which has a coastline of 45 miles on the Beauly, Inverness, outer Moray Firth and Cromarty Firth and Easter Ross, which is bounded by the Cromarty Firth, the Moray Firth and the Dornoch Firth and ends in the long peninsula of Tarbat Ness. Along the innermost tips of the three deep-thrusting firths, from Beauly through Muir of Ord, Dingwall, and Ardgay, lies 'brae' or upland country on the edge of the northern Highlands.

The mountains, overtopped by Ben Wyvis (3,429 feet) are never very far away, but there is a great extent of rich and famous arable country in the two peninsulas and along the northern shore of the Cromarty Firth. At Muir of Ord, three miles north of Beauly, there is a sense of frontier for here on one side the A832 strikes off to the west and the Atlantic coast, and on the other side it pushes out across the Black Isle to Munlochy, Avoch, Fortrose, Rosemarkie and Cromarty. The point where this lateral highway from Cromarty to Gairloch bisects the A9 on its way to the far north is very much the Charing Cross of the northern Highlands.

An 18-hole golf course now straddles the A9 south of the village and occupies the lion's share of the former Market Muir, where the historic Beauly market was transferred last century, but cheek by jowl with it is an industrial estate with several engineering and contracting firms, while behind it is the permanent showground of the Black Isle Farmers' Society and nearby there is the Ord Distillery. The population is about 1,000. Muir of Ord is in the parish of Urray which in 1600 was united to another parish on the east, Kilchrist of Tarradale. It varies in altitude from sea level to ridges of 3,400 feet and was the scene in fairly recent geological time of a strange case of river capture. The River Orrin which now sweeps north-eastwards to join the River Conon and swell the waters of the Cromarty Firth originally turned in the opposite direction and flowed south to augment the River Beauly and its firth.

The ancient pre-Reformation church of Tarradale or Kilchrist, said to have been built about 1235, was converted into a mausoleum and reroofed at the end of the nineteenth century. At Tarradale House in 1792 was born Sir Robert Impey Murchison, pioneer of geological science. Murchison's niece, Miss Amy Frances Yule, bought Tarradale House and began amassing there a library of 5,000 volumes. When she died she bequeathed the house "to be preserved forever to the use and enjoyment of my countrymen" and it is now a field centre and residential school administered by the Geography Department of Aberdeen University. Miss Yule was a great character and many stories are told of her foibles. She was seldom punctual and could be heard shouting to the station-master to hold back the train for her as her carriage rumbled into the village. The Highland Railway always obliged. She doted on the military, presented battle scenes to the village school, and insisted that 24 June, the anniversary of the battle of Bannockburn, must be celebrated by the flying of the Scottish saltire from the flagpole.

From the early seventeenth century the dominating power in the parish was provided by the Mackenzies of Seaforth and Kintail and their cadet branch the Mackenzies of Ord. It was the first Earl of Seaforth who in the seventeenth century built Brahan Castle on the north side of the Conon River. It was a battlemented stronghold with a courtyard that could hold 1,000 men. In the Jacobite rebellions it was garrisoned by government troops. It became the birthplace of the Seaforth Highlanders, was a hospital in World War I, and a headquarters for Norwegian troops in World War II. The

battlements were removed in a nineteenth-century reconstruction and today it is a massive but truncated ruin. The
former stables have been converted into a pleasant manor
house for the present laird, Captain A. P. Matheson of
Braham. Ord House, which also dates from the seventeenth
century, is happily in fine preservation. Just off the Muir of
Ord road to the west is another historic building—Ord
Cottage. Long, low and picturesque, it dates from 1717 and is
probably the only chapel of the Scottish Episcopal Church
from the time of the penal laws which still survives. It has
now been converted into a charming dwelling-house.

Thanks to the industrial boom in the western Moray Firth,
both Muir of Ord and Conon Bridge, three miles to the
north, have seen fairly massive housing development in recent
years. It was Thomas Telford's bridge, built in 1809 to carry
the Great North Road over the Conon, which brought the
latter village into existence. Today its population is around
700 while Maryburgh, just across the bridge, has another 500.
The Holmes Report suggested that Maryburgh and Conon
Bridge could be extended on flatter land to the south and west
to take a total population of 3,000. A fish-processing plant
intended to give work to around 100 is Conon Bridge's latest
acquisition, but apart from its shops, garage and smithy that
is virtually the only industry. "I have no doubt," I was told
by one local observer, "that in fifty years' time this lovely
corner of Ross, so ideal for human settlement, will be
booming, but what we need is employment now". The kind
of industry required is light, otherwise the beauty of this
sylvan spot would be wrecked, a fact of which Mr Gerald
Laing, the sculptor, who besides splendidly restoring Kinkell
Castle, a mile south-east of the village, has given a good
example by establishing a tapestry workshop in the old
schoolhouse at Loch Ussie, a couple of miles to the west,
where three tapestry-makers working on his designs are
employed.

Conon Bridge, like Muir of Ord, is a gateway to the Black
Isle (Gaelic: Eilean Dubh), a fertile peninsula which probably
derives its name from the rich darkness of its soil, and is
centred by the Millbuie ridge that runs for 18 miles from
Muir of Ord to Cromarty, rising in the centre of its length to
a height of 838 feet, though its average altitude is about 500

feet. In the land that rises up behind Conon Bridge to this ridge there is a remarkable profusion of cairns and stone circles, testimony that even in the Bronze Age man found the locality one of great attraction. In the medieval period there were two parishes here, Urquhart and Logie Wester, which merged to form the civil parish of today. After the Reformation two dominating families emerged—the Mackenzies of Gairloch and the Forbeses of Culloden.

The Mackenzies were descended from Red Hector, third son of Alexander Mackenzie of Kintail, who flourished in the first quarter of the fifteenth century. It was his descendant, John Rory Mackenzie, who built the Z-plan castle of Kinkell in 1594, a date inscribed in a sculptured panel above the fireplace in the great hall. Mr Laing took over the much altered building in 1968. As a sculptor he recognized its essential character and swept away the later accretions which were disguising its true provenance, built up the modern windows, exposed the gunloops and laid bare the outlines of a warlike fortalice of the sixteenth century. For Laing, the reconstruction of the castle was not merely an antiquarian exercise. He admired the medieval castle as a fine piece of sculpture in its own right and in a book on his experience at Kinkell he relates it to the movements of contemporary art in which "we are allowing the magic, the spiritual and the unknown back into our lives. In this," he adds, "we are closer to the Middle Ages than we have been for four hundred years."

In the eighteenth century the Mackenzies of Gairloch moved down from Kinkell Castle to the lower ground and in 1760 built a gracious Georgian mansion with an imposing pedimented main block and semi-circular pavilions—Conon House—occupied today by Brigadier and Mrs W. A. MacKenzie.

The present Church of Scotland in Conon Bridge is called Ferintosh church, a reminder of the part played in the community by the barony of Ferintosh, a detached portion of Nairnshire in the Black Isle. It extended to 5,973 acres, acquired by the Forbeses of Culloden whom we have already met in the last chapter. Because of their loyalty to the Government in the Claverhouse Rebellion, pro-Jacobites laid waste the Forbes lands, and in 1690 the Scots Parliament, seeking to compensate them for their losses, gave special exemption from duties of excise to whisky distilling from grain grown in Ferintosh. This unique privilege lasted for nearly 100 years, being repealed in 1786 when the Forbeses were given compensation of £20,000, certainly less than the losses they had sustained through loyalty to the Hanoverian regime in the 'Fifteen and 'Forty-five Risings.

Kinkell was only one of the castles built to guard the fertile Black Isle from invasion from the west, as we shall see as we now move round the peninsula parish by parish. Two more Mackenzie strongholds designed to bar the way to reivers and raiders lie south-east of Kinkell virtually in a straight line across the neck of the territory, and both are in the parish of Killearnan. The B9162 road from Conon Bridge to North Kessock and the A832 from Muir of Ord to Cromarty both pass within a mile of Kilcoy, a Z-plan castle with two round towers built by Mackenzies of Kintail, which bears the date 1679 on the hall mantelpiece, where there are three well-preserved coats of arms of the family. There are two mermaids playing with harps at each end of the series together with a carving of a hare at one end and a greyhound at the other. The castle has been ruinous for over a century. Farther south is Redcastle, on the shore of the Beauly Firth. This massive pile was visited by Mary Queen of Scots in 1562 but was modernized in the nineteenth century. It is close to the parish church and a small hamlet. A road along the coast continues eastward to North Kessock which is in the parish of Knockbain, running six miles north-eastward to the deep inlet of Munlochy Bay. Kessock, much developed by private enterprise house-builders, is virtually a suburb of Inverness and will have increased importance when the £20,000,000 Kessock Bridge gets under way in 1978.

B9161 links up with the A832 road at Munlochy village at the head of the bay, which despite its name is more of a sea loch or fjord. The main road then runs inland for three miles to emerge on the coast again at Avoch (pop. 900), a characterful fishing village much expanded by new housing. Avoch (pronounced Och) has a history of 200 years as a fishing community and refuses to succumb to pressure for centralization. Its fleet of over a dozen modern boats fishes from Mallaig on the west coast but comes home at the weekends to its home port administered by local trustees. 'Avoch' is said to mean 'shallow water'. A mile south of the village on the coast stood the medieval Castle of Avoch on the Lady Hill, with fortifications 360 feet long and 160 feet broad, which after the forfeiture of the earldom of Ross was given by James III to his second son, Duke of Ross and Marquess of Ormond, the castle being renamed Ormond Castle. On the heights above the village arose another castle, the Tower of Arkindeath, remains of which still stand almost buried in undergrowth.

It is uncertain when fishing started in Avoch or where the first fishers originated, though the family names in the Sea-town have been for at least a century Patience, Jack, McLeman and Reid. There is however one clue. There was in the past a tendency among them to contract a form of St Vitus dance called McLeman's disease which has only been traced to one other locality in Britain, Boston in Lincolnshire.

The Bay of Avoch, with its harbour built 150 years ago, is backed by wooded ridges of steeply rising ground, and this type of coastline continues for the next two miles till we reach Fortrose, where the hill of Fortrose rises up behind the town to an altitude of 629 feet. Approaching along the narrow coastal terrace with rocks and woods on one side and the quiet waters of the Firth on the other, on a sunny summer weekend, you will find the sea speckled over with white sails, for the little harbour is the headquarters of the Chanonry Sailing Club and the whole expanse will be dotted with sailing dinghies, from the long curving promontory of Chanonry Point, facing across the narrows to Fort George, on the east, to the hills around Munlochy Bay on the west.

At one time the club was only one in this inner enclave of the Moray Firth, but, founded in 1956, it has gone ahead with gathering momentum ever since, and its near neighbours, the Ness Sailing Club and the Beauly Firth Sailing Club, both decided to merge their resources and join up with the Chanonry organization. As a consequence it soon had a membership of 150, over 60 per cent of whom were from the Inverness side of the firth. Anticipating an eventual membership of around 400, it embarked on a joint scheme of improvements to the harbour in conjunction with the local authority.

This is a symptom of the escalating popularity of Fortrose, which has become an embarrassment to the planners. Fortrose was a police burgh formed by the joint resources of the two ancient communities of Chanonry and Rosemarkie, separated by less than a mile of open country along the broad base of the cuspate foreland ending in Chanonry Point. Ever since 1851 when it had a population of 1,148 the numbers had been declining and it was thought that by the 1970s it would fall below 800. But after falling to 878 in 1931 it started to rise and by 1971 had reached 1,081. This was due to a spate of private house-building and since the industrial boom at Invergordon and Nigg, due to the aluminium smelter and oil-related developments, the trend has intensified until today there are about 1,300 residents. A public meeting was held by the planning authority to plan for expansion, but the feeling of the existing residents was that Fortrose should not be allowed to grow any bigger. They thought their little paradise was perfect as it was, and that more and more incomers would only spoil things. It had already been decided in principle that the whole of the Black Isle must remain a 'green belt' between the industrial areas to the north and the south.

The attractions are obvious. Who would not want to live in a quiet 'cathedral city' which has the added appeal of superb beaches, a wonderful little harbour for pleasure sailing, a first-class golf course, glorious hill walks, secondary educational provision second to none in the North, a southern exposure and that fabulously mild and sunny climate peculiar to the 'dry' area of the Moray Firth? Many of the newcomers are commuters with cars, who find it no obstacle to travel to work on the north side of the Cromarty Firth.

Not for nothing was the motto of the royal burgh of Fortrose "From Age to Age Endure". It celebrated its quincentenary in 1955 and marked the occasion by restoring five 300-year-old houses. Its ancient ruined cathedral of dull red sandstone is set like a jewel in the centre of a charming green or cathedral close, formerly surrounded by the manses of the canons, now mostly replaced by gracious villas. Only one of the cathedral manses survives—on the south-eastern boundary of the green. Of the cathedral itself all that survives is the south aisle of the chancel and nave and a detached chapter house. But, however fragmentary, the old shrine gives a dignity to the little town which has besides long rows of venerable cottages whose tiny front gardens are a mass of flowers.

Curiously enough, of the twin villages, Rosemarkie, on the east, is the more ancient. It was the site of a chapel of St Moluag of Lismore and the tradition is that he died there on 25 June 582. In the parish churchyard is a Pictish sculptured stone, a cross slab with elaborate Celtic ornamentation. The first title of the Bishops of Ross was "of Rosemarkie", and it may have been in 1227, when the small chapter of Rosemarkie was enlarged, that the cathedral was moved to its present site in Chanonry, the western village. The lower portion of the chapter house belongs approximately to this period. A chapel said to have been dedicated to St Nicholas, it is vaulted in six bays, groined and with six bosses including a fine multi-petalled rose.

The cathedral itself, of which the main part is represented now only by the ground plan filled in with gravel, was a splendid building in the pure Early Decorated style of the fourteenth century. The surviving south aisle was built by Euphemia, Countess of Ross, a grand-niece of Robert the Bruce, perhaps in contrition for the sacrilegious misdeeds of her second husband, the notorious Wolf of Badenoch. The countess was buried in her aisle and the easternmost of the three canopied tombs within is thought to be hers. Fortrose Academy, founded in 1791, is now the secondary comprehensive school for the whole of the Black Isle, with a roll of 400. Pupils from the Academy were responsible for casting a plaque which identifies the stone at Chanonry Point, alongside the lighthouse, which commemorates the death by burning there of Kenneth Mackenzie or Coinneach Odhar, the Brahan Seer, whose feats of second-sight and prophecy have sent a shiver down the spines of generations of Highlanders. The tradition is that he overstepped the mark by predicting that "the long descended line of Seaforth will end in extinction and sorrow" and—though the prophecy was later vindicated by the event—was put to death for his temerity. Today the Chanonry Point peninsula is occupied partly by a fine 18-hole golf course and partly by new bungalows. From it one gets a splendid view across the firth to Fort George and to Whiteness Head beyond it, where the skeletons of successive oil production platforms under construction are plainly visible. Nobody on the Black Isle, indeed, can fail to be aware of the North Sea oil boom, for while one production platform can be seen from Fortrose, another dominates the skyline at Cromarty on the north side of the peninsula, which lies directly opposite the yard at Nigg.

From Rosemarkie, with its narrow old-world main street from which a succession of lanes run down to the sea-front and to a beach and bathing lido sheltered by trees from the steep hillside at Kincurdy, the A832 road turns inland and climbs up the defile of a burn on to the central ridge of the Millbuie Forest on its way to Cromarty. Here it might be appropriate to interpolate that one derivation of that mysterious term 'Black Isle' is from the black uncultivated moorland in the interior, once largely treeless but now very largely covered with Forestry Commission and private plantations. Another name for the spine of the Black Isle is Ardmeanach—the 'yellow headland', from the vast stretches of bright golden gorse which still delight the eye there.

After traversing nine miles from Rosemarkie the road reaches the plateau behind Cromarty, one of the most fascinating little towns in Scotland. Before descending into the town it might be a good idea to turn aside into the clifftop cemetery above Kirky Brae dominated by the tall column topped by a statue of Hugh Miller (1802-56) who has brought it perhaps its greatest fame, though it would be unforgivable to forget Sir Thomas Urquhart of Cromarty (1613-60) the eccentric genius whose English translation of Rabelais will never be equalled. It perhaps tells us something about Cromarty that both these men were in very different ways radical individualists. Both died in early middle age: Urquhart as an exile on the Continent for his royalist convictions, in a fit of laughter on hearing of the Restoration of Charles II, and Miller in Edinburgh by shooting himself when the balance of his mind was disturbed.

In his first book *Scenes and Legends of the North of Scotland* (1835), which is subtitled "The Traditional History of Cromarty", Miller described the dramatic situation of his native town, which lies just within the gateway to the Cromarty Firth, a natural postern scooped out of the middle of an immense wall: "a wall of brown precipices beetling for many miles over the edge of the Moray Firth and crested by dark thickets of furze and pine". In this wall there is a gap flanked by two headlands, the North and South Sutors, and as Miller put it:

> The huge projections of cliff on either hand, with their alternate masses of light and shadow, remind us of the outjets and buttresses of an ancient fortress, and the two Sutors, towering over the opening, of turrets built to command a gateway. The scenery within is of a softer more gentle character. We see hanging woods, sloping promontories, a quiet little town, and an undulating line of blue mountains, swelling as they retire into a bolder outline and a loftier altitude until they terminate some twenty miles away in snow-streaked, cloud-capped Ben Wyvis.

Cromarty, the "quiet little town", built on a long tapering triangle jutting out into the narrows near the mouth of its firth, is the third to be built in the vicinity, the first two having been eroded away and submerged by the sea. Tides of prosperity and depression have washed over it also. Its destiny was from the beginning linked with the sea. Before the Act of Union in 1707 it was a prosperous seaport trading with the Continent. Then, under the changed conditions of landward trade with England, it sank into a decline and, as Miller put it, had sunk to the status of an insignificant village by 1750. After this, aided in particular by the exertions of a new landowner, George Ross, who bought the Cromarty estate in 1722, it began to revive. Ross launched a factory for processing hemp which employed hundreds of workers, built a large brewery, a nail and spade factory, and imported lace makers from England. He persuaded the Government to subsidize the building of a pier.

Miller described the third town of Cromarty as "irregularly built, exhibiting in the more ancient streets and lanes that homely Flemish style of architecture characteristic of all our older towns in the north, and displaying throughout that total disregard of general plan which is said most to obtain in the cities and villages of a free country". But this is perhaps to underestimate the orderly progress which resulted in "stately merchants' houses of three storeys with wide steps rising to well-proportioned front doors", as well as "the humble cot-

tages of the fisherfolk, with their gables to the sea and their
tiny windows peeping at one another across the vennels".

Special distinction was given to the town by two fine
buildings which Ross had built: the Sheriff Court-House
(1782) with its cupola and clock which has a large hall in the
first floor and prison cells below, and the Gaelic chapel (1783)
on the high ground beside the cemetery, designed to serve the
Gaelic-speaking immigrants from the Highlands who flocked
into the town to find work in the new factories.

In another of his books, *My Schools and Schoolmasters* (1852),
Miller described what it was like to be a boy in Cromarty in
the first decade of the nineteenth century:

> As the school windows fronted the opening of the Firth, not a
> vessel could enter the harbour that we did not see . . . there was
> perhaps no educational institution in the kingdom in which all
> sorts of barques and carvels, from the fishing yawl to the frigate
> could be more correctly drawn on the slate . . . Further the town,
> which drove a great trade in salted pork at the time, had a
> killing-place not thirty yards from the school door, where from
> 80 to 100 pigs had sometimes to die for the general good in a
> single day . . . All the herring boats during the fishing season
> passed our windows . . . We could see, simply by peering over
> book or slate, the curers going about rousing their fish with salt
> . . . bevies of young women employed as gutters, and horridly
> incarnadined with blood and viscera, squatting around the heaps,
> knife in hand, and plying with busy fingers their well-paid
> labours, at the rate of sixpence per hour.

But Cromarty's fortunes changed again. Steam looms
displaced the hand-loom weavers; the fishing declined; the
railway age destroyed the coastal shipping trade. From the
1840s when the town had a population of over 2,000 a decline
set in which has resulted in the reduction of its folk to the
pitiful 484 of 1971. But not perhaps so pitiful, as much of the
building heritage has survived, and first the colourful Fishertown and then High Street and Church Street were scheduled
as a conservation area. Hugh Miller's birthplace, the old
thatched cottage built by his buccaneering great-grandfather
John Fiddes in 1711, has been open to the public since 1900
and was acquired by the National Trust for Scotland in 1938.
The lovely old court-house has been externally restored, and
between it and the thatched cottage, Miller House, a two-

storey sandstone villa built by Captain Miller, the father of Hugh, but never actually occupied by him owing to a financial crisis caused by the loss of his brig, has been restored by the Trust and recently received a special commendation by the Saltire Society.

All these features are in Church Street, where there is also to be seen Forsyth House, the red sandstone mansion of William Forsyth, an eighteenth-century merchant benefactor of the town who instituted a bounty for herring catching and stimulated linen spinning. At the end of Church Street is the remarkable parish church built in 1700, with its box pews and lairds' and poors' lofts—a survival from the old town that was swept away by the sea.

Back in the cemetery overlooking the town, we have a reminder that for a brief period in the present century Cromarty was once more a hub of seafaring activity. This was shortly before and during the First World War when the British Home Fleet used the Cromarty Firth as its base, and many a sailor who had lost his life on service was buried here, in a peaceful plot high above the town under the Miller Monument which looks so like the Nelson Column.

On leaving school Hugh Miller apprenticed himself as a stonemason but had to give up the trade when it threatened his health, and he gravitated to literature and journalism. He became a key figure in the Disruption of the Church of Scotland and edited *The Witness,* the newspaper of the Free Church party. At the same time he made his name as a geologist by identifying new species of fossil plants and animals and the publication of his book *The Old Red Sandstone* in 1841. He remained a rugged individualist familiar to Edinburgh society by his eccentric dress of rough tweed with a shepherd's plaid. He was in fact the typical Scottish self-made genius or 'lad o' pairts'. All the aspects of his work—scientific, journalistic and theological—are illustrated in the thatched cottage museum in Church Street.

Despite a flood of temporary residents brought to Cromarty by the proximity of the Nigg platform yard and the revival in the 1970s of the ancient Nigg Ferry, the future of the little town remains problematical. As a conservation area of remarkable character, it could become a booming resort, for, as Miller put it, its hinterland is "rich in prospects which combine the softer beauties of the lowlands with the bolder graces peculiar to an alpine district"; but these days are still in the future.

The Hill of Cromarty behind the town rising to 500 feet has fine views over both Cromarty and outer Moray Firths. On the west, the B9163 road along the northern coast of the Black Isle, hugging the shore of Udale Bay, crosses the long parish of Resolis to Conon Bridge, which it reaches in 16 miles. The little hamlet of Jemimaville, about five miles from Cromarty, owes its name to Jemima Poyntz, the Dutch-English wife of an eighteenth-century laird of Ardoch. The laird renamed his house Poyntzfield in her honour, and the Post Office frank for the area is still 'Poyntzfield'. It is here that the novelist Jane Duncan lived by the firth, and readers will find a description of childhood on a Black Isle croft in her book *My Friends the Miss Boyds* and in her autobiography *Letter from Reachfar*.

At Balblair there is a ferry across less than a mile of firth to Invergordon. The old ruined kirk of Urquhart lies close to the firth. In the kirkyard can be seen a monument to John Macdonald, a Gaelic preacher whose itinerant evangelistic campaigns irked his Presbytery. At the Disruption he seceded and became the first minister of the handsome Ferintosh Free Church higher up the slope.

From Maryburgh, just across the new bridge on the Conon River which supplanted Telford's 1829 bridge in 1969, it is a short run of two miles to Dingwall, the county town of Ross, a royal burgh for 700 years, and the administrative hub of the Cromarty Firth growth area.

It may seem almost paradoxical that while a few miles away, under the pressure of the increasing industrialization, Alness is promised an eventual population of 16,000 and Tain is set a target of between 10,000 and 20,000 in the next two decades, Dingwall was offered a modest 7,000 by the planners' blueprints. But its role is quite different from these growth points. It will be bypassed by the eventual realignment of the A9 trunk road, but will remain, as it has been for centuries, a great market town, the administrative capital of the larger part of the northern Highlands, a home for top executives, businessmen and civil servants, and most important of all, a services and shopping centre, with a fine pedestrian precinct in part of its High Street. This limitation of function was a deliberate planning decision. As the Holmes Report put it: "if the town were allowed to grow so large that the central area would have to be remodelled . . . its character would be destroyed, and the efficiency of its special functions impaired rather than improved".

Dingwall (Norse: Thingvollr, the parliament wall) was a Viking colony in the eleventh century, in the time of the Orkney Jarl, Thorfinn the Mighty. A clump of trees on the Green Hill at the west end of the town is pointed out as Thorfinn's 'thing-wall' or 'parliament-seats' where his chieftains and freemen sat to mete out justice. Later twelve earls of Ross in succession held the Castle of Dingwall, and confirming charters by James IV and James VI defined Dingwall's status as a royal burgh. The stones of the castle were used in the eighteenth century to construct the tolbooth tower which still forms the central feature of the otherwise modern municipal buildings in the High Street. This dates from 1777, while a flanking tower is all that remains of the castle.

Among the listed buildings in the town one of the most attractive is the Georgian parish church built in 1801, and it is generally agreed that some of the late eighteenth-century and early nineteenth-century buildings, mainly in the High Street, have a vigorous and quite original quality in detail and preserve the flavour of an old-world rural market town.

The beautiful wooded plain, between two ridges of hills, on which the town stands was once a swampy marsh, but since 1817, through drainage and spirited agriculture, has become one of the loveliest valleys in the north. On the south it is overlooked by the tall, square tower of the Sir Hector Macdonald monument on the summit of the Mitchell Hill, now an attractive public park, while on the north the splendidly wooded Tulloch Hill (800 feet) crowned by Tulloch Castle, has been utilized for well-planned housing development and public buildings. The castle itself, former home of the Bains and later the Davidsons of Tulloch, is now a hostel for girls attending Dingwall Academy, itself rebuilt and resited on the lower slopes of the hill. Dingwall's population in 1971 was 4,232, but it has probably gained another thousand since then.

The lush valley of the little Peffery River on which Dingwall stands, fringed by venerable rows of poplars, extends westward for five miles from its present outfall on the Cromarty Firth to the spa of Strathpeffer. Its form can be better understood when one realizes that at one time the firth itself extended this far inland. Above the waters on the south were the heights of Knockbain, the long ridge of the Cat's Back and the Hill of Knockfarrel. On the north were the steep slopes of the Heights of Brae, the Heights of Fodderty, Inchvannie, Keppoch and Auchterneed, a continuous range forming the edge of the elongated bulk of Ben Wyvis. On these slopes both to north and south are a profusion of cairns, chambered tombs, hut circles and standing stones.

Almost due north of Strathpeffer, about a mile from the holiday village with its seven hotels and fifteen boarding houses, is Castle Leod, the home of the Earl of Cromartie, whose ancestor Sir Roderick Mackenzie acquired it in 1606. Originally flat-roofed with a battlemented parapet, it was rebuilt in its present form with corbelling, angle turrets, decorated dormers and other details of richness and variety. The year 1777 was important for the whole area, for in that year the son of the attainted third Earl of Cromartie regained possession of the Cromartie estates which had been forfeited after the 'Forty-five Rebellion. His family have occupied Castle Leod ever since. In that year also the first of the Strathpeffer mineral wells, the Castle Well, was roofed in. The spa itself developed in 1819 with the building of the Pump Room and the crusading zeal of a certain Dr Thomas Morison. An army surgeon who suffered from rheumatoid arthritis, he came to Strathpeffer, took the waters and devoted the rest of his life to singing the spa's praises. Four springs were tapped and their waters piped to the Pump Room.

By 1909 the cult of the spa was at its height. A fifth well was brought into service and a series of baths—peat, immersion, douche, Russian and Nauheim—was offered. While the wells are not now so much lauded, the holiday magic of Strathpeffer remains. There is a fine Spa Pavilion and the Square at Strathpeffer, with its ten shops, is one of the most charming in the Highlands. The planning authority in 1974 produced an ambitious blueprint for further development on sports centre lines. If the population increases envisaged for the Cromarty Firth industrial area materialize, there will certainly be a future for the old spa.

North of Dingwall the trunk road at first clings to a narrow platform between steep hill slopes and the Cromarty Firth. At Ardullie, about four miles on, a causeway is being constructed across the firth to carry the rerouted A9 highway, which, crossing the Kessock narrows by the new bridge, will cut across the Black Isle via Tore to shorten the distance to the north. Three more miles bring us to Evanton which was singled out by the Holmes Report as a springboard for expansion. "Evanton," this stated, "is contained by woods, and to the north-east by potential industrial development on 350 acres of flat land, and by the slopes of Cnoc Mhabairn to the north and west. Part of the new town would lie on the south slope between the Rivers Glass and Sgitheach. It is linear and could, within its boundaries house 22,000."

That was in 1968. Since then, despite the new factor of the North Sea oil boom, the plan for Evanton has been revised downward. The target now is a population of 10,000. Industrially very positive gains have been registered. A small engineering firm which began by manufacturing steel lobster pots graduated into oil-related contracts. A box factory also expanded into new fields, and steel, engineering and plant hire companies also moved in.

There is no doubt that Evanton could be a delightful place to live and work in. Before it lies the firth and behind it the mountains, with wooded slopes leading upwards to the ridge of Ben Wyvis, with its perpetual snowfield, from which the Munro barons of Foulis were, as direct tenants of the sovereign, expected on demand to provide "one snowball on the longest day of summer". Evanton is in the parish of Kiltearn, of which Foulis Castle, about a mile south-east of the village, is the chief mansion and the ancestral home of the chiefs of the Munro Clan.

In the Jacobite era the Munros stayed loyal to the Hanoverians and suffered severely for it. Sir Robert Munro, sixth baronet, after leading his Highlanders to triumph in the Battle of Fontenoy, died on the field at Falkirk in 1746 in a heroic last stand. Foulis was plundered by the Jacobites, but Sir Harry, the seventh baronet, rebuilt Foulis Castle in a Dutch courtyard style, for as a Latin scholar he had studied at Leyden. It survives in fine preservation today.

The present village of Evanton dates from 1810. It was laid

out on a triangular plan at the apex of which, around 1816, was built a handsome United Secession church. The old parish church of Kiltearn, now unroofed, stands close to the firth. It was associated with the Rev. Thomas Hog, a Covenanting martyr of the Second Episcopacy.

In four more miles we reach Alness, the model 'new town' designed to house the great bulk of the workers in the Invergordon industrial area. Its optimum size will be a 16,000 community spread over four centres—Teaninich, Obsdale, Culcraggie and Struie—each with its own centre, with a primary school, local shops, meeting rooms and a public house, so designed that the furthest house in each locality will be around ten minutes' walk from a local bus stop. At present the Teaninich/Coulhill area has been completed. It is laid out on a succession of southward-facing slopes giving views over the firth, while on the west the view is towards Cnoc Fyrish, crowned by the fantastic Gates of Negropatam, an Indian city captured by General Sir Hector Munro of Novar after a month-long siege in 1781.

The new Alness is not sprouting out of a complete vacuum as many new towns do. Alness is a historic community with a long story behind it, although most of the houses of the present village, strung out along the A9 road, are comparatively modern. The sheer physical spread of the new town is more impressive than mere population figures suggest. Every newcomer to the town receives a copy of a bulky 'information kit' containing a guide called *About Alness,* a street plan, an Alness Directory, a list of Alness clubs and societies, and a transport bulletin with details of bus, train and air services.

There is just the danger that so much emphasis is placed on the 'new town' aspect of Alness that its historical roots will be forgotten. It is divided into two by the River Averon. Alness parish lay on the west side with the parish church surrounded by open country, while the main part of the village, paradoxically enough, grew up on the east, in the parish of Rosskeen, which also includes Invergordon, which lies three miles farther east. This odd dichotomy has been obliterated by the new development. The once isolated parish church is now surrounded by the housing estate of Kirkside, backed farther up the hill slope behind by two more housing schemes at Coulpark and Coulhill. Rosskeen parish church and hall are now incorporated in the eastern half of the village, which also boasts along the line of the High Street a public hall, post office, library, community centre, masonic hall and the district office of the local authority, while there is a golf course along the left bank of the river. In the haughland below the town are the two old distilleries, Teaninich and Dalmore. About a mile west of the built-up area the A836 road, nicknamed 'the Struie', provides a drastic shortening of the A9 route to the north by climbing over the desolate hills and moorland via Altnamain (684 feet) to the Dornoch Firth, which it reaches in fourteen miles.

The Ness of Invergordon, which the A9 now traverses, is a headland jutting out into the central portion of the Cromarty Firth and forming the apex of a fertile triangle of almost flat country at the base of the Ross-shire hills. The name Invergordon was adopted by Sir William Gordon, first baronet of his line, on the creation of his baronetcy in 1704. Pennant, who first visited the place in 1769, predicted Invergordon's future as a naval base. Of the Cromarty Firth he wrote: "The whole bay is the most capacious and secure of any in Great Britain. Its whole navy might lay there with ease, and ships of 200 tons may sail up above two-thirds of its length. The projecting hills defend this fine bay from all the winds." Early in the nineteenth century Invergordon became a thriving port and before the railway came in 1863 there were steamer services to London, Aberdeen and Leith. In 1864 the little town, which then had a population of 1,122, became a police burgh. The Town Hall was built in 1871, its classical pediment appropriately showing a sculptured figure of Neptune, while in 1875 the oldest part of Invergordon Academy was built in the Romanesque style.

In 1907 the Admiralty decided that calls would be made by the Home Fleet at Invergordon twice yearly, a routine not finally abandoned until 1959. The great period of Invergordon's naval role was the First World War. At its height 20,000 servicemen were based in the town. On the last day of 1916 the town was shaken to its core when the battle cruiser *Natal* blew up and sank at her moorings. In 1931 occurred the Invergordon Mutiny when 8,000 sailors refused to man their ships in protest against reductions in pay.

By the time of World War II it was decided that Invergordon was too vulnerable to air attack to serve any longer as a principal base and the Fleet went to Scapa Flow. Nevertheless it was used at later periods for occasional exercises and as a NATO rendezvous. When the last naval presence had departed the little town settled down to look for new industry and it did not have to wait for long. Its development since then has been in three phases. In 1960-61 came the Invergordon Distillery, at first employing 400 men in grain and malt whisky production—the largest plant of its kind in Europe. While there are eighty or ninety malt distilleries in the country there are only about a dozen grain distilleries, and their output is correspondingly greater—at Invergordon it reached 11,000,000 gallons. There was a reduction later, but by then Phase Two, the establishment of the British Aluminium Company's smelter, giving initial employment to about 450 men—with the plant working at only half its capacity—was in prospect. Finally, in the 1970s came the North Sea oil boom, bringing to Invergordon the massive complex of M. K. Shand, whose role was the coating of submarine piping with the protective shell which enables it to lie on the sea bed and bring ashore the crude oil from the Forties, Brent and Ninian Fields, as well as the gas from the Frigg Field—all of them between 150 and 200 miles offshore.

There were in addition numerous auxiliary enterprises connected with the North Sea developments. These have fluctuated in profitability. But the harvest of the North Sea oilfields will continue till the end of the century and as its greatest concentration is in the far north, particularly in the East Shetland Basin, Invergordon is favourably placed on the oil boom map. The smelter with its six tall chimneys lies well inland from the town at Inverbreakie, but its spectacular access jetty strikes deep into the Firth and from it a gleaming overhead corridor conveys the ore from ship to smelter automatically on an endless chain system. The output of aluminium is around 100,000 tons per annum in the form of sheet, bars, sections and foil.

At the last census Invergordon had a population of 2,352, but this was before the peak of the oil-related development had been reached. No attempt has been made to concentrate workers' housing in the town. Travel-to-work was the assumption on which the residential provision for the coming boom was made at Alness, Tain, and the small coastal villages of the Easter Ross peninsula. The A9 leaves the town on the north-east hugging the coast through the pleasant suburb of Saltburn with an attractive promenade along the seafront and in eight miles reaches the Nigg Station road which runs south-east to Ankerville Corner and a choice of roads to the platform site on Nigg Bay.

Nigg is a four-letter word that for five years has electrified the northern quarter of Scotland. It derives from the Gaelic *an eag*—a cove, a place separate and apart. But today Nigg is not separate and apart. It is the symbol of North Sea oil and what it is doing for the economic life of the Highlands. When I visited the yard a short time ago 2,500 men were working at the fabrication yard of Brown and Root-Wimpey who had formed a consortium to build a series of platforms designed to operate in BP's Forties Field at a water depth of 416 feet. The structures were made to withstand 93-foot waves and wind speeds of 130 mph. The principal part of the platform is called the jacket, which is secured to the sea floor by piles. Deck sections are then placed on the jacket, from which the drilling and production of the oil takes place. The jacket is 460 feet high and 300 feet by 250 feet at base, and tapers to 180 feet by 175 feet at deck level. Until completed it lies horizontally and when launched is towed on a specially built flotation tank to the site in the oil field. After piling, the flotation tank is removed and brought back to Nigg to be used again on the next job.

The huge manpower pool employed fluctuates according to the urgency of the work and the stage it has reached. On the site there is a permanent staff of 1,500 most of whom have found settled homes in the Easter Ross area. Until more conventional housing was available two large luxury liners were hired by the consortium to house the temporary work force and moored off the site in Nigg Bay. Apart from that, commuters from as far north as Helmsdale and Brora in Sutherland, and as far south as Inverness, travelled daily by bus to the site. Workers were recruited from the remotest work-hungry areas of the Highlands. Some 300 men migrated from Caithness and as many again from Lewis and Harris.

In 1974 a Tain observer told me: "Four years ago the average young man's wages in the Highlands were between

£20 and £25 a week. Today they are between £60 and £100." Inflation will have produced some escalation since then. No injection of industry and unaccustomed opulence can take place without some unpleasant side-effects. But when Brown and Root came on the scene in Easter Ross there were 700 unemployed. To most men activity is the key to happiness. Nigg has given profitable activity to many who lacked it.

Nigg is a very beautiful and historic parish nearly six miles long and three miles wide, covering an area of 9,000 acres. Of this the platform site occupied originally 150 acres, later expanded by another 70 acres. What interested the oil men was the Sands of Nigg—a unique topographical feature which was being exploited for industrial purposes 200 years ago. During high water they are covered by the sea to a depth of from four to eight feet, but at low water they are dry. During the eighteenth century they were excavated to uncover layers of shells used to manufacture lime of a superior quality. Today their value was simply to provide a sheltered location in close proximity to deep water, within easy towing distance of the North Sea oil fields—and they were only selected after six possible alternatives in five different countries had been considered. To create the graving dock (1000 feet by 600 feet by 50 feet deep) Wimpey reclaimed over 100 acres from sand dunes and estuary and dredged 1,250,000 cubic yards of material which was used in the extension of the yard into Nigg Bay.

Two worlds subsist in Nigg today side by side. Before the platform came Nigg was known to the wider world as the home of a famous herd of shorthorn cattle, for flocks of North Country Cheviot sheep, and for seed potatoes. Probably the most serious side-effect of the new development is that farm workers and tradesmen have been tempted away to the big money of the platform site. Yet up on the plateau above the bay all is still lapped in rural peace. Eric Linklater's old home, Pitcalzean House, out of sight of the platform, is well cared for as a guest house for VIP visitors. Nearby is the old parish kirk of Nigg, built in 1626 and still in use one Sunday in the month. The other three Sunday services are held in the more modern church of Chapelhill, a former Free Church with an imposing Norman-style tower.

Under a canopy at the east gable of the old parish kirk is the Nigg sculptured stone—often described as the finest Pictish cross slab in Scotland. One side shows the cross surrounded by snakes and bosses intricately worked; the other shows a harp, dog-like animals and a man with cymbals. There were similar cross slabs at Shandwick and Hilton of Cadboll on the other side of the Hill of Nigg some four miles away. The Hill of Nigg is the name of the great cliff-like bluff, 666 feet high, which terminates in the North Sutor of Cromarty and runs for four miles along the Moray Firth coast to the north of it. Both Shandwick and Hilton, which before the oil boom had populations of 100 and 230 respectively, have swelled perceptibly as the oil men find new homes there, while Balintore, with a population of 369 in 1961, which lies between them, has had a massive injection of new housing in the sheltered valley behind the original seafront village. Its population has probably been trebled. Facing south across the Moray Firth all three villages were popular summer resorts in a modest way before recent developments; now they are becoming dormitories for the platform site workers.

From Balintore the B9166 road strikes north-west across the Easter Ross farmlands to Fearn, with its abbey—of which the chapel survives, somewhat mutilated, as the parish church. The abbey, dedicated to St Augustine, had been first founded at Edderton, ten miles to the north-west on the Dornoch Firth, in 1221 but was moved to Fearn in 1338, where it was hoped it would be less subject to the depredations of 'wild Highlanders'. The interior of the abbey church is impressive with walls of yellowish stone and lancet windows. It was rebuilt in 1772 after a disaster thirty years earlier when the stone vaulted roof of the nave fell in during a service, killing forty-four people. The village Hill of Fearn, with a pleasant village green, was the birthplace of Peter Fraser, Prime Minister of New Zealand (1940-49). It was suggested in the Holmes Report that Fearn would be suitable for large-scale residential development, but only modest growth has taken place since.

At Fearn the B9165 road leads north-west to Tain or north-east to Portmahomack, on the northern shore of the Tarbat peninsula, a wonderfully characterful old fishing village near the mouth of the Dornoch Firth. In 1971 it had a population of 226 and has since expanded as a result of the oil boom, which has brought several new settlers. As it faces north it is more exposed to cold winds, but it fronts a grand semi-circle of sand and enjoys a fine view of the mountains of Sutherland, blue across the firth. Its old cottages and warehouses (one of the seventeenth century with crow-stepped gables) are full of chacacter, as is the old parish kirk of Tarbat on a high road above the village. There are two inns, and a massively constructed old harbour with a long pier designed by Telford. This, like Cromarty, is a haven which must appeal to the artist and the antiquarian. A minor road recrosses the peninsula for the remaining three miles to Tarbat Ness with its lighthouse (1830), said to be the second tallest in Britain. Nearby is the tiny hamlet of Wilkhaven, while at Blindal a track of about a mile in length leads to Ballone Castle, a finely decorated Z-plan tower house of the Rosses of Balnagowan with unusual corbelling, but long in ruin.

There is a daily bus service from Portmahomack to Tain, the 'second capital' of Ross-shire which has been recompensed for the loss of its agricultural marts to Dingwall by extra-ordinary residential expansion as a result of the oil boom.

"Tain," wrote the compilers of the Holmes Report, "is a charming old royal burgh with extensive views over the Dornoch Firth. In the longer term it could be readily ex-panded to about 7000 persons mainly employed in Invergor-don." But that was in 1968. Invergordon is thirteen miles away, but in 1971 came the Nigg development, from which Tain is only nine miles away, and Tain has shifted its sights dramatically upwards. "In the longer term", it now aims at an eventual population of 20,000. By 1974 a staggering total of 823 new houses were either being built or had been planned for in the town, which at the 1971 census had a modest population of 1,942, which was nevertheless higher than it had been for over a century. One of the wonderful things about the expansion of the town is the compact pattern, almost perfectly circular, that is emerging as it stretches out. To make this complete a feasibility study was commissioned to reclaim 800 to 1,000 acres of foreshore on the shallow Dornoch Firth. The reclaimed land would be used for industrial, residential and recreational purposes.

Even the most casual visitor to Tain, as he sights the

spectacular red sandstone tolbooth tower embellished with quaint corner turrets, clock and steeple, and the golden lion of Ross above its arched entry, must guess that here is an old town with a long pedigree. Tain, like Dingwall, derived its name from the Orcadian-Norse occupation of northern Scotland. Both were the sites of 'things' or parliaments in the age of Thorfinn the Mighty. And it must have been during this occupation that there was born in Tain—allegedly on the site of the chapel on the Links that subsequently bore his name—the Celtic saint Dubthack or Duthus. Marvellous tales were told of his sanctity and almost two centuries later (in June 1253) his remains were moved from Armagh in Ulster to his Scottish birthplace, there to be revered and frequented by king and commoner alike for the next three centuries.

The arrival of the relics resulted in the creation of a garth or sanctuary-of-refuge where fugitives from the violence of their enemies' or the power of the civil authority were, under the protection of the Church, at least nominally safe. In 1307 the wife, sisters and daughter of King Robert the Bruce sought this sanctuary, but were dragged forth by the Earl of Ross and handed over to the tender mercies of Edward I of England. At a later date the parish church of Tain was dedicated to St Duthus. To the old chapel on the links King James IV made regular pilgrimages.

In 1487 St Duthus Church, which stands in the centre of the town behind the High Street, was raised to collegiate status. A Papal Bull of confirmation issued by Pope Innocent VIII and dated four days before his death in 1492 is preserved in the Tain Council Chambers. The church, in the Decorated Gothic style, was restored in the nineteenth century to become the memorial church of St Duthus and is held as a non-denominational shrine under the care of the Tain Guildry Fund.

It had of course been the parish church at the time of the Reformation, and in recognition of Tain's zeal in that movement, the Regent Moray presented to it an elaborately carved oaken pulpit claimed to be the finest of the kind in Scotland. The old building was abandoned in 1815 when another parish church was built, and the pulpit suffered some damage. But a public fund secured the restoration of both church and pulpit. The roof and buttresses were renewed along with the magnificent windows, and the walls were used to frame memorials to the illustrious dead of Easter Ross—from Patrick Hamilton of Fearn, the first of the Reformation martyrs, down to the fallen of the two world wars.

Tain Royal Academy dates from 1813 and was housed in a fine Georgian building before it moved to a new site in 1971 where there was room for the inevitable expansion. As the crow flies Tain is only five miles almost due south of Dornoch, the county town of Sutherland, on the other side of the Dornoch Firth. Some three miles to the north-west the Meikle Ferry formerly plied across half a mile of water to Ferrytown, connected to Dornoch by a road across the links. A disaster occurred at the ferry on the morning of 16 August 1809, when the overcrowded boat with 100 on board overturned and sank. A laminated timber girder bridge to span the firth was designed by Robert Stevenson in 1830. It was never built, but a model of it is shown in the Royal Scottish Museum, and as Sutherland casts envious eyes on the East Ross industrial boom, proposals for a bridge at this point have been revived. It would bring Dornoch within 14 miles of the Nigg platform site and greatly shorten the trunk road to the north, for at present it makes a detour of 22 miles around the firth, crossing the Kyle of Sutherland at Bonar Bridge. Here a bridge designed by Telford survived until 1892 when it was swept away in a spate. An iron bridge replaced it and this in its turn has now been supplanted by a suspension bridge.

Over nine miles of very beautiful country lies between Meikle Ferry and Ardgay at the head of the Dornoch Firth, where road and railway run side by side along the fertile shelf between the upland plateau, rapidly rising to 1,000 feet, and the firth-side shore. The hamlet of Edderton, five miles west of Tain, has a handsome modern parish church dated 1842, but more interesting is its predecessor, about a mile to the east on the bank of the Edderton Burn. Here in the kirkyard is a Pictish slab with a wheel cross in relief on one side and a horseman on the other. The Balblair Distillery adjoins Edderton Station, and nearby is another Pictish stone of earlier date, bearing incised symbols and known as the Clach Beorach. Soon the road is running under the forested slopes of Struie Hill, and at Fearn Lodge joins the A836 or Struie road, descending from the Cadha Mor pass.

Before we reach Ardgay the old parish kirk of Kincardine is passed on the south of the road. Its kirkyard includes a most unusual recumbent Pictish stone. Ardgay village, though a tiny place today, was created a burgh of barony under the name of Bonarness in 1686. A moving account of his boyhood in Ardgay was given by Alasdair Alpin MacGregor in his book *Land of the Mountain and the Flood*. Comparing this country with that of the west coast, he wrote: "About the colours of Easter Ross and Easter Sutherland there is something vivid, outstanding and unmistakable deriving from a richer soil ... Unless you have actually seen the real thing upon the hills of parishes such as ours you might think their bluey-purple crude and fanciful in some coloured reproduction." This is very true. The Dornoch Firth has a beauty akin to the great sea lochs of the west but it does not look so barren. Its slopes are clothed with heather. Its trees are more substantial and its haughlands are fertile in a way that is absent in the west with its greater rainfall and grassy mountainsides. There is a sharper, clearer atmosphere and a sense of well-being which grows with closer acquaintance.

# CHAPTER IX

## SUTHERLAND AND CAITHNESS

A ROAD a mile and a half long terminating in the new suspension bridge connects Ardgay with the long, straggling village of Bonar Bridge (pop. 437), one of the most strategic and populous centres in Sutherland—that huge county with an area of 2,125 square miles but only around 13,000 inhabitants. Its emptiness appals but its beauty is haunting. Bonar Bridge is all the more remarkable in that its population has actually increased by nearly 100 since the end of last century. From Bonar the A9 runs along the high north shore of the Dornoch Firth with a succession of fine views, passing the picturesque hamlet of Spinningdale on the left, and Skibo Castle, on the right—home of Andrew Carnegie. At Evelix, the A9 swings north while B9167 continues eastward for two more miles into Dornoch. One might pardonably paraphrase John Betjeman to catch the essence of this golfers' paradise:

> Ah! seaweed smells from sandy coves,
>     And woods and fields and moors around;
> The long Firth stirred by gentle waves
>     And Dornoch's mellow towers behind;
> Lark song and sea sounds in the air
> And splendour, splendour everywhere.

There is a mildness in the air which quite distinguishes it from its Scottish east coast peers in the golfing world. Two fingers of mellow yellow sandstone signal one's approach to Dornoch from any angle—the tower of the cathedral with its squat spire, and the soaring five-storey keep of Dornoch Castle, originally the bishop's palace and now a hotel. The cathedral with its kirkyard stands on an island site between High Street and Castle Street, from which it is separated by a lawn, and faces directly towards the castle, alongside which is a range of buildings including the Sheriff Courthouse and Tolbooth —here known as the Old Jail. To the east of the Old Jail, Castle Street then opens out into a spacious square lined with modern buildings with timber gables in the Old English style which yet succeed in blending pleasantly with the whole municipal layout.

Dornoch has never been more than village-size. In 1971 it had 838 folk and that was more than in any previous census except 1961, when it achieved 933. But it has a large tourist and holiday influx every summer. The two magnificent golf courses lie one to the north on the Moray Firth coast and the other to the south of the town on the extensive links west of Dornoch Point. The name 'Dornoch' first appears on record in 1138 when the Scots king sent a mandate to the earls of Orkney and Caithness to protect the monks of the place. In the next century, Gilbert de Moravia, Bishop of Caithness and Lord Treasurer of the North, moved his see from Halkirk in Caithness to Dornoch and built it next to the ancient church of St Barr.

When completed it consisted of a nave with two transepts, a choir and a massive tower supported by four fine clustered pillars and pointed arches richly moulded. The only parts now visible are the four great piers and bearing arches of the tower with the walls and windows of the choir. All the rest has either been destroyed in the many vicissitudes of history or obscured by the 'restoration' carried out by the Countess-Duchess of Sutherland and her architect William Burn of Edinburgh in 1835-37.

The castle of today is a part of the fifteenth-century bishop's palace, a large and stately building with three towers forming a courtyard. Like the tower of the cathedral, it withstood the Sack of Dornoch in 1570, when the town was given to the flames by the wild Mackays of Strathnaver. Golf on the Old Course of Dornoch is first mentioned in 1616 and it is thus the third oldest course in the world, after St Andrews and Leith. The Witch's Stone at Dornoch marks the spot where the last witch-burning in Scotland took place in 1722.

Three miles north of Dornoch on the Moray Firth coast is the fishing hamlet of Embo where a chambered cairn has been excavated showing the remains of two burial chambers built of upright stones roofed by a large capstone. Originally they were covered by an oval cairn and entered by short passages. Built about 2000 BC, they were reopened for later Bronze Age burials. Embo was also the site of a semi-fabulous battle between Norse invaders and Scots around 1259, during which the Earl of Sutherland is said to have seized a horse's leg after being disarmed, and used it as a weapon to good effect. It is claimed that the horse shoe which is the principal symbol of the Dornoch coat of arms derives from this incident. There is at least some tangible evidence of the battle in the sarcophagus and sculptured effigy of Sir Richard de Moravia, brother of Gilbert de Moravia, who fell at Embo and is buried in Dornoch Cathedral.

From Evelix the A9 road runs north for five miles to the shores of Loch Fleet, a lagoon-like inlet formerly a normal sea loch which became obstructed and almost cut off from the sea by a sand bar extending south from the Golspie area. It is crossed near its head by The Mound, an embankment 995 yards long, and a bridge of four arches and sluices, built to carry the main road to the north in 1816 at a cost of £12,500. The neck of the Fleet between the lagoon and the sea is said to be the only spot in the kingdom where angling for salmon is successfully carried out in salt water.

Golspie (pop. 1,167) is Sutherland's second largest town and chief administrative centre. Behind it towers Ben Bhraggie (1293 feet) crowned by the giant statue of the first Duke of Sutherland (Lord Stafford the 'Leviathan of Wealth') who elevated the village from a collection of "rude and primitive" fishermen's huts into what was intended as a model resettlement area for the population moved from the deep inland glens that were being converted into sheepwalks. It was intended to be a fishing port and for well over a century it was so, though the number of fishermen was never very large. As late as 1929 there were still forty-five Golspie fishermen going to sea in their little motor-boats. But today it sees its main role as a services centre, a tourist resort and an educational capital.

Its beautiful situation was eulogized by an Oxford observer eighty years ago in these words:

At Golspie we found all that we had craved. On the north of the bay, where we first sought it, there was just sand enough—we had not yet seen the miles of smooth sand which lie south of the village. Before us across the steely sea rose far and dim the line of the Moray hills, while in front of us the seabirds swam, wheeled and settled. Behind, brown kye and snowy geese were dotted over a broad belt of green pasture. To the left stood the woody heights and gleaming turrets of Dunrobin Castle. To the right swept a low shore backed by a crescent of mountains, and the Golspie Burn with its beautiful fall, babbling rapids and clear pools of brown water, its rocks and trees and ferns and mosses . . .

Golspie has a breezy 18-hole golf course on the links.

The new high school at Golspie looks after the senior secondary education of the whole of young Sutherland, and the Sutherland Technical College also serves the whole region. It has been in existence for seventy years. Golspie parish church is full of interest. Its pulpit canopy, box pews and massive Sutherland Loft all date from 1738-39.

Dunrobin Castle has been occupied by the earls and dukes of Sutherland since the fifteenth century and the present palatial building is of many periods. To the medieval keep additions were made by Earl John in the seventeenth century, by Countess Elizabeth around 1785, and again in 1835, when Sir Charles Barry designed the façades on the north and east which encased the original keep and wings. The castle was ravaged by fire in 1915 but restored after the First World War under the direction of Sir Robert Lorimer.

A couple of miles east of Dunrobin A9 enters the parish of Clyne, the only one in the shire in which there has been no overall decline in the number of inhabitants for a century, but this is entirely due to the growth of Brora (pop 1,256) compensating for the drain on its rural hinterland. Brora has grown to five times its level at the middle of last century and is Sutherland's biggest town and only industrial centre. Unfortunately its most colourful industry, coal mining, was hit by manpower competition from the oil boom in 1973 and a remarkable co-operative venture ended. After having been worked sporadically since 1529, Brora's mine was saved from closure in 1961 by co-operation between the Highland Fund and local miners. When I visited the Ross Pit in 1964 I found twenty-five miners themselves running the mine. To see the lorries of the Highand Colliery filling up with their freight of coal to distribute to Sutherland and the north was an inspiring sight, but in 1973 the venture ran into difficulties through loss of workers to oil-related industries, and the mine was sold to an English firm. Brora's other industries include a wool mill, a distillery, a brick works and a radio station.

In 1961 too, Brora was a pioneer in the 'community school'. With its own exclusive headquarters in a small adult wing containing common room, library and offices, the community centre expanded by night into the whole of a well-equipped new school with assembly hall, gymnasium and teaching rooms so that the leisure activities of the whole community could be catered for.

Brora has built up its industries with no loss to its Highland picturesqueness. Its river, teeming with salmon, flows to the sea from a noble loch through a tree-girt gorge which has been an obvious bridging point from the dawn of history. Its name, the 'Bruar-A' of the Norsemen, means simply 'bridge water'. Once a herring port with three curing stations, Brora harbour is only usable by large boats at high tide but I found two local seine-net boats, the *Girl Anna* and the *Provide,* at the grass-grown quay preparing to go to sea.

There was golf on Brora Links long before the first formal course was laid out in 1892. Then in 1924 the present 18-hole course was designed by James Braid. It was one of his masterpieces. Along a dozen miles of coast north of Brora the hills come close to the shore and rise steeply to the 1,000 foot contour, but in the days following the Clearances crofts have been carved out wherever the terrain would permit and at one point a new channel was cut for the River Loth through a rock 20 feet high, so that a swamp could be drained and its bed converted into rich arable carseland. At the foot of Glen Loth is a stone to commemorate the killing of the last wolf in Sutherland in 1700. After passing the hamlet of Portgower the A9 sweeps down to the mouth of the Strath of Kildonan and enters Helmsdale by a box girder bridge opened in 1972. With its accompanying road works it cost £460,000. Upstream is the shapely two-arched stone bridge designed by Telford and a handsome war memorial clock tower on the knoll which overlooks it.

The village of Helmsdale (pop. 800) stands at the mouth of the Helmsdale River on a series of terraces overlooking the quiet harbour and the mountain stream. Its connection with the Strath of Kildonan is not merely coincidental. From that strath and from the sudden emergence of the herring boom in the year 1814 it took its origin. Behind the excitement of the herring boom there lay the shadow of a tragedy—the Sutherland evictions. Between 1811 and 1821 the population of Kildonan parish dropped from 1,547 to 565, and by 1831 it had fallen to 257. Nor did this change take place gradually. Donald Sage recorded: "The whole north and south sides of the Strath from Kildonan to Caen on the left bank of the river and from Dalcharn to Marrel on the right bank, were at one fell swoop cleared of their inhabitants. The measures for their ejectment had been taken with such promptness, and were so suddenly and brutally carried out as to excite a tumult among the people."

Omitting all reference to the ruthlessness of Patrick Sellar and William Young on this occasion, the Second Statistical Account states merely:

> The decrease is accounted for by the change that occurred in the rural economy of the parish by the substitution of Cheviot sheep for Highland cattle ... The system of small holdings and sub-letting previously common was thereby altered, and no part of the parish being adapted for new settlements, the bulk of the original population were settled in the coast-side parishes, and in particular in the village of Helmsdale.

Today the hamlet of Kildonan has a population of 22. The Kirk of St Donan, where the pulpit of Donald Sage's father still stands, bears a plaque recording how John Diefenbaker, Prime Minister of Canada, sought there the memory of his ancestors. Many of the evicted people emigrated. A number settled on the Red River in what is now the Canadian province of Manitoba:

> Fair these broad meads—these hoary woods are grand;
> But we are exiles from our fathers' land.

It was never of course the intention of the Countess–Duchess of Sutherland to evict her peasant sub-tenants and squatters so as to force them to emigrate. 'Removals' not 'evictions' was the word used, and the theory was that all could be resettled on the coast where they could eke out the poor reward of small crofts by fishing. But although this grandiose scheme of social engineering was inadequately implemented the effect on Helmsdale was electric. Between 1811 and 1821 the population of the parish of Loth shot up from 1,330 to 2,008 and by 1831 had reached 2,234. "The increase," wrote the parish minister, "is to be attributed to the successful establishment of the herring fishery at Helmsdale, and to the settlement of several small tenants in that track of improvable land ... near the coast from Port Gower to Navidale." Herring fishing began in 1814 and the 'town' of Helmsdale was first laid out in 1818. The first year's fishing produced 5,318 barrels of cured herring. By 1831 the figure had reached 46,571.

For sixty years the herring brought great prosperity to Helmsdale. Coopering and curing yards employed many people and in the season (July and August) herring boats came from all quarters. Older folk can recall seeing the harbour literally packed with boats. About the turn of the century however conditions began to change. Herring became less plentiful on the inshore grounds and boats had to go farther afield. The sale of herring by auction in the larger ports like Wick proved more popular to fishermen than the old bounty system, and the small harbours declined. Coopering continued at Helmsdale until 1914 but there was no resumption after World War I. White fishing remained. During World War II and for a few years after it there was a further boom. Today only five of the larger boats, with several small lobster craft, use the port.

As the result of the coming of the railway in 1874 with its long detour inland across the Caithness moors to Wick and Thurso, Helmsdale acquired a locomotive power depot which employed over seventy men, but this was closed in 1963 and now the staff consists of two signalmen and thirteen trackmen. So there is now much travel-to-work as far south as Brora and Golspie—and even to the Nigg platform site.

Tourism becomes increasingly important. There are six sporting estates in the depopulated Strath of Kildonan. In 1971 the Highlands and Islands Development Board produced a report on the Strath and recommended the escalation of tourism and recreation. It suggested that tourists could be interested in an unusual form of holiday here—panning for gold in the Helmsdale River and the Suisgill Burn, which was the scene of a famous gold rush in 1868. Some miles up the Strath the road sign Baile-an-Or, 'the town of gold', recalls that here in 1868-69 there was a huge prospectors' camp. During the short but hectic scramble 500 to 600 prospectors were earning from 5s. to 35s. per day. The largest nugget panned was valued at £20.

There is still alluvial gold in the Suisgill Burn. I found two devotees of the sport from Cheshire, members of the North-West England Lapidary Society, gloating over their day's haul—forty tiny grains of gold held in suspension in a test-tube. They told me that the pursuit of precious metals is a very popular hobby with scores of affiliated clubs all over Britain. There is certainly scope for these enthusiasts in Kildonan.

On its 36-mile coastal route to Wick the A9 highway crosses into Caithness at the Ord four miles north of Helmsdale in truly spectacular fashion. At Navidale, the last hamlet in Sutherland, it is already high above the rocky coast, looking down on the little cove with its mansion and hotel from an altitude of 435 feet. But that is only the beginning. The road continues twisting and climbing and when it reaches the county boundary it is already 747 feet up with the 1288 foot Hill of Ord towering above it on the left. One has the impression that a real frontier is being crossed. Groome in his *Ordnance Gazetteer* (1890) defined the Ord as "an abrupt, broad, lofty granite mountain overhanging the sea", adding: "the old road over it, formerly the only land ingress to Caithness, traversed the crest of its stupendous seaward precipices at a height and in a manner appalling to both man and beast".

The modern road exhilarates rather than terrifies. Here we see the Moray Firth at its grandest, for the higher the road climbs on the coastal escarpment the more the surface of the sea comes into view, until we seem to be looking down into an infinite mirror. In contrast, the deep defile into which the road must dip at Berriedale seems almost claustrophobic, but the effect is softened by the picturesque little village. Just before reaching it there is a very fine view on the left up the Langwell Glen to the conical summit of Morven (2313 feet) with Scaraben (2054 feet) on the right. Near Berriedale are

Langwell House and the ruins of two old castles. On the greensward above the inn, near the kirkyard, is the Long Grave—over nine feet long. It is said to have been marked out by a warrior called Big William Sutherland, who on setting out on a foray lay down on the grass and had it marked out—on the assumption that he might never return alive.

On the coast, about a mile south of Dunbeath, is Dunbeath Castle. It stands on the top of a rocky promontory with the sea on three sides—a gay, fairy-like structure with flanking and angle turrets suggestive of the influence of the French *château*. It had a part to play in history in 1650. In the early spring of that year the Marquess of Montrose, proclaiming himself Charles II's lieutenant-general, landed with 2,000 men at Duncansby and occupied Thurso. Sir John Sinclair of Dunbeath galloped off to Edinburgh to inform the Covenant regime of this royalist invasion. Montrose and his army marched south along the coast and his second in command, General Hurry, laid siege to Dunbeath. Lady Sinclair and her servants surrendered after a brief resistance, on condition that their persons and property would be respected.

A small royalist garrison was left to hold the castle while Montrose and his men marched on to their doom at the Battle of Carbisdale, after which the wounded marquess was betrayed in Assynt and beheaded in Edinburgh. For the Covenant regime General Leslie and the Earl of Sutherland then marched into Caithness and invested Dunbeath Castle. The royalist defenders, under Major Whitford, put up a stout resistance, but their water was cut off and they were forced to capitulate. The castle is still in full and fine preservation.

Dunbeath, the native village of the novelist Neil M. Gunn, is vividly described in several of his books. Once a flourishing herring port and the setting for *The Silver Darlings*, it is now almost purely residential with a harbour which has decayed to the point of collapse, but its surroundings are still beautiful and recall the *Highland River* which Gunn so movingly depicted.

All this country at the southern end of Caithness is in the parish of Latheron and beyond Latheronwheel we come to the handsome parish church with its domed belfry. Before this was added to the building the people were summoned to worship by a bell tower, which still stands 500 yards to the north, on the other side of the A9 road. Between the two are ruins of an Iron Age broch—one of 149 such cylindrical dry-walled structures in Caithness.

At Latheron, the A895 road strikes north and, crossing a 500 foot col, traverses desolate moorland to Georgemas and Thurso. A9 continues along the coast, now cliffed by dark sandstone of Caithness slabs and penetrated by rugged 'goes' or inlets, to reach Lybster village with its long and broad main street stretching south for nearly a mile—from the road to the rockbound harbour which was once the centre of a great fishery district.

In 1838 the parish minister of Latheron listed the fishing 'stations' of the district with the boats attached to each as follows: Dunbeath 76, Latheronwheel 35, Forse 32, Swiney 10, Lybster 101, Clyth 53 and East Clyth 18. There was a total of 325 boats, 1,321 fishermen, 106 coopers (to make the herring barrels), 737 women packers, 178 labourers—in all 2,540 persons—besides about 50 fish curers. In a year 39,093 barrels of herring were cured and the average price per cran (roughly equivalent to a barrel) of 'green' or uncured fish was 9s. This observer, the Rev. George Davidson, added:

> It is difficult to say which of the sights is most pleasingly interesting to a stranger, that of beholding, the whole coast as far as the eye can reach, covered with human beings in their little barks, as they issue forth from every creek and disperse in different directions full of life; or that of attending in the morning at one of the stations, and witnessing the return of 40, 60 or 100 boats all crowding in to one creek, most of them laden with fish to the gunwale ... It is not unusual for the crew to engage in worship after shooting their nets. On these occasions a portion of a psalm is sung, followed by prayer, and the effect is truly solemn and heart-stirring as the melodious strains of Gaelic music carried along the surface of the waters spread throughout the whole fleet.

Though the days of its glory as a herring port have long gone, Lybster, which has a population today of around 550, has been given a measure of new life by its five seine-net boats. Two and a half miles beyond Lybster is Clyth Ness with its lighthouse. Two more creeks on the coast that now trends north-eastward to Wick and is virtually an unending succession of 'goes' are Whaligoe and Sarclet Haven, where the harbour has been almost destroyed by the sea.

Beyond the sea-lashed castle of Old Wick the foreland of South Head guards the entrance to Wick Bay. To the north of Wick the great green promontory of Noss Head can well be counted the final bastion of the northern flank of the Moray Firth, for here beyond the lighthouse the coast turns almost due west to the wide sandy sweep of Sinclair's Bay. As it does so however there is a final flourish of rocky splendour and human pretensions. Few castles can have a more arresting situation than Girnigoe, the ancient stronghold of the Sinclairs, earls of Caithness. The mighty medieval keep, built towards the end of the fifteenth century, stands on a long narrow rock running diagonally to the shore, which is flanked on either side by similar promontories from 50 to 60 feet high.

High isolated stacks of rock stand above the waters like advanced outworks of the fortress. The castle rock is cut through in two places by great ditches at the base and in the centre. The keep occupying the full breadth of the rock stands on the seaward side of the central ditch. Castle Sinclair, really a modern extension of Girnigoe, was built on the landward side of the ditch in 1606 but ceased to be inhabited in 1690 and has fallen into complete ruin. From Girnigoe the turbulent Sinclairs sallied forth to scour the country far and near. "For generations," say MacGibbon and Ross, "the name of the castle was one of terror all over the North of Scotland." The blackest of Girnigoe's black chapters was written between 1572 and 1576 when there languished, until he was ultimately murdered, John Garrow, the Master of Caithness, a victim to the hatred of his unnatural father, who revelled in the chambers above while his son was perishing in the dungeons below.

# CHAPTER X

# THE FUTURE OF THE FIRTH

THREE GOVERNMENT decisions announced in the spring of 1976 confirmed what had been temporarily in doubt—that the growth policy for the inner Moray Firth initiated by the Highlands and Islands Development Board will go marching on.

In February one of the Ministers of State in the Scottish Office announced that it was intended to start work on the construction of the Kessock Bridge across the narrows of the firth between Inverness and the Black Isle early in 1978. This would cost between £20,000,000 and £40,000,000 and work on the bridging of the Cromarty Firth may begin earlier.

In March the Secretary of State for Scotland approved the Cromarty Petroleum Company's application to build an oil refinery at Nigg Bay, alongside the existing platform yard there, at a cost of £150,000,000. A few days later another Minister of State (Mr Bruce Millan, now the Secretary of State for Scotland) announced that British Rail had been authorized to restore a second running line on a large part of the Highland Railway between Perth and Inverness which had been felled by the Beeching axe.

Of these the oil refinery decison was the most important. In 1974 when I visited the platform yard at Nigg I saw the blueprint for the refinery, but I knew that it would have to face intense scrutiny and much opposition before it could be implemented. The planning inquiry in 1975 lasted for five weeks and 500 objections were lodged, mainly by environmentalists. The reporter appointed by the Secretary of State concluded that, although there were no insurmountable objections on the grounds of controlled pollution, noise, navigational safety or agriculture, there was no evidence of need sufficiently great to warrant overriding the objections. The Secretary of State did not accept this. He saw the development as one that must be accepted if the growth policy was to continue.

The HIDB, the Highland Regional Council and other bodies who had supported the refinery project were delighted. Several of the regional councillors were soon arguing that the Dornoch Firth should also be bridged. Objectors continued to fear that the environment would suffer and wild birds would be driven from their haunts.

The building of the refinery will involve a work force of 1,500 and an operating force of 450. Petro-chemical complexes ancillary to the refinery may well follow. Underground storage is provided for and the single visual blemish on the landscape will be a chimney 500 feet high.

Safeguards against pollution are embodied in seventy planning conditions. Meanwhile the Nigg platform yard, having completed three platforms for the Forties Field, is at work on a steel platform for Chevron's Ninian Field, and Highlands Fabricators have plans for expansion to the tune of £1,000,000 and the construction of a metallurgy laboratory. They intend to diversify by entering the concrete platform market. On the opposite side of the Firth at Whiteness Head, McDermott's 1,600 work force is completing a third large platform—for Union Oil's Heather Field. Their skills are also being used on other contracts and the object of both great enterprises is to continue viable after the more pressing needs of North Sea oil have been met in the 1980s.

The great majority of the people who live in the Moray Firth area are not opposed to development. As the chairman of the Highland Regional Council, the Rev. Murdo Nicolson, puts it: "Some small price in conservation will have to be paid, but the Highlands are large enough to sustain it." For some like the late Eric Linklater, it meant the sacrifice of a loved home and cherished acres of land. "But," as he told me, "could I weigh that against men who have been idle for years? Spoil the Highlands? There's an awful lot of them to be spoiled."

In its long history the Moray Firth has seen tides of industry flow and ebb. If boom times have now come to its inner heart, its exposed extremities are still suffering from the ebb that succeeded the herring bonanza of last century. Stubbornly the fisher folk of Rosehearty, Gardenstown, Sandend, Portsoy, Cullen, Portknockie, Findochty, Portgordon, Portmahomack, and many another little haven cling to their old homes and prefer the ardours of long-distance travel-to-work to the alternative of desertion. By doing so they make the firth a fascinating place for the visitor and demonstrate that they had discovered the Window Concept—of living-places with a panoramic view from firth-slopes—before it became a catchword patented by the planners.

It is greatly to be desired that the delectable Brae Country —as Scots call the uplands between the Laich and the mountains—should be appreciated as it deserves. Certainly the curious tourist will not find the firth less interesting because it nourishes more folk. Nor will he have far to go to find still empty glens, and what Stevenson called "the trance of silence":

> Lo! for there among the flowers and grasses
> Only the mightier movement sounds and passes;
>> Only winds and rivers,
>> Life and death.

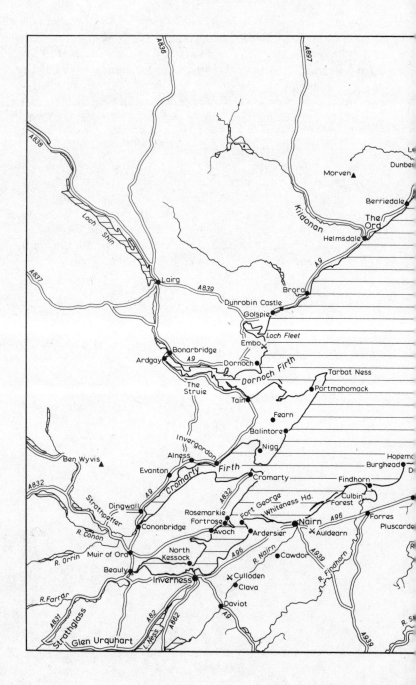

Noss Head

A9

Wick

Ibster

Miles
0                    20

'A' roads                ====
Battle sites              ✕

FIRTH

RAY

Portknockie

siemouth          Findochty      Cullen                Troup Head    Rosehearty      Sandhaven    Fraserburgh
ingston        Buckie        ✕                Portsoy   Whitehills    Crovie    Pennan                              Cairnbulg Pt.
rmouth                    Sandend                Banff        ✕                Dundarg
                Portgordon      A98      Fordyce          Macduff    Gardenstown    ✕        Inverallochy
lanbryde                                                            A98
        Fochabers
                A96
                        A95          A97
                                                Turriff                          A950

                                                                        A948    A92
Craigellachie                    R. Deveron

                        Huntly
                                    A96          A947
A941

# BIBLIOGRAPHY

Anson, Peter F., *Fishing Boats and Fisher Folk on the East Coast of Scotland* (Dent 1971)

Bain, George, *A History of Nairnshire* (Nairn 1893)
—— *The River Findhorn (Nairnshire Telegraph* 1911)

Bain, Robert, *A History of the Ancient Province of Ross* (Pefferside Press, Dingwall 1899)

Barclay, William, *Banffshire* (Cambridge 1922)

Barron, Evan M., *Inverness in the Fifteenth Century* (1905)
—— *Inverness Courier Guide to Inverness* (Carruthers, Inverness 1950)

Brereton, Henry L., *Gordonstoun, Ancient Estate and Modern School* (W. and R. Chambers, Edinburgh 1968)

Calder, James T., *History of Caithness* (Rae, Wick 1887)

Cant, Ronald G., *Old Moray* (Elgin Society 1948)
—— *Moray in Scottish History* (Elgin Society 1952)
—— *Historic Elgin and Its Cathedral* (Elgin Society 1974)

Cruden, Stewart, *The Scottish Castle* (Nelson 1960)

Forsyth, Isaac, *A Survey of the Province of Moray* (Aberdeen 1798)

Garry, Flora, *Bennygoak and Other Poems* (Rainbow Books, Aberdeen 1975)

Groome, Francis H., *Ordnance Gazetteer of Scotland* in 10 vols (William Mackenzie, London 1895)

Gunn, Rev. Adam, and Mackay, John, *Sutherland and the Reay Country* (Mackay, Glasgow 1897)

Gunn, Neil M., *Highland River* (Porpoise Press, Edinburgh 1937)
—— *The Silver Darlings* (Faber 1941 and 1969)

Henshall, Audrey Shore, *The Chambered Tombs of Scotland* (Vol. 1, 1963, Vol. 2, 1972, Edinburgh University Press)

Highlands and Islands Development Board: *Reports* No 1—No 6 (Bridge House, Inverness)

Holmes Group: *The Moray Firth, A Report to the Highlands and Islands Development Board* (Jack Holmes Planning Group, March 1968).

Innes, Cosmo, *The Family of Kilravock* (Spalding Club 1848)

Laing, Gerald, *Kinkell: The Reconstruction of a Scottish Castle* (Latimer, London 1974)

Maclean, Loraine (ed.), *The Hub of the Highlands* Inverness Field Club Centenary Volume (Albyn Press, Edinburgh 1975)

McDowell, R. J. S., *The Whiskies of Scotland* (John Murray 1967)

MacGregor, Alasdair Alpin, *Land of the Mountain and the Flood* (Michael Joseph 1965)

Miller, Hugh, *My Schools and Schoolmasters* (Edinburgh 1854, popular edition Nimmo, Hay and Mitchell, Edinburgh 1893)

—— *Scenes and Legends of the North of Scotland* (1834, Centenary Edition 1902)

—— *The Old Red Sandstone* (Edinburgh 1841)

Milne, John C., *Poems* (Aberdeen University Press 1964)

Murison, David D., 'Local Dialects' in *The North-east of Scotland* (British Association, Aberdeen 1963)

Nicolson, James R., *Beyond the Great Glen* (David & Charles 1973)

Prebble, John, *The Highland Clearances* (Secker 1963)

Richardson, J. S., and Mackintosh, H. B., *Elgin Cathedral* (H.M.S.O. 1968)

Robertson, Alan G. R., *The Lowland Highlanders* (The Bookshop, Tain 1971)

Shaw, Lachlan, *The History of the Province of Moray* (Hamilton, Adams, London 1882)

Simpson, W. Douglas, *The Ancient Stones of Scotland* (Hale 1968)

—— *Portrait of the Highlands* (Hale 1969)

—— *Dundarg Castle* (Aberdeen University Studies No 131 1953)

Statistical Accounts of Scotland: *Sir John Sinclair's* (O. S. A. 1799, 21 vols). *The New* (N. S. A. 1845. Separate volume for Aberdeenshire; Banff, Elgin, Nairn; Inverness and Ross and Cromarty; Sutherland and Caithness—Blackwood, Edinburgh). *The Third* (3 S. A., Aberdeenshire 1960, Banffshire 1961, Moray and Nairn 1965, all edited by Henry Hamilton; Collins). These volumes, which have no parallel in the literature of any other country, present a total picture of the area, parish by parish.

Steers, J. A., *The Coastline of Scotland* (Cambridge 1973)

Stuart, John, *The Sculptured Stones of Scotland* (Spalding Club 1856)

Taylor, Iain Cameron, *Culloden: A Guide* (National Trust for Scotland 1965)

Thompson, Francis, *The Highlands and Islands* (Hale 1974)

—— *Highland Waterway: The Caledonian Canal* (Graphis, Inverness 1971)

Vallance, H. A., *The Highland Railway* (David & Charles 1964)

Waterston, Charles D, *Hugh Miller, The Cromarty Stonemason* (National Trust for Scotland 1961)

Watson, J. and W., *Morayshire Described* (Elgin 1868)

Youngson, A. J., *After the Forty-Five* (Edinburgh University Press 1973)

# INDEX